Library of
Davidson College

THE SUBURBAN TREND

Harlan Paul Douglass

ARNO PRESS
&
The New York Times
NEW YORK · 1970

Reprint Edition 1970 by Arno Press Inc.

Reprinted from a copy in The University of Illinois Library

LC# 73-124478
ISBN 0-405-02450-9

THE RISE OF URBAN AMERICA
ISBN for complete set 0-405-02430-4

Manufactured in the United States of America

THE
SUBURBAN TREND

THE SUBURBAN TREND

BY
HARLAN PAUL DOUGLASS
Author of "THE LITTLE TOWN," etc.

THE CENTURY CO.
New York & London

301.36
D737s

Copyright, 1925, by
THE CENTURY CO.

PRINTED IN U. S. A.

79-7467

PREFACE

Of any sociology which this book may contain, much the greater part has been drawn from the author's experience. No one who, for years, has shuttled daily back and forth between suburb and city can have escaped the frequent necessity of formulating his *apologia* for suburban life. One covers a matter of a quarter of a million miles of distance in about twenty years of fairly average commuting. It is not too much to estimate that at least once for every two hundred miles the commuter has been challenged to defend his faith. Some of these occasions arise incidentally out of friendly exchanges between fellow-commuters. Here is the questioning brother who is doubtful whether or not to give it up and move back to the city; here, on the other hand, the rampant assurance of the neighbor whose zeal for suburban life is still more assertive and robust than one's own. Challenges of another sort come from the commiserations or pleasantries of city dwellers, who keep on contrasting their own happier lots, in season and out. All told, the confirmed suburbanite is virtually compelled to develop a sort of social philosophy about which his numerous observations tend to organize themselves. Enough commuting anecdotes have fastened upon the Erie Railroad alone to supply the essence of quite a respectable suburban sociology. It is in such informal materials that the book has its origins.

Beyond this, however, the author confesses his long-time conviction that the intermediate aspects of our civilization afford especially penetrating clues to its tendencies and meanings. His volume on "The Little Town" (1919) was something of a pioneer in its field. It interpreted the town as a sort of half-way house between country and city, which is exactly what the suburbs, at first glance, appear to be. This explains the primary theoretical interest of the author's mind in them.

The present work has been compelled to conclude, however, that the suburbs, in the main, are intermediate in form rather than in significance. In essence they are parts of the evolving cities and in sharp contrast with the original rural pattern of social experience.

Nevertheless, in a subordinate sense, the suburbs do function as an in-between type, particularly with reference to the modified rural civilization which is just now forming over large areas of the nation. This is the particular warrant for including their story in one of the Century Country Life Books.

Specifically, the present study has discovered—as genuinely suburban in many of its aspects—a widening geographical zone around cities and definitely within the sphere of urban influence, which is characteristically devoted to the production of food from the soil and is dominated by a type of life unmistakably rural in its major quality. It is a sort of rural life, however, which can be described and understood only with reference to the city which it surrounds. Its variant qualities are the direct creation of the city. Here the very stuff of

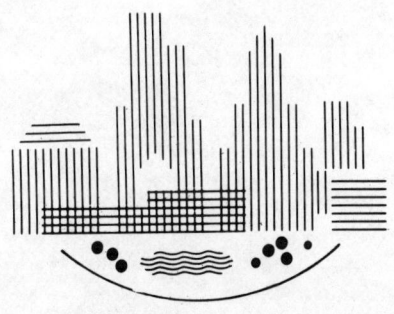

THE RISE OF URBAN AMERICA

ADVISORY EDITOR
Richard C. Wade
PROFESSOR OF AMERICAN HISTORY
UNIVERSITY OF CHICAGO

PREFACE

which the metropolis is made is found in direct contact with the most aboriginal rural processes.

Both the fact and the extent of these contacts have largely escaped those accounts of the suburban situation which have started with city centers. It is equally legitimate to approach the problem from the side of the open country and to work in toward the center. This method reveals a suburban phase which is definitely intermediate between country and city. No comprehensive version of urban and rural relationships can omit it. It is a phase destined to be still more important in the future. It is a form of rural centralization corresponding to and involved in urban decentralization. It constitutes one of the most interesting aspects of the suburban trend.

In the matter of method, it will be observed that the book makes frequent, though obviously limited, excursions into the realm of quantitative measurement and comparison. This has been done primarily in order to illustrate the place and possibilities of a statistical treatment of the field and to indicate specific aspects of it to which statistics might fruitfully be applied. Any more extensive or rigid statistical processes were judged out of place in a work designed to be somewhat popular in presentation and attempting to open up the field at many points rather than to exhaust it at any.

The maps and charts which accompany the text were executed by Miss Gladys McNair of the Institute of Social and Religious Research from the author's designs.

H. P. D.

Upper Montclair, N. J.,
December, 1924.

CONTENTS

CHAPTER		PAGE
I	Cities and Their Suburbs	3
II	Measuring the Suburban Trend	38
III	The Major Suburban Types	74
IV	Other Varieties of Suburbs	93
V	The Cost of Suburban Living	123
VI	Suburban Society and Institutions	164
VII	Suburban Society and Institutions (Continued)	194
VIII	Suburban Social Deficiencies	215
IX	The Rural Side of the Suburban Trend	239
X	The Deliberate Decentralization of Cities	271
XI	The Suburban Evangel	304
	Appendix I	329
	Appendix II	331
	Bibliography	335

CONTENTS

CHAPTER		PAGE
I.	CITIES AND THEIR SUBURBS	3
II.	APPROACHING THE SUBURBAN TREND	23
III.	THE MAJOR SUBURBAN TYPES	46
IV.	OTHER VARIETIES OF SUBURB	88
V.	THE CENSUS SUBURBAN TREND	127
VI.	SUBURBAN SOCIETY AND INSTITUTIONS	164
VII.	SUBURBAN SOCIETY AND INSTITUTIONS (CONT.)	195
VIII.	SUBURBAN SOCIAL PATHOLOGIES	216
IX.	THE RURAL SIDE OF THE SUBURBAN TREND	240
X.	THE DELIBERATE DECENTRALIZATION OF CITIES	267
XI.	THE SUBURBAN TREND	294
	APPENDIX I	326
	APPENDIX II	331
	BIBLIOGRAPHY	335

LIST OF CHARTS

CHART NUMBER		PAGE
I	Relative Density of Population New York and Environs, and Area of Daily Delivery of Merchandise by a Representative Department-Store	11
II	Railroad Commuting Time, New York and Environs	13
III	Percentage Excess of Families over Dwellings for 21 Cities and Their Suburbs by Size Groups	22
IV	Suburbs Growing Faster than Cities	41
V	Growth is Greatest Where Congestion is Least	48
VI	Suburban Opportunities Within the Limits of a Crowded City	53
VII	Percentage of all Incorporated Places of 500 to 100,000 Population which are Suburban to Cities of 100,000 and Over, by Size Groups	59
VIII	Massing of Rural Population in the Vicinity of Cities	62
IX	A Continuous Urbanized Area	66
X	Varying Space Requirements of Industries	83
XI	Percentage of Industrial Wage-Earners in Total Population	88
XII	Excess Over Parent City of Foreign-Born Population in Exceptional Industrial Suburbs and of Negroes in Exceptional Residential Suburbs of Chicago and New York	98

LIST OF CHARTS

CHART NUMBER		PAGE
XIII	Percentage of Population which is 45 Years of Age and Over in Chicago and New York and in Exceptional Residential and Industrial Suburbs	100
XIV	Percentage Distribution of Number of Rooms Per Family in New York City Apartments	125
XV	Percentage of General Municipal Expenditures Going to Specified Departments of Government by Size of Cities	134
XVI	Percentage of Married Population 15 Years of Age and Over	170
XVII	Average Number of Churches in Suburban and Non-Suburban Communities by Size Groups	204
XVIII	Contrasting Urban and Suburban Church Tendencies, St. Louis 1899–1919	205
XIX	Suburban Success and Failure: Home Ownership Compared with Infant Mortality	213
XX	Average Size and Value of Farms as Affected by the Proximity of a City	251
XXI	Percentage of Receipts Drawn from Different Types of Farm Products as Affected by Proximity of a City	253
XXII	Apartment-House Type of Suburban Development	283
XXIII	Mill Green Housing Project, United States Housing Corporation	287
XXIV	Standard Types of Industrial Housing, Five- and Six-Room Houses	294
XXV	Standard Types of Industrial Housing, Four-Room Houses	295

THE SUBURBAN TREND

THE SUBURBAN TREND

CHAPTER I

CITIES AND THEIR SUBURBS

OUT toward the fringes and margins of cities comes a region where they begin to be less themselves than they are at the center, a place where the city looks countryward. No sharp boundary line defines it; there is rather a gradual tapering off from the urban type of civilization toward the rural type. It is the city thinned out.

Confronted with the expanding cities the adjacent country also begins to look cityward. The result is not, however, a compromise of equals. The original movement was, and the major movement is the city's. The suburb is a footnote to urban civilization affecting the near-by country-side. It is not a true mediating type. The town is such a type. It stands between the country and the city, partaking somewhat equally of the nature of both. Even so the town's primary relationships are rural. It is the country thickened up. But the suburb does not mediate in a similar sense between the city and the country-side. It is a part of urban civilization. Even though it is a town in form, the brand of the city is stamped upon it. It straddles the arbitrary line which statistics draw between the urban and rural spheres; but in reality it is the push of the city outward. It makes physical compromises with country ways but few compromises of spirit. It is the city trying to escape the consequences of being a city while still remaining a city. It is urban society trying to eat its cake and keep it, too.

The View from Eagle Rock Park

What does an actual sample of suburbs look like? Probably the world's greatest panorama of a metropolitan area is that of New York and its suburbs seen from New Jersey from a vantage-point on the "First Mountain."

In the foreground, glimpsed at intervals through the green of trees, winds a historic thoroughfare skirting the base of the mountain. Mansions and villas creep up its lower slopes. On the middle horizon are silhouetted the city's towers, accenting the most marvelous sky-line ever made by man. To the right lies the faintly gleaming bay with ships moving across the background of Staten Island. Between the two opens the unseen gateway to the Atlantic and to all the world. To the left the back slopes of the Palisades stretch in long unbroken line.

Between the mountain and the city a spacious suburban area is spread out. The dominant impression it makes is that of roominess. Its spaces seem more open than occupied. Its habitations, half buried in foliage,

CITIES AND THEIR SUBURBS

are uncrowded. In the immediate foreground lies the Village. Its three spires lift their points, and one who knows can pick out the school, the Woman's Club building, the cluster of stores, and the plaza of the railway station.

Beyond the Village is the Town, its few tall apartment-houses competing with the church towers. Still farther away lies the Minor City, one of the great ones of America if it were not overshadowed by giant New York. A cathedral crowns its heights and the smoke of its factories ascends endlessly. At the extreme left sprawl the industrial cities par excellence—Paterson, Passaic, their characters accented by the thickets of smoke-stacks towering with almost monumental aspect.

The lesser suburbs, too numerous to count, spot the picture. Ranging the open spaces, the eye passes from the white-walled college to the red-roofed country-club house and smooth golf-links; then over peach-orchards, market-gardens, forest-patches, to the gray-green marshes which the sea here interposes between the city and suburb.

The mountain ridge on which one stands separates the first line of suburbs from the second. It was George Washington's first line of defense during the Revolutionary War. The later suburbs lie more thinly scattered, less connected with the city, maintaining more of the old rural traditions. They thin out in turn into a region of great country estates encroaching upon old-time farms. In the valleys are factory villages adjoining which immigrant workers are buying the old farms and cutting them up into peasant holdings. Beyond, in the farthest zone immediately touched by the city, are forested watersheds, Alpine lakes, the playground and the scenic background of the Colossus of urban civilization.

Ribbons of gleaming rails, often obscured by trails of smoke, and highways filled with processions of motor-cars, turn the panorama into a living picture and tie its parts together.

A First Approach to the Suburban Problem

Such is the rich and bewildering reality which the environs of a great city present. Seeking to reduce it to terms which the mind can grasp and discuss, the common device is to conceive of a metropolitan or complete urban area as consisting of three zones: (1) The urban zone in the narrow sense; that is to say, the city itself or the closely related cluster of cities. (2) The suburban zone proper. (3) The rural zone within which the countryside is modified by considerable urban contacts and which is suburban in a secondary sense.

In the most general sense the suburbs are thus a belt of near-by but less crowded communities which have "close connections" with the city, made possible by physical arrangements for the rapid transfer of people and goods between the two. It is the area within which many people go to the city to work and come back at night, the area within which numerous shoppers flock to city stores which make daily deliveries of purchases.

The rural suburbs have no such complete system of daily interchange. They have fewer and slower trains. Their populations do not experience a daily change of environment by going to work and returning at night. Their characteristic type of economic activity is not urban. They have not even the detailed dependence upon the city which the more distant open country has upon its village or town centers. But the city greatly affects the temper and in considerable degree transforms the life of the rural suburb. It seems merely the frame of a rural picture preserving all the glow of the original coloring, while in reality it gives an entirely different balance and focus to the composition.

The three zones just described are not accurately defined by political lines. "City" in the sociological sense may not stop with the municipal limits and may not go as far as the limits. The urban core of the vast metropolitan district of Greater New York includes Jersey City, Hoboken, Newark, and several smaller municipalities in Hudson County, New Jersey; but properly speaking it excludes, for example, the old Quaker town of Flushing with its strongly marked local traditions, as it does large portions of Queens and Richmond boroughs which lie within the political city.[1]

Tracing the Suburban Pattern

If political boundaries are not sufficient to define the suburbs, how then shall they be defined? Many considerations must be canvassed and many points of approach utilized before this question can be fully an-

[1] The inadequacy of political boundaries to define the suburb as a social phenomenon is discussed in numerous connections. See pp. 39, 47.

swered. A start in the direction of precise definition may, however, be made in two ways: (1) by measuring relative densities of population, and (2) by measuring facility of transportation in terms of distance and cost.

(1) The suburbs are less densely populated than the city. That belt of population which lives under distinctly roomier conditions than is the average lot of city people, but under distinctly more crowded conditions than those of the adjoining open country, is suburban whether lying within or outside of the city.

(2) Those communities within the total metropolitan area which have a suburban density of population, and from which in addition, the heart of the city can be reached conveniently, quickly, and at low cost (in contract, it may be, with others of equal distance) are suburban.

Now, from neither standpoint does the suburban zone define itself as clear-cut, continuous, and equidistant at every point from the center of the city. The *average* character of this zone meets these specifications, but many areas within it will not do so. The first reason is that few cities develop in complete and regular form from inside to outside. The very features of physical advantage which locate the city in the first instance—its harbor, a river-gorge with falls for water-power, its high elevation above a swamp—generally constitute barriers to equal growth in all directions. Expansion involves many deflections. A city is forced to conform to its physical site. Topography may pull it out into a lozenge-shaped area along a waterfront as in the cases of

Philadelphia, Chicago, and St. Louis, or may cut it into intricate, irregular patterns traced by river and sea as in those of New York, San Francisco, and Seattle.

Urban Radial Expansion

In seeking to avoid natural barriers, original highways seek out and follow lines of least resistance, utilizing passes and tracing aboriginal trails along water-levels and across divides. These natural lines of communication radiating from cities are later taken over by railways and other transit routes, which in turn determine the location of industries. The routes which are earliest developed, and which turn out to be permanently the best located, provide the skeleton of metropolitan plan and determine the major lines of suburban growth. Populations expand decade after decade along such radiating lines originally dictated by topography. They press out along the major axes of the city's structure, aided by cheap and convenient facilities for carrying goods and people.

At strategic points within the sphere of metropolitan influence minor cities spring up, as Paterson did at the falls of the Passaic River. The intervening territory now thickens with population and now thins out. Between the major lines of development, and often far nearer in miles to the heart of the city than are the minor centers, lie rural areas like islands in an urban sea. Their life is profoundly modified by the proximity of the city, but they are not fully suburbanized. They are generally unincorporated and are still largely devoted to farming. The peculiarities of these areas has already been touched upon and will have full discussion in a special chapter on the rural suburbs. It is enough for the moment to note that every great city has such near-by undeveloped areas lying comparatively close to it but somewhat off of the main lines of suburban growth. They are relatively lacking in urban contacts, although geographically nearer than many full-fledged suburbs.

The Urban Core and Its Circumference

In attempting to comprehend the suburbs the mind must therefore seek a middle way between the two extremes. It cannot get along merely with the broad generalization which divides the metropolitan district into the city, suburbs, and rural suburbs. Neither can it deal with the infinite complexity of the actual structure of the area, based as it is on topography, facilities of communication, the composition of communities, their prestige, prejudices, and a whole welter of other modifying factors. It must therefore devise a more accurate system of expressing the facts, which shall both simplify their statement and recognize their diversity.

As developed by the city planners, the device commonly used for this purpose is a series of geographical charts and diagrammatic maps. For example, such a series of maps was prepared by the Plan of New York and Its Environs organization on the basis of the 1920 census. A map showing density of population (Chart I) uses the county as a unit where its distribution is fairly uniform; otherwise it breaks up counties into districts.

CITIES AND THEIR SUBURBS

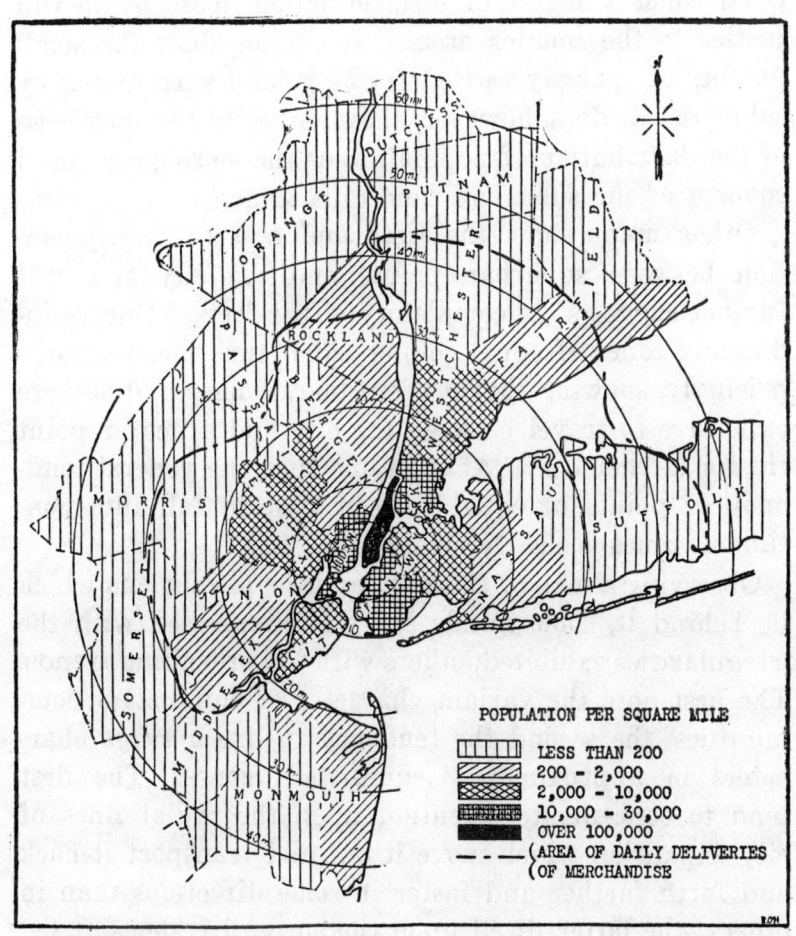

RELATIVE DENSITY OF POPULATION, NEW YORK AND ENVIRONS

Also area of daily delivery of merchandise by a representative department-store.

(Adapted from "Plan of New York and Environs," Maps and Diagrams, p. 9.)

Often such a degree of discrimination does not do full justice to the smaller areas. It cannot show the small patches of sparsely settled farming land surrounded by suburbs. It does, however, show correctly the spottiness of the distribution of population as the mere generalized concept of the suburban zone fails to do.

Other maps show the time and cost of transportation between suburban points and the city and still further suggests the complexity of the facts. Curves indicating zones of equal cost or equal time meander surprisingly, showing that it often takes longer and is more expensive to travel between the city and a nearer point than a farther one. At the same time the general tendency of points of equal time or cost to fall into continuous zones is clearly evidenced.

Observing a map of this sort, and the phenomena which lie behind it, some minds are most impressed with the irregularities exhibited, others with the prevailing trends. The first note the variant character of equidistant communities, the second the tendency to like *average* characters in approximately equidistant zones. The first tend to concentrate attention upon the radial lines of city expansion which move it out and transport it back and forth farther and faster in some directions than in others; the latter dwell upon the successive zones of development which surround it. These differences pass over into the realm of city planning, giving us the "radial" school, which conceives of the city's pattern as a star and wants to push the points out indefinitely, maintaining permanent the wedges of agricultural land between; and the "ring" school, which would encircle the

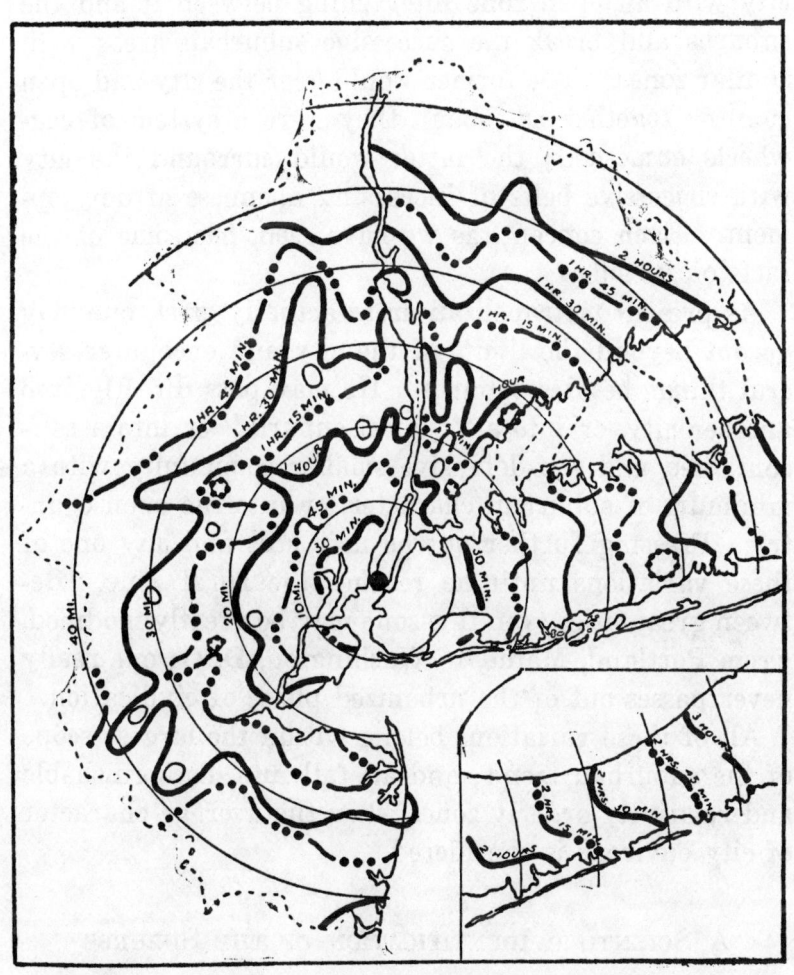

RAILROAD COMMUTING TIME, NEW YORK AND ENVIRONS

Shown by 15-minute intervals from city terminals.
(Adapted from "Plan of New York and Environs," **Maps and Diagrams,** p. 27.)

city with an open zone intervening between it and the suburbs and break the successive suburban areas with similar zones. The former would gear the city and open country together as though they were a system of cogwheels enmeshed; the latter would surround the city with successive belts of increasing openness of development. Each concept, as we have seen, has some of the facts on its side.

As present metropolitan areas actually exist, one may go out beyond the limits of the city and encounter several things besides suburbs. He may pass directly into another city, or into a "typical suburb," or into a self-contained and self-defensive smaller community with a minimum of suburban character, or into the open country. Pressing further out he may still find any one of these variations until he reaches the rural zone. Between great cities even this zone may be greatly modified. From Portland, Maine, to Washington, D. C., one really never passes out of the urbanized phase of civilization.

All of these variations belong within the largest scope of the suburban trend; and all fall into distinguishable and relatively orderly zones when the average character of city environs is considered.

A Scientific Identification of the Suburbs

Even such devices as have just been illustrated do not make it easy for one to go about attaching the right labels to the different communities found within metropolitan districts. One who would speak accurately of "city," "suburbs," or "rural suburbs" must discover some more precise criteria for defining them. Just what is a suburb? How much difference in the ways already suggested must it develop before it ceases to be part of the city? What determines where the city leaves off and the suburb begins? When does a suburb begin to be rural? When is one beyond the metropolitan area altogether? The transitions from one of these phenomena to the other are so gradual that more precise and if possible quantitative measures of difference are demanded.

These can only be discovered by further analysis and the attempt to use any available data which appear competent to throw light upon the vital differences we are trying to understand.

Urban Struggle for Space

In the search for a more precise definition a fresh start may be made by returning to the fact that the suburb is less densely populated than the city. The special mark of the city is the economical use of land. The rural suburbs, on the contrary, use land extensively. There is plenty of room in the country. Suburban use of land falls between the two extremes. Compared with the city's, the plots into which it is divided are large; compared with the country's, they are small. The city measures in feet, the suburbs in rods, the country in acres. A foot in the city is worth more than a rod in the suburb and far more than an acre in the country. Furthermore the value of land both in suburbs and rural suburbs is based upon the expectation of a more intensive use of their land as the city grows.

THE SUBURBAN TREND

The city has many people within a small space. These people are doing many things of many sorts. They and their activities compete with each other for room, for air-space, for freedom to move about, for the right of way, for places for the feet of man, for the foundations of structures, for the storage of goods. The uses to which land is put compete with one another. Factories struggle to locate where homes now are. Railroads want to take streets, and business infringes upon parks and play-spaces. The available surface of the earth gets closely occupied.

The first stage of this urban filling-in process is marked by the covering of the entire surface of the city lot by structures. Thus the house at 28 East Twentieth Street, New York, in which Theodore Roosevelt was born, stood tight between two other houses but boasted a flight of steps in front. He describes the middle room on the first floor, a library, as "without windows and consequently available only at night." There was, however, a diminutive yard at the rear of the house to which the conscience-stricken culprit once fled after biting his sister.[2]

Alternatives in Intensive Occupancy of Space

In the intensive occupancy of city land, surrender of the door-steps and the back yard follows later than the acceptance of the dark middle room. But even before the tendency to occupy the entire surface of the city

---

[2] Theodore Roosevelt, "Autobiography," pp. 6 and 10.

CITIES AND THEIR SUBURBS

reaches its practicable limits there are set up the two great alternative processes by which the city attempts to satisfy its demand for space, namely, by going up and by going out. The first process attempts to provide more space by building one house upon another and another upon that until the city becomes many storied. It towers above the earth, which was not roomy enough for its immediate uses until the danger of literally breaking in the earth's crust comes seriously to be considered. The second alternative attempts to provide more space by lateral expansion and annexation of territory. There is unoccupied space outside the city, if not within it. The city therefore reaches at and takes over a larger and larger superficial area, finding room at its edges for the open lot and cottage house which the crowding of the center forbade.

These two tendencies fix the visible contours of virtually every American city small or large. They are high at the center, low at the circumference. They go up, and they go out.

In contrast with the going up at the center, all the goings out of cities illustrate the suburban trend. The suburbs proper are simply the more radical expansions of the area of occupancy where room is secured at cost of inconvenient distance from the center and where distance is overcome by transportation facilities. They mark the extremes to which the going-out process may go without the loss of "close connection" with the center.

Such is the general philosophy of the suburb. Our attention next turns to some of its concrete manifestations in the United States.

CONTRASTING OCCUPANCY OF LAND

By building story upon story the going-up process economizes land. On the contrary, the suburbs, in the desire to be uncrowded, make large demands upon land. The difference between the two with respect to the occupancy of land (measured in terms of the areas recognized as metropolitan by the 1920 United States census for the cities of 100,000 population or over) is as follows: [3]

	Included in metropolitan district	
	Population	Acres
Within 68 cities	27,429,326	2,038,020
In adjacent suburban territory	9,457,635	21,428,598

The suburbs of the sixty-eight greater American cities thus contain about one third as many people as inhabit the cities themselves, using about ten times as much land. This fairly characterizes the suburban situation as a whole and justifies the outstanding popular distinction between the congested cities and the roomy suburbs.

CONTRASTING CONGESTION OF DWELLINGS

In order to appreciate what this condition means to the individual family, let us consider some additional facts drawn from the census. If, for example, every house in New York City was occupied by a single family, 71.4 per cent of all families would be homeless. There is this enormous discrepancy between the number of dwellings and the number of families. But in New York suburbs with populations of 2500 to 10,000 every house could have a single family to itself and only 16.3

[3] Fourteenth Census, Vol. I, p. 75, Table 42.

CITIES AND THEIR SUBURBS

per cent. of all families would be left homeless. In rural America the average house does have a single family to itself, the number of families and dwellings being substantially equal. Even the smaller suburbs therefore turn out to be a little crowded compared with the country town, though very uncrowded compared with the city.

The successive steps by which city congestion gives way to suburban roominess are illustrated for Greater New York in the following table:

TABLE 1—RATIO OF FAMILIES TO DWELLINGS IN THE NEW YORK METROPOLITAN AREA

Suburbs by size of population	Families per dwelling	Percentage of excess of families over dwellings
2,500– 10,000	1.19	16.3
10,000– 25,000	1.43	31.0
25,000–100,000	1.76	43.2
City		
New York	3.49	71.4
Richmond Borough	1.30	23.2

As would be expected on the basis of experience, the larger suburbs are more congested than the smaller ones. Some of them are cities in themselves. Richmond Borough, however (consisting of Staten Island), an integral part of the city of New York, is less congested than any group of its suburbs, except those of less than 10,000 population.

Parts of cities then may be and frequently are less crowded than some suburbs. The broad contrast, however, stands, the roominess of the suburbs decreasing as they increase in population.

Scaling Down from the Parent City

Such immense contrasts in congestion as pertain between New York and its smaller suburbs do not exist in all cities. In Philadelphia, the least crowded of the larger cities, the scaling down of congestion is but slightly more than 50 per cent. even in the case of the smallest suburbs, as is seen in the following comparison:

TABLE 2—RATIO OF FAMILIES TO DWELLINGS IN THE PHILADELPHIA METROPOLITAN AREA

	Percentage of excess of families over dwellings
Philadelphia	12.4
Suburbs by population groups	
25,000–100,000	10.8
5,000– 10,000	8.7
2,500– 5,000 (16 cases)	5.1

Philadelphia has but two suburbs of from 10,000 to 25,000 population which are actually less congested than the average of the next smaller group. They do not, however, disprove the general tendency.

Average Congestion of Cities and Suburbs

It was noted that Philadelphia itself is less congested than the smaller New York suburbs as a group. Its own smaller suburbs are still more roomy than those of New York, though not proportionately so.

To realize on what different scales the tendency to decreasing suburban congestion works out in different cities is more important than to construct a composite

CITIES AND THEIR SUBURBS

measure of this phenomenon for all suburbs in contrast with all cities. A certain interest, however, attaches to the average excess of families over dwellings, worked out for a sample of the twenty-one large cities which have suburbs of 25,000 population and over. Congestion in these cities is compared with congestion in all their suburbs of the size just indicated and in a considerable number of their smaller suburbs. In the following comparison the results are expressed in medians rather than in mathematical averages:

TABLE 3—EXCESS OF FAMILIES OVER DWELLINGS IN 21 LARGE CITIES AND THEIR SUBURBS

Cities and Suburbs	Number	Percentage of excess of families over dwellings		
		Median	Range Smallest	Largest
Cities with suburbs of 25,000 population and over	21	34.7	6.5	71.4
Suburbs by size of population				
50,000–100,000	20	33.6	10.7	71.0
25,000– 50,000	44	24.4	5.8	59.0
10,000– 25,000	9	21.4	0.7	54.5
5,000– 10,000	16	7.0	2.9	36.0
2,500– 5,000	23	7.9	0.7	17.6

In a previous comparison we found the suburbs occupying ten times as much land as the cities for one third of the people. We now find a group of twenty-one parent cities with nearly five times the average congestion of their smaller suburbs. It is also to be noted that there is little difference in average congestion between the twenty suburban cities of from 50,000 to 100,000 population and the twenty-one parent cities of over 100,000 population; and also that the two smallest groups average close together though their range shows large variation.

Are Large "Suburbs" Suburban?

Since the largest subordinate cities are almost as crowded as the parent cities about which they cluster, it is fair to raise the question whether they should be

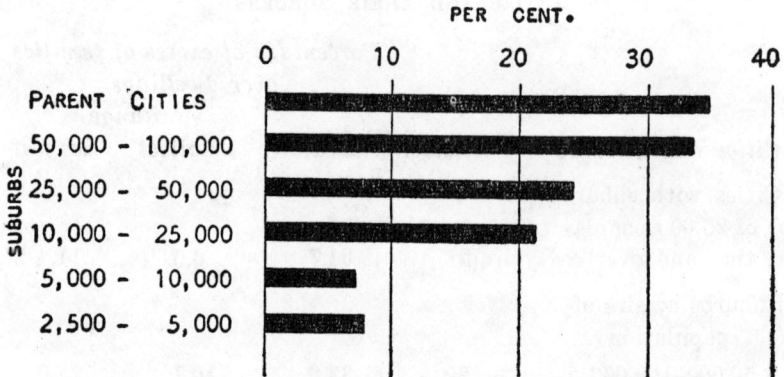

PERCENTAGE EXCESS OF FAMILIES OVER DWELLINGS FOR 21 CITIES AND THEIR SUBURBS BY SIZE GROUPS

called suburbs. We have shown that a basic distinction between city and suburb is between the more or less intensive use of land. From this point of view it is obvious that they classify themselves with the city. They have "gone up" almost as high, and whatever "going out" tendencies they once had are now entirely outstripped by the contrary tendency. The best term for these congested suburbs is perhaps "satellite cities."

It is beyond the purpose of this book to discuss at length why cities so frequently exist in clusters. The fact remains, however, that immediately adjacent populations, living under strictly urban conditions, do not always organize themselves under single political units. Generally a physical barrier is involved; sometimes a political difficulty like a state boundary line. For the present it is only necessary to insist that the relation between clustered cities is not always that of central city and suburbs. Satellite cities are not suburbs unless they exhibit suburban characteristics, of which roominess in comparison with the congestion of the central city is chief. Suburban communities may be found within the limits of cities. Purely urban character may likewise be found beyond their limits in satellite cities.

The satellite city is generally larger than the true suburb; but this is not invariably so. Very congested communities of from 10,000 to 25,000 population and even smaller are sometimes found immediately adjacent to a large city, of which they are simply extensions under separate political control. Such urban fragments may be discovered immediately across the Hudson River from New York at a point just opposite Grant's Tomb. When such small but crowded suburbs are surrounded by large areas of truly suburban territory the general character of which they are not able to change, they may properly be considered as exceptions within a suburban whole. When, however, they immediately join parent cities they are more correctly assigned to the urban than to the suburban category.

Laws of Suburbanization

We have noted the varying degrees to which urban populations thin out in the suburbs of different cities. New York contrasts strikingly with Philadelphia in this point as well as in the degree of central congestion. Such contrast suggests the inquiry whether any distinguishable principle governs the degree of suburbanization. Why does one city have more suburbs than another? Can we discover an empirical law which shall serve at least as a starting-point for our understanding of the matter?

A very elementary examination of the facts reveals two laws: (1) going out is proportionate to going up, and (2) the closeness of relation of the suburb to the city varies as its distance from the center.

Central Congestion Creates Suburbs by Reaction

An urban area generally has suburbs in about the proportion that it has an overcrowded center. Population is pressed out into the suburbs by the unusually severe struggle for space within the city. While people show considerable elasticity with respect to living arrangements and expect some degree of urban crowding, their capacity to endure congestion has limits. Consequently, when central crowding is excessive, the going-out process increases somewhat proportionately.

Convenient proof of this generalization is found by comparing the ratios of urban and suburban population for the sixty-eight American cities of 100,000 population and over (arranged by the census in fifty-eight metro-

CITIES AND THEIR SUBURBS

politan districts) and the excess of families over dwellings in the same cities, as shown in the following table:[4]

TABLE 4—CORRELATION OF SUBURBANIZATION AND CONGESTION IN LARGE CITIES

1—*Suburbanization Proportionate to Congestion*

A—To High Degree			B—To Considerable Degree		
Cities	Congestion	Rank by Suburbanization	Cities	Congestion	Rank by Suburbanization
Albany	1	1	Lowell	2	1
Providence	1	1	Norfolk	2	1
Springfield	1	1	Pittsburg	2	1
Boston	1	1	Worcester	1	2
Hartford	1	1	New York	1	2
Cincinnati	1	1	Fall River	1	2
New Haven	1	1	Los Angeles	3	2
Akron	2	2	Nashville	3	2
Louisville	2	2	Memphis	3	2
Atlanta	2	2	Washington	2	3
Bridgeport	2	2	Seattle	2	3
Syracuse	2	2	San Francisco	2	3
Fort Worth	3	3	Salt Lake City	4	3
Portland, Ore.	3	3	Grand Rapids	4	3
Spokane	3	3	Houston	4	3
Indianapolis	4	4	Toledo	4	3
Dallas	4	4	Des Moines	4	3
New Orleans	4	4	Omaha	4	3
Columbus	4	4	Kansas City	3	4
			San Antonio	3	4
			Rochester	3	4
			Denver	3	4
			Baltimore	3	4

[4] Calculated from Fourteenth Census, Vol. I, Tables 40 and 41, and Vol. II, p. 1271.

II—Suburbanization Not Proportionate to Congestion

A—More than			B—Less than		
Cities	Congestion	Rank by Suburbanization	Cities	Congestion	Rank by Suburbanization
Scranton	3	1	Buffalo	1	3
Birmingham	3	1	St. Louis	1	3
Youngstown	3	1	Detroit	2	4
Trenton	4	2	Minneapolis	2	4
Dayton	4	2	Richmond	2	4
Philadelphia	4	2	Chicago	1	4
Reading	4	1	Cleveland	1	4
Wilmington	4	1	Milwaukee	1	4

Counting the number of cities in the respective columns, one finds nineteen cases in which suburbanization is directly proportionate to congestion (Group IA) and twenty-three additional cases in which the tendencies of the two phenomena are to keep relatively close together (Group I-B). This gives a total of forty-two cases, or more than five out of every seven, in which going out is somewhat definitely proportionate to going up. In sixteen cases it is not proportionate (Group II). Eight are cities which have relatively larger suburbs than their central congestion calls for and eight cities which have relatively small suburbs considering their central congestion.[5]

[5] The method of reaching this correlation is as follows: The cities were ranked separately by percentage of suburbanization and congestion and divided into fourths on this basis. Those

CITIES AND THEIR SUBURBS

Turning to these cities which show exceptions to the general tendency, one comes upon ready explanation by merely reading down the columns. In the cases where suburbanization is relatively less than congestion (Group II-B), it is clearly topography which is to be reckoned with. Among them are Buffalo, Milwaukee, Chicago, Cleveland, and Detroit, all of which are limited in expansion by location on the Great Lakes, and St. Louis, Minneapolis and St. Paul (considered by the census as a single urban unit), and Richmond, all of them limited in expansion by the physical barrier of a sundering river. In three of these cases, while central congestion is above average, it is not extreme. This leaves but five cases in which extreme pressure at the center has failed to be accompanied by more than average dispersal of population. Four of these are limited by their sites to a semicircular area within which only is it possible to expand. Generalizing the case, one concludes that some cities thin out easily in all directions because noth-

---

marked 1 on either phenomenon belong to the upper fourth, that is, they show the highest degree of suburbanization or congestion; those marked 2 belong to the second fourth and show these phenomena in more than average degree; those marked 3 in less than average degree, and those marked 4 least of all. In Column 1 the degrees are exactly proportionate. Highest rates of suburbanization go with highest degrees of congestion, high with high, low with low, and lowest with lowest. In Column 2 the ranking numbers are never more than a single unit apart, thus showing corresponding tendencies. In Columns 3 and 4, however, the ranking numbers are separated by one or two intervals, thus showing widely deviating tendencies in the two phenomena compared.

ing restrains them. With others the suburban tendency is dammed up by physical barriers on one or more sides.

Again, the dominant industries of some cities make heavier demands upon space and necessitate larger areas than those of others. Reading down the column of cities which have relatively larger suburbs than their central congestion calls for, the influence of this factor is clear (Group II-A). Mining is such an industry. It is easy to see why so much of the Scranton district's population is in the surrounding coal-fields and so much of Birmingham's in the coal and iron towns and villages on either side of the city, in spite of the fact that neither city is itself crowded. The heavy steel industry of Youngstown has likewise spread over a large district, pulling population after it without the excuse of great central pressure. Ship-building, wharves, and heavy industries have also caused Philadelphia and Wilmington to sprawl out beyond any necessity based on central congestion. Virtually all the cases in which the suburban population is greater than the crowding of the city explains, are to be accounted for on this score.

Our generalization should therefore be amended to read: In urban areas of similar topographical and economic character, going out is proportionate to going up. Except where physical barriers prevent the equivalent spread of a city, or where, on the other hand, the nature of its economic life facilitates or compels its spread, cities with the greatest excess of families over dwellings tend to show the higher proportion of suburban population and vice versa.

To the law as thus corrected very few exceptions, if

CITIES AND THEIR SUBURBS 29

any, will be found. Such exceptions, if they occur, must be charged to combinations of factors, partly psychological, whereby unusual prestige may get arbitrarily attached either to city or to suburb to a degree which checks the operations of the major forces above disclosed.

DISTANCE AND DEPENDENCE

Our second major generalization is: The more distant from the city the less closely related a suburb is and the more independent is its community life. The reverse is also true.

Even a crude handling of limited data discovers this second empirical law. The same qualification must be made as in the case of the former one: the law applies to suburban communities which are similar to one another in character. Its operation may be seen in the Long Island suburbs of New York City. These are relatively homogeneous residential communities, manufacturing having chiefly developed in other directions. A comparison of sixty-two of these suburbs,[6] located beyond the area of active street-car commutation and dependent upon a single railway, reveals that the proportion of commuters to total population averages about 20 per cent. at fifteen miles, 15 per cent. at twenty miles, and 10 per cent. at twenty-five miles. In other words, as evidenced by this criterion and within these distances, every additional five miles decreases the economic de-

[6] Based upon reports of the Long Island Railway of the average number of commuters for 1922.

pendence of the suburb upon the city at a geometrical rate.

This result does not contradict our earlier discovery that, with respect to distance from the center, the suburban zone is fluctuating; and also that facility of transportation is ever present as a determining factor of the degree of relationship to the city. It merely shows the average results for homogeneous suburbs whose relation to the city would naturally be alike except for the fact of distance.

Classes of Exceptions

The exceptions revealed by this calculation show, as our previous analysis foresaw, that equal distance does not always mean equal urban dependence. In the sixty-two cases, five classes of exceptions were found:

(1) Communities devoted to agriculture. Here, for example, within the most intensive commuting area, lies a little community specializing upon the raising of bulbs and flowers. In spite of the fact that towns lying just beyond it have upward of fifty trains per day, few of them stop here. Few of its people commute because the direct economic relations of most of them are with the soil rather than with the city.

(2) Old and self-contained communities, with venerable historic traditions and exceptional wealth, are not attached to the city as closely as others at the same distance which were built up by the overflow of city people. The former knew the city when it was young. Their

CITIES AND THEIR SUBURBS

attitude toward it is that of the old home town toward a son who has become famous; respectful but not overawed. They maintain their old traditions and peacefully go their own way, while newer suburbs are mere dependent creations of the city with no separate history or strong self-consciousness.

(3) A political capital, like Mineola, the county-seat of Nassau County, New York, has 50 per cent. fewer commuters than neighboring towns of similar size and with the same train service. Here is something of a local trading-center, the seat of many county institutions and of the administration of special agencies, like the county Y. M. C. A. and Red Cross. This gives it a complexion and life of its own and makes it less suburban than its neighbors.

(4) Suburban communities chiefly populated by mechanics rather than by business people, and generally on a lower economic level, have relatively fewer commuters. One may guess that this is because, unlike the clerk's or business man's work, the mechanic's job is now here and now there. Accordingly his dependence upon the city for work is fluctuating and not fixed by any single place. It does not take him over the repetitious path of the commuter. Perhaps he is himself engaged in suburban building operations. Possibly, not going and coming regularly, he boards the street-car inconveniently instead of becoming a regular commuter by train.

(5) The relation of the summer-resort suburbs to the city is equivocal. Their permanent residents are not

largely commuters. Their seasonal population also does not go back and forth with proportionate frequency because it is on vacation. There are, to be sure, vast numbers of summer commuters; but their roots are not permanently fixed in the resort suburb, and they do not link it to the city by regular ties. As a net result such suburbs are not as closely related to it as their distance would suggest.

With these exceptions, the tendency which makes closeness of relation to the city proportionate to the distance of the suburbs apparently works out for the New York metropolitan area for suburbs like those of Long Island up to a distance of twenty-five miles. Beyond this distance the suburbs are fewer and dependence does not seem to vary directly as to distance. The factors of transportation and the character of the individual community dominate but do not develop any general trend.

Summary

We may therefore assert that the process of suburbanization has laws: (1) that its magnitude is generally proportionate to the congestion of the city center, and (2) that its relation to the city tends to vary directly as its distance from that center. Variations in the character of individual suburbs modify the ways in which these principles work out, yet their operation creates the skeleton of outlying metropolitan structure upon which suburban life and character forms itself.

CITIES AND THEIR SUBURBS

Social Consequences of the Suburban Trend

Merely articulating the skeleton of the suburbs fails, however, to reveal their heart. They are far more than a certain physical dispersion of population in areas relatively near to city centers. Distance and spaciousness in contrast with nearness and congestion are only the conditions of suburbanization. The important fact is the increasing social separateness and the consciousness of independence which arise within the continued fact of dependence upon the city and the continued realization of it. That such an increasing separation, both in practical relations and in thought and feeling, accompanies every successive degree of departure from the city in distance and in difference of physical character, is the essence of the suburban trend. Within this trend a suburb may be defined as a community in which the social consequences of these separations from the city have become clear and demonstrable. It arises, in other words, only when these consequences have definably registered in such a way that they can be recorded. A suburb is more than a distant fringe of the city. It is a community developing according to a distinctive social pattern which it more or less distinctly realizes.

At what distance and in connection with what degree of spaciousness, in contrast with city congestion, such a pattern will arise, differs from suburb to suburb. Examples already noted make this fact obvious, and a subsequent chapter, showing how suburbs differ from each other, will suggest abundantly the reasons why. For the present it is important only to insist that in the suburbs one finds a social structure differing even from that of the outlying parts of the city, accompanied by a special type of community consciousness. Only when these things are encountered can one find a true suburb.

So much might be presumed on the strength of the previous analysis of the suburban trend. The soil and the pavements grow different crops, even though the soil is cut up into minute suburban plots. The actual explanation, as subsequent chapters will show, lies, however, in the difference between the total elements which make up the city and the part which gets transplanted to the suburbs. The things which are in the city, which go on in the city, which *are* the city, have a very unequal capacity for decentralization. Some can be suburbanized and others cannot. It is by studying these "cans" and "cannots" that one comes to understand the suburb as a social fact and the accompanying mind of its people.

Psychological Selection of Suburbanites

The people of the residential suburbs, at least, live where they do by reason of natural selection based on a peculiar psychology and motivation. This is a second major clue to the heart of the suburban situation. As between families equally in position to exercise choice, some are naturally responsive to the suburban trend and others are not. The former desire to escape from the city or wish to preserve town forms in connection with urban opportunities; primarily, one assumes, for the sake of family privacy and independence. Again, they may have a sort of esthetic affinity for a suburban environment. In any case they are a chosen people separated from their fellow city-men by the strength of a particular group of inner attributes.

The Social Bases of Suburbs Narrower than Those of Cities

Both materially and humanly, then, the suburbs, all told, contain only part of the elements found in the city. They represent selection. Out of the particular elements which can be and actually are decentralized they build a peculiar community life. The stuff which they have to use is limited both in quantity and adaptability. Their materials are urban fragments rather than urban wholes. They must make what they can out of what they have, meanwhile remaining dependent upon the central city for what they have not.

The particular elements which are or are not available differ from suburb to suburb. Consequently the social results differ; the outcome is sometimes fortunate and at other times not. Hence no generalization is possible, as, for example, that the suburbs are better or worse than the city. On the whole it is easier to build a true and self-conscious community out of the available materials than it is to do so out of the complex and conflicting materials of the city; but much harder than in the independent town of equal size. The sifting out for decentralization of a limited number of functions and of peculiar types of people does not often result in a good collection of elements for an all-round community life. On the other hand the suburb's materials are simpler than those of the city. In many respects it is fortunate not to have to deal with the whole mass of urban factors at once. As a community the suburb is more homogeneous. Furthermore it is newer than the city and hence more plastic, more likely to be tractable. It uses the old forms of village and town life to which human nature is accustomed because it was created in them. They are less of a strain upon it. Consequently in the suburbs it should show its better aspects.

The Suburbs the Hope of the City

Because they constitute an unscrambling of an over-complex situation, because they are largely composed of like-minded people to whom coöperation should not be difficult, and because of the environmental advantages of roominess, the suburbs, in spite of their limitations, are the most promising aspect of urban civilization. By the very experience of revulsion by which they have taken themselves out of the central congestion of city life they are committed to finding or creating a solution of the city's problems as well as of their own. Formed out of the dust of cities, they wait to have breathed into them the breath of community sentiment, of neighborly fraternity and peace. They reflect the unspoiled and youthful aspect of urban civilization, the adolescent and not yet disillusionized part of the city, where, if at all, happiness and worthy living may be achieved, as well as material well-being.

Summary and Review

This the opening chapter of the story of the suburbs has described and analyzed them and offered certain more general clues to the viewpoint of the book. The next step is to measure their present extent and their growth. Following this, the third and fourth chapters show how they vary and suggest why. Already the discussion has found itself compelled to enter the realm of economics. It therefore goes on to discuss the costs of suburban living and how they are met. It has touched upon the peculiar psychology of the suburban people and suggested special aspects of social life and organization which rear themselves upon the suburban ground pattern. It has noted the special character of the rural suburb as a metropolitan fringe rather than a continuous suburban zone. It has assumed the desirability of decentralization, of which the suburbs are the essential expression, and will naturally be concerned with deliberate attempts to facilitate and accelerate the process. Finally it has ventured to believe that the suburbs are in great measure the hope of the future city.

These various suggestions and outlooks constitute major topics for the subsequent chapters of the book.

CHAPTER II

MEASURING THE SUBURBAN TREND

THE rapid growth of American cities compared with and largely at the expense of country population has impressed the imagination probably more than any other contemporary social tendency. Commonplace as the fact has become, it remains a staggering commonplace, one challenging repeated attention. From the standpoint of the present discussion, urban growth comprehends two tendencies, one central, the other peripheral. The first relates to the cities proper, the second to their suburbs.

In order to comprehend the growth and extent of the urban trend as a whole, one needs to compare the two tendencies with one another and with the total growth of population.

This the present chapter seeks to do summarily. It considers the past, present, and future of suburban growth. It first examines the rate of suburban growth in recent years. Second it measures the extent of the suburbs today. Finally it touches upon the contemporary trend as prophetic of the still larger suburbs of to-morrow.

THE GROWTH OF SUBURBS

Are any means at hand for the accurate measurement and comparison of suburban growth? A general

MEASURING THE SUBURBAN TREND 39

difficulty confronts one at this point. In the previous chapter we have been at great pains to insist that cities do not end nor suburbs begin with legal boundaries; and furthermore, that true suburbs are specific social structures built upon the foundations of certain limited aspects of the city which have been decentralized.

When, however, one attempts to measure the suburbs he has only the data of the Federal Census. This is based either upon political units or upon a confessedly arbitrary definition of "metropolitan districts" and "adjacent territory." The former include "those suburban areas which lie within approximately ten miles beyond the municipal limits and in which the density of population is 150 per square mile or more." The "adjacent territory is the total suburban territory regardless of its density of population which lies within a distance of approximately ten miles of the central city."

Metropolitan districts, as above described, are recognized only in the cases of cities of 200,000 population and upward; while the population of suburban adjacent territory is also given for all cities of 100,000 population and upward.

The census does not systematically explain or defend the grounds of its distinction nor does it give reasons for not recognizing suburbs of still smaller cities. That they are more likely to have large elements of purely rural population within ten miles of their municipal limits is incidentally pointed out.[1] It is evidently not believed that the influence of the smaller city, within the same distance zone, is as great or exactly of the same

---
[1] Fourteenth Census, Vol. I, p. 63.

sort as the influence of the larger one. Its suburbs are not suburban in the same sense as those of the larger cities. The making of this distinction is a significant attempt to reflect some of the actual differences which the analysis of the first chapter discovered. Defining the suburbs in this way we may measure their growth. The categories used, though arbitrary, are the only ones available and undoubtedly present a rough quantitative expression of the suburban trend.

Increase of Suburban Population, 1910–1920

Combining the sixty-eight American cities of 100,000 population and upward in 1920 into sixty-two urban communities, the census finds a gain of about 2,133,714 suburban inhabitants during the previous decade. The rate of increase is 25.5 per cent. in the central cities and 29.1 per cent. in the adjacent suburbs.

This more rapid growth of the suburbs as compared with the city is true, however, only of the cities of above 200,000 population. Considering the sixty-eight cities in two groups gives the following results:

Table 5—Increase of Metropolitan Population, 1910–20

	Percentage of increase
A—Cities of 200,000 population and over	
Central city	25.1
Metropolitan district outside central city	32.7
Adjacent territory	30.3
Total	26.5
B—Cities of 100,000–200,000 population	
Central city	30.9
Adjacent territory	19.0

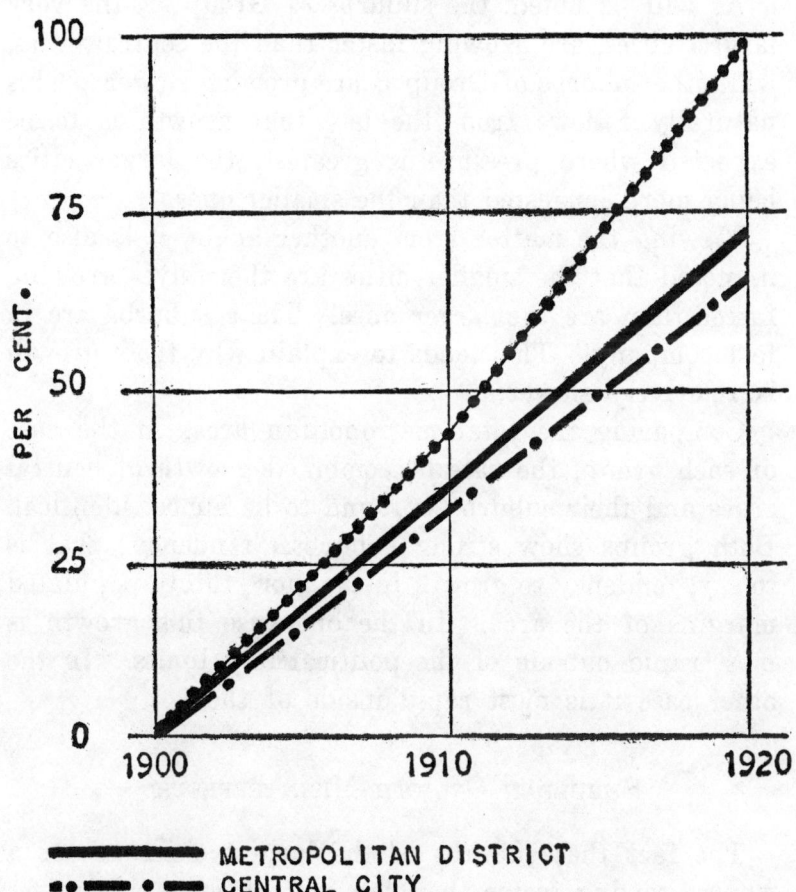

SUBURBS GROWING FASTER THAN CITIES

Percentage increase of city and suburban population, 1900 to 1920, compared with increase of population of total metropolitan districts for 28 cities of 200,000 population and over in 1910.

As will be noted, the suburbs of Group A, the very largest cities, are growing faster than the central cities, while the suburbs of Group B are growing slower. This naturally follows from the law that growth is to be expected where pressure is greatest, the larger cities being more congested than the smaller ones.

Viewing the matter from another angle, it is also to be noted that the smaller cities are themselves growing faster than are the larger ones. Their suburbs are in fast company. This tends to explain why their growth is relatively slower.

Comparing the total metropolitan areas in the case of each group, the rate of combined growth of central cities and their suburbs is found to be almost identical. Both groups show strong suburban tendency; that is to say, tendency to growth in the more thinly populated margins of the area. In the one case this growth is most rapid outside of the political city limits. In the other case it is most rapid inside of them.

Suburban Growth Misinterpreted

The fact that suburbs of the largest cities are as a whole growing faster than the central cities themselves largely explains an anomaly in the census showing, namely, the unusual growth of cities of 25,000 to 100,000 population. These cities have increased their population by almost exactly one third, while those of over 100,000 population have increased by only about one fourth. Examining the matter more closely, one finds, however, that nearly one third of all cities of 25,000 to

MEASURING THE SUBURBAN TREND 43

100,000 population are suburbs. Their growth is the spill-over of great cities and part of the metropolitan movement. This is what brings up their statistical showing. The independent small city is not exceeding the larger city in rate of growth.

A similar "joker" appears in census figures purporting to show the increase of rural population in certain highly urbanized States like Connecticut and New Jersey. The farms of these States have not increased in number nor changed in size, while the average size of the rural family is virtually stationary. It is obvious, therefore, that the rural growth which is statistically shown is non-agricultural. It is, as a matter of fact, suburban. Suburban growth thus appears at many points and enters into unexpected relationships where it greatly needs to be recognized.

Substantially the same rate of excessive suburban growth was going on between 1900 and 1910 as during the last decade.

As a net result of the uneven growth of urban communities of various sorts and sizes the large city now holds a slightly smaller fraction of the total population of the nation than in 1910, while the suburbs—and the total metropolitan areas because of the suburbs—hold an appreciably larger one.

URBAN AND SUBURBAN GROWTH OF INDIVIDUAL CITIES

Appendix, p. 331 summarizes the growth of metropolitan centers of 200,000 population and over, and their suburbs. These illustrate immense variations in the rate of growth which the averages previously used fail to suggest. Of the thirty-two cities of this size, Louisville, with an increase of but 4 per cent., shows the slowest growth, and Akron, with an increase of 201 per cent., the largest growth of the central city. Baltimore, by reason of the annexation of a large suburban area, registers a loss of 49 per cent. in suburban population, while on the other hand Detroit gained 255 per cent. The most frequent rate of urban growth is between 20 and 30 per cent., with the median rate of 22 per cent. illustrated by Milwaukee. The most frequent rate of suburban growth is between 30 and 40 per cent., with a median of 32 per cent. illustrated by Columbus and Kansas City. In other words, the respective contributions of the cities of the generalized result above noted is so uneven that only a study of the actual data city by city can unravel the texture of the facts.

Why Suburbs Grow

Passing on to an attempt to explain why suburbs grow, one is thrown back upon the hypothesis offered in the previous chapter: suburbs grow because cities grow and because cities grow more crowded. Both homes and industries are increasingly crowded out, the severest pressure being experienced now by the one, now by the other. As a net result "going out," we found, was roughly proportionate to "going up."

A study of facts from the standpoint of growth generally confirms the previous conclusion. In more than

MEASURING THE SUBURBAN TREND 45

half of the cases, cities of over 200,000 population which are growing rapidly within the political city are also growing rapidly in the suburbs. The trend is clear. Flagrant exceptions where "inside" growth has been arbitrarily accelerated by wholesale annexation have already been illustrated in the case of Baltimore. Such apparent exceptions do not affect the principle.

Other exceptions are apparently to be explained by the factor of time. They are, in the main, cities which were already highly congested previous to 1910 but which physical barriers held back from earlier suburban expansion. During the decade the dam has broken and population has overflowed.

The specific cause is frequently the belated provision of transit facilities. Such facilities are not infallibly forthcoming the moment they are needed, as the experience of many a city can testify. Hence, within a given decade, the rate of growth may not exactly reflect the degree of internal congestion, though it would in all probability be found to do so if compared for a larger number of cities over a longer period of time.

Studying the matter from the standpoint of congestion, the census enables one to discover whether a rapid increase in crowding is immediately reflected in a corresponding increase of suburban population. Here the bare statistical results appear more dubious. It should be obvious, however, that in thinly populated cities a great percentage of increase in the excess of families over dwellings might take place without bringing the city as a whole to the point where suburban growth results. They are in position to take care of a strong "going out" tendency within their political limits. In the case, however, of cities which are already congested the response of the suburban process is clear. In proportion as congestion increases beyond the average, the suburban movement is accelerated and with but little delay.

WHERE SUBURBS GROW

Because so many of the most rapidly growing "suburbs" of the largest cities are themselves cities in size and character, doubt has been expressed as to whether the suburban growth shown by census statistics is not mainly that of close-in and relatively congested and urbanized communities not yet annexed to the city, rather than in true suburbs. "We need," says the objector, "some more accurate measure than is contained in these data before we can safely conclude that there is any definite tendency toward living in the less congested parts of our metropolitan areas."[2]

The census has somewhat forestalled this objection by lumping the population of suburbs of over 100,000 population with those of the parent cities in some of its calculations. Thus Cambridge is combined with Boston, Oakland with San Francisco, Camden with Philadelphia, and its four larger suburbs with New York. In other

[2] Warren S. Thompson, "Growth of Population in Outlying Parts of Metropolitan Districts," "Journal of the American Statistical Association," Vol. XVIII, p. 578.

MEASURING THE SUBURBAN TREND 47

words, the census recognizes that these are not true suburbs; consequently it excludes them before attempting to measure suburban growth.

This, however, only begins to clear up the matter; and, since a calculation for all suburban communities would go beyond the method open to the present discussion, a limited sample has been examined from New York, St. Louis, and Washington. This probably illustrates sufficiently the dual suburban trend, namely, that within and that without the city boundaries.

WHERE SUBURBS GROW MOST RAPIDLY

For New York City the smaller and less crowded suburbs are growing very much faster than the larger ones, as shown by the following table, which adds a column covering relative degree of congestion:

TABLE 6—INCREASE OF POPULATION COMPARED WITH CONGESTION IN NEW YORK METROPOLITAN AREA

New York City suburbs by population	Percentage of increase of population 1910–20	Percentage of excess of families over dwellings
2,500– 10,000	43.5	16.3
10,000– 25,000	31.6	31.0
25,000–100,000	21.2	49.0
All suburbs	24.2	43.2
New York City	17.9	71.0
Richmond Borough	35.6	23.2

This table is strong evidence that both in the city and in its suburbs, the rate of growth is greatest where congestion is least. It is especially noteworthy that one of the five boroughs of the city proper has less congestion than any of the suburban size-groups except the smallest one; also that it grew faster than any except that particular group. As is well known, Manhattan Island actually lost population during the last decade, and the fear that the showing of suburban growth was really that of large and urbanized suburbs is definitely disproved.

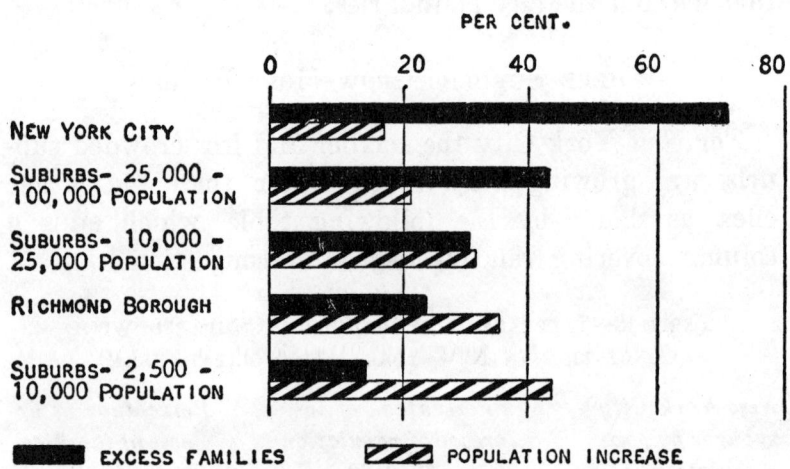

GROWTH IS GREATEST WHERE CONGESTION IS LEAST

Percentage excess of families over dwellings in New York City, Richmond Borough, and suburbs by size groups compared with increase in population, 1910–20.

WASHINGTON

The available data for Washington, though not based on identical or exactly comparable periods, demonstrates the same tendency.

MEASURING THE SUBURBAN TREND 49

TABLE 7—INCREASE OF POPULATION IN "OLD" WASHINGTON, IN THE DISTRICT OF COLUMBIA, AND SUBURBS

Area	Percentage of gain or loss in population	Average population per acre
1907–15		
Original area covered by L'Enfant's plan	6.5 loss	89.5
Remainder of the District of Columbia	48.7 gain	7.0 [3]
1910–20		
City of Washington	32.2 gain	—
Suburbs outside of the District of Columbia	39.6 gain	—

In the case of Washington, the "suburbs within the city" (of which the outlying portions of the District of Columbia has many) were growing more rapidly up to 1915 than were the suburbs outside of the city for the census period. Undoubtedly a considerable proportion of this growth was in an essentially urban environment. Nevertheless, from both standpoints, the major phenomenon is the actual decrease of population in the most congested portion of the city and the very large growth of the more roomy portion of the metropolitan area both within and without the District of Columbia. Both mark a genuinely suburban trend.

ST. LOUIS

The data for St. Louis distinguish within the city the

[3] Bulletin of Children's Bureau, U. S. Department of Labor, "Facilities for Children's Play in the District of Columbia" (1917), p. 9.

districts east of Jefferson Street, generally including the wards touching the river and roughly defining the old city, and the newer districts touching the western boundaries. The situation is shown in the following table:[4]

TABLE 8—INCREASE OF POPULATION IN THE ST. LOUIS METROPOLITAN AREA

St. Louis, 1910–20 Within the city	Percentage of gain or loss in population	Range of gain or loss
Districts east of Jefferson St.	6.2 loss	29.3 loss—0.3 gain
Districts touching western boundaries	30.0 gain	19.0–43.0 gain
City and suburbs		
City	12.5 gain	—
Adjacent territory	26.4 gain	—

As in the other cases, St. Louis shows a rate of increase in the more open parts of the city itself somewhat beyond that of the suburbs in general. This is not strange, since the suburbs within the city are naturally the first expression of the suburban trend. Many such areas, indeed, are true suburbs in character. They afford an advantageous compromise even when they do not attain the full advantage of the independent suburbs. On the whole it strengthens the evidence of the suburban trend to show that it begins within the city, as our previous analysis prophesied. The going-out process is essentially of one piece. To be sure, some of the rapidly growing areas within the city limits are by no means

[4] Douglass, "The St. Louis Church Survey," p. 303.

MEASURING THE SUBURBAN TREND

suburbs in character. Others, however, are distinctly so both in social functions and conditions of living.

A Widely Distributed Sample

Still further statistical evidence as to the incidence of rapid growth is found in a sampling of 108 suburbs of ten representative cities of 100,000 population and over. In the case of the suburbs generally it was proved, as in the case of New York City, that the larger ones have a higher average of congestion. The calculation sought to determine whether or not they were also growing faster. For the 108 suburbs the median excess of families over dwellings was 18 per cent., which is just about half the average excess for the parent cities. Dividing the 108 suburbs into two equal classes gave fifty-four with more than 18 per cent. more families than dwellings and fifty-four others had less than 18 per cent. more families than dwellings. The growth of the two groups between 1910 and 1920 is compared in the following table:

Rate of Growth and number growing or not growing	*54 more congested suburbs*	*54 roomier suburbs*
Median percentage of growth	32	41
Number growing 100 per cent. or more	7	12
Number growing 50 per cent. or more	15	23
Number losing population	3	0

This conclusively shows a much higher percentage of the more roomy suburbs growing and growing rapidly, while none are losing population. The above sample covers nearly one tenth of the total number of incorporated suburbs and is ample to demonstrate the trend. The conclusion is that suburban growth as measured is most largely in the more open and least congested suburbs and that the fear that the statistics are not true to the facts is quite unfounded.

Extent of the Present Suburbs

The present suburban population of the United States may be estimated in round numbers at fifteen millions, or about 15 per cent. of the total population of the nation in 1920.

To reach this estimate, one starts with more than ten millions of suburban population tributary to cities of 100,000 population and over as recognized by the census. He must then add:

(1) A fair estimate for the suburbs of still smaller cities.
(2) An estimate for the population of true suburbs within city boundaries.
(3) An estimate for suburban population of very large cities beyond the ten-mile limit of the census.

He must then subtract:

An estimate for the non-suburban population within the ten-mile limit of certain cities.

MEASURING THE SUBURBAN TREND

SUBURBAN OPPORTUNITIES WITHIN THE LIMITS OF A CROWDED CITY

The specific process of carrying out these additions and substractions throws such light upon the suburban problem that they are worth tracing in some detail.

Extent of the Suburbs According to the Census

Table 9 shows the facts as the census reveals them:[5]

Table 9—Total City and Suburban Population of Cities of 100,000 Population and Over

	Total	200,000 and over	100,000–200,000
Number of cities	62	32	30
Aggregate city population	26,254,645	22,111,380	4,143,265
Suburban population	10,632,316	8,077,163	2,555,153

Of the 8,077,163 people living in the suburbs of cities of over 200,000 population, 7,127,202 live under density conditions of more than 150 per square mile, while the remaining 949,961 live within ten miles of the city boundaries but not under urban conditions of density.

Suburbs of Still Smaller Cities

To the above more than ten millions of suburbanites we have agreed to add a fair estimate of suburbs of still smaller cities. The aggregate population of cities of the three size-groups below 100,000 as enumerated by the

[5] Fourteenth Census, Vol. I, p. 63 and 72. The totals in this table (for sixty-two cities) differ from those given on p. 18 (for sixty-eight cities) because in this the census counts as suburbs the other six cities of 100,000 population and over which are very much smaller than their parent cities. The aggregate of metropolitan populations is of course the same.

MEASURING THE SUBURBAN TREND 55

census was about seventeen million in 1920, divided as follows:

NUMBER AND AGGREGATE POPULATION OF CITIES OF 10,000 TO 100,000 POPULATION

Population range	Number of cities	Aggregate population
50,000–100,000	76	5,265,747
25,000– 50,000	143	5,075,041
10,000– 25,000	459	6,942,742

With respect to the suburbs of these cities two questions arise: first, how small a city can have suburbs? and second, how can one estimate the number of suburban people for the descending size-groups when the census has not counted them directly?

As already noted, the census implies that even cities of 100,000 to 200,000 population do not have suburbs in the same sense that the largest cities do. A subsequent chapter will characterize the suburbs of these smaller cities, showing why suburban life cannot mean exactly the same thing that it does in larger ones.[6] The question, however, has no absolute answer. It is obvious that some of these smaller cities have genuine suburbs. Since no considerable number of them have been studied directly, it is necessary to set an arbitrary limit for the purposes of the present calculation. The line will accordingly be drawn at cities of 25,000 to 100,000 population. It is assumed that the 219 cities of this size may have suburbs, while it is doubted whether the 459 cities of from 10,000 to 25,000 population have suburban population in any considerable number. That

[6] Page 116.

the later should not be entirely ignored in our thinking is obvious, since in experience one frequently finds industrial or foreign communities adjoining cities of this size, which have all the traits of genuine suburban dependencies. Our purpose, however, is merely to make a reasonable guess of the total suburban population, and for this purpose the limitation above suggested may properly serve.

How many suburbanites, then, are there living on the margins of the 219 cities of from 25,000 to 100,000 population? One may roughly estimate about two millions. He will reach this conclusion by observing the proportion of suburban population to the total metropolitan population in cities where its size is known. This is shown in the following table:

TABLE 10—PERCENTAGE OF POPULATION OF METROPOLITAN AREAS OF VARIOUS SIZE WHICH IS SUBURBAN

Population of city and adjacent territory	Percentage suburban
1,000,000 and over	29.8
750,000–1,000,000	20.2
500,000– 750,000	25.2
200,000– 500,000	26.0
150,000– 200,000	24.2
100,000– 150,000	20.1

On the whole the smaller the metropolitan population the smaller the proportion of it which is found in the suburbs. The general trend is slightly downward, though its course is not exactly regular. Following this trend one reaches the conclusion that suburban population of cities under 100,000 population will likely be

MEASURING THE SUBURBAN TREND

somewhat less than one fifth of the total population of city and suburbs. For the more than ten and a quarter millions of people of these 219 cities we may therefore count approximately two millions of suburbanites.

Adding these to the more than ten and one half million population suburban to the larger cities gives an estimated total of more than twelve and one half millions.

Further Additions and Subtractions

Lacking a complete study of the density of population and character of community life in the outlying portions of political cities, one can only resort to a very rough estimate as to the number of suburbanites which they contain. General knowledge of cities, however, suggests that these "suburbs within the city" are fairly extensive [7] and it will be entirely conservative to add two millions more population from this source to swell the suburban total.

The area comprehended within the "Plan for New York City and Its Environs" has nearly a million more population than the suburbs of New York as recognized by the census. The determination of the territory to be included was the result of most careful and scientific analysis of populations and their relations to the central city. A number of the most distinctive suburbs of Chicago are beyond the arbitrary ten-mile limit as fixed

[7] As for example in Los Angeles, Baltimore, and Rochester, to say nothing of Queens and Richmond Boroughs of New York City.

by the census, and Chicago's new regional planning reaches fifty miles out. Speaking as a city planner, George B. Ford of the Technical Advisory Corporation illustrates the extent of the suburban zone for cities of different sizes as follows: for New York, forty to fifty miles; for Boston, Buffalo, Cleveland, and St. Louis, twenty to twenty-five miles; for New Haven, Norfolk, and Omaha, fifteen miles.

Some of this additional population will be offset by people living near to the smaller cities who are not really suburbanites though counted as such by the census. As a result of give and take between the two factors, one will be safe in making a net addition of a million population to the suburban estimate, bringing the total up to fifteen million of our fellow-citizens. This is no mean fraction of the nation. The lives and fortunes of this multitude must be granted every value that attaches to any other portion of the American people. Thus considered in themselves alone the suburbs present a significant phenomenon. Furthermore they constitute an extension of the urban problem of the most instant and impressive importance.

Incorporated Suburban Communities

The extent of the suburbs may be measured much more accurately in terms of places than in terms of people. The sixty-eight cities, with populations of 100,000 population and over, include within their surburban areas 1025 incorporated towns and cities of 500 population and upward. The following table shows the size-groups into which these communities are divided and the percentage of all communities in the United States of similar size which are suburban:

TABLE 11—NUMBER AND PERCENTAGE OF ALL TOWNS AND SMALL CITIES WHICH ARE SUBURBAN TO CITIES OF 100,000 AND OVER

Population	Number suburban	Percentage of total which are suburban
500– 1,000	165	5
1,000– 2,500	324	11
2,500– 5,000	216	15
5,000– 10,000	152	21
10,000– 25,000	102	22
25,000–100,000	66	32

As previously noted, virtually one third of all cities of from 25,000 to 100,000 population are themselves suburban. Over one fifth of all towns and cities from 5000 to 25,000 population are suburban. Combining

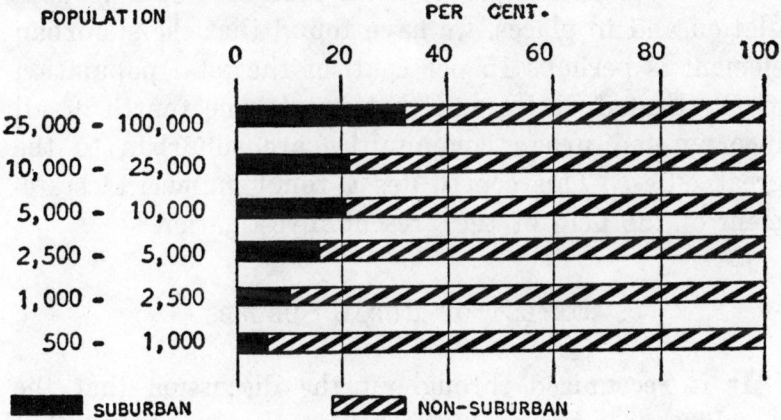

PERCENTAGE OF ALL INCORPORATED PLACES OF 500 TO 100,000 POPULATION WHICH ARE SUBURBAN TO CITIES OF 100,000 AND OVER, BY SIZE GROUPS

all groups of urban size according to the census definition, that is to say, about 2,500 population, one finds nearly one fourth of all urban incorporated communities are suburbs of the great cities. No one has counted how many more are suburbs of smaller cities. The total in any case would not cover all the solidly built and densely inhabited areas adjoining cities, since exceedingly large numbers of them are unincorporated. The calculation only shows therefore that a very large fraction of smaller American communities of any considerable size cluster around cities, as do a much smaller but still significant percentage of strictly rural ones.

Thus New York alone has 129 incorporated suburbs, Pittsburg 71, Chicago 67, Philadelphia 57, Boston 55. The distribution of the entire 857 incorporated suburbs with respect to their parent cities is shown in Appendix I.

Summing the matter up with reference both to population and to places, we have found that the suburban element is perhaps 15 per cent. of the total population of the United States and that nearly one fourth of all incorporated urban communities are suburban to the great cities. This constitutes a rough numerical statement of the field of the present investigation.

Extent of Rural Suburbs

It is recognized throughout the discussion that the rural suburbs are not suburban in the same sense that the true suburbs are. A separate chapter is given to their discussion; and while their extent cannot be definitely measured the problem should be contemplated independently. Naturally they cannot be measured in number of incorporated places since well over four fifths of rural population lives outside of such places in hamlets or in the open country.

Speaking positively, the extent of the rural suburbs can only be suggested by illustrating the surprising fashion that rural population has of massing about great cities. Not only do the cities go out with a subsidiary form of urban civilization, but they draw about them relatively dense agricultural populations. Instead of being competitive with agriculture in their immediate vicinity, the great cities actually create the conditions under which increasing agricultural populations are brought in to people the rural suburbs.

This is well established by the census, though unfortunately not exactly measured. It stands out even in the most general statistics. Thus the Middle Atlantic States with the smallest percentage of rural population compared with urban have at the same time the greatest density of rural population per square mile. In other words, such country people as they have tend, throughout the whole region, to be piled up thick about the urban populations.

The same phenomenon is shown in greater detail by the census mapping of rural population per square mile by counties. Even a superficial study of this map shows the massing of rural population about virtually every great city. How much of it falls to the smaller suburban towns and how much to actual farm population is not directly indicated anywhere by census data. Interesting bits of evidence, however, exist. A recent religious survey of Worcester County, Massachusetts, for example, began by isolating the twenty-six rural towns of the county from the thirty-two industrial im-

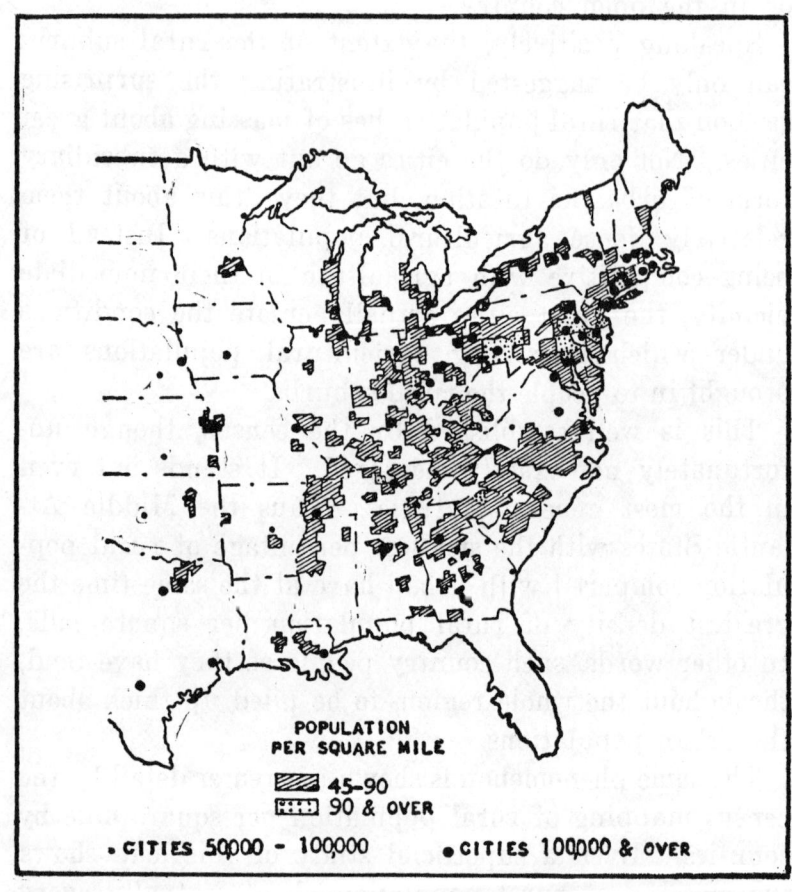

MASSING OF RURAL POPULATION IN THE VICINITY OF CITIES

Counties in the Eastern half of the United States with a rural population of 45 per square mile and over.

(Adapted from Fourteenth United States Census, Vol. 1, p. 89.)

MEASURING THE SUBURBAN TREND 63

mediately surrounding the cities in order to study the social and religious needs of farm population. The surprising discovery was then made that the industrial towns had more farmers per town than the rural ones. In other words, the place to study the mass of Worcester County farmers was in the rural suburbs where the majority were.

Again we have fragmentary evidence that actual farm population adjacent to cities engages very extensively in urban pursuits. A census monograph entitled "Farm Population of Selected Counties" shows the following variations for eight counties:

TABLE 12—PERCENTAGE OF FARM POPULATION ENGAGED IN NON-AGRICULTURAL PURSUITS

Types of counties	Number	Percentage
With no cities	4	5– 7
With small cities	3	10–15
With large city (Seattle)	1	24

Here are virtually a fourth of the people of the farms adjoining Seattle engaged in business other than farming. This is especially frequent among males from farm-owner families and females from farm-labor families. The men work as carpenters and machinists; in shipyards and sawmills; in lumber-camps; as railroad and highway laborers; as salesmen, commercial travelers, and deliverymen. The women go most frequently into domestic service, next into clerical work, teaching, telephone service, and nursing. It is not proved how many are actually working in Seattle or that the same percentage would hold for other cities. It undoubtedly reveals, however, what more extensive statistics would show conclusively; namely, the very extensive economic contacts between members of families actually living on farms and opportunities of employment in the adjacent city.

Genuine Suburbs with Rural Characters

One must reckon therefore with very large rural populations included in the more distant suburban area and in part actually commuting to the city daily for work, while the major relations of the families to which it belongs are still with the land. Much of the population of the rural suburbs is of course non-agricultural, inhabiting small towns surrounding cities but away from the points of rapid transit and close urban connections. As already indicated, no accurate means exist of measuring this element in the suburban situation. For this reason it is all the more necessary to visualize it clearly. The city has wide influence on adjacent population. It does not leave it scattered out in a normal density but pulls it in and banks it heavily around itself. It is not therefore an ordinary rural population but a massed population, subject to intimate urban contacts and relationships. The rural suburbs, in other words, are genuine suburbs, though not in the same sense that the residential and industrial suburbs are.

MEASURING THE SUBURBAN TREND

Extent of Metropolitan Population

Popular thinking is so addicted to the use of the categories "urban" and "rural" that it is well to consider that large parts of the United States, especially in the northeastern section, are so dominated by metropolitan conditions that the entire fabric of civilization is changed. There are cities and suburbs, but there is no rural territory left in the sense that the major part of the area of the nation is rural. In other words, the network of urban communities leaves little space for anything else. Cities of 100,000 population and over with their suburbs absorb 63 per cent. of the total population of the Middle Atlantic States and 60 per cent. of the population of the New England States. Here the people are dependent not merely upon cities but upon big cities. No less than eight States are affected by this condition, as is shown in the following comparison:

TABLE 13—STATES HAVING OVER 50 PER CENT. OF THEIR TOTAL POPULATION IN CITIES OF 100,000 AND OVER AND THEIR ADJACENT TERRITORY

States	Percentage
Rhode Island	87.3
Massachusetts	78.4
New Jersey	77.8
New York	73.4
Delaware	61.6
Maryland	60.0
Connecticut	56.0
California	52.0

THE SUBURBAN TREND

A sound understanding of the social structure of these States is not gained by the conventional categories "urban" and "rural." They are all more than one half metropolitan, the rest being divided between small cities and towns and the open country.

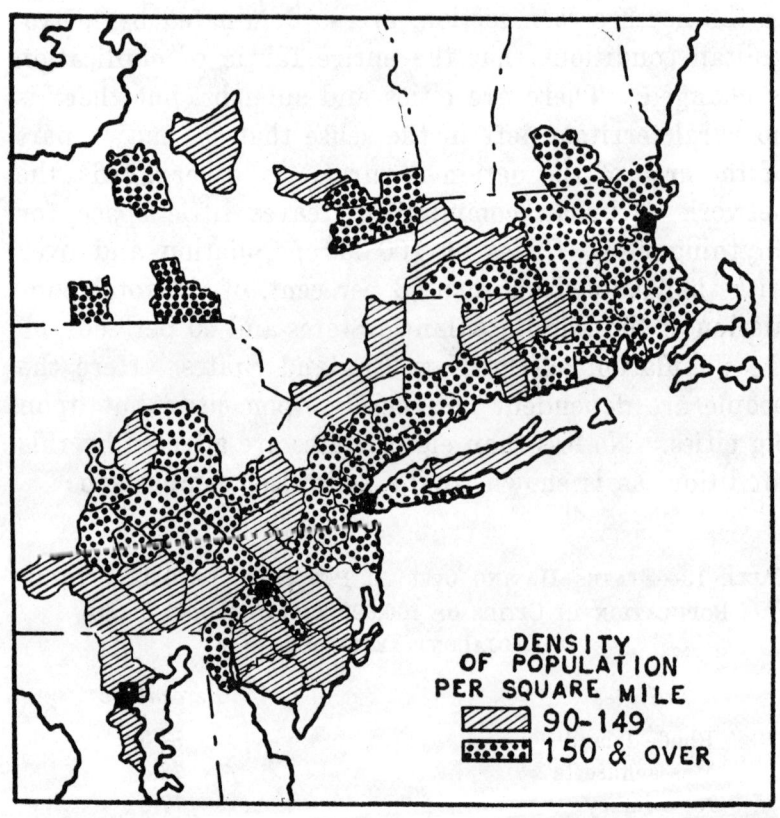

A CONTINUOUS URBANIZED AREA

Contiguous counties with relative congestion of population forming a continuous zone through nine states.
(Adapted from Fourteenth United States Census, Vol. 1, p. 88.)

SUBURBAN COUNTIES

To realize how nearly metropolitan population exhausts the total population of considerable political areas it is only necessary to consider the matter in terms of counties adjacent to or containing large cities.

Of 132 such counties including cities of 200,000 population and over, or parts of such cities and their suburbs, the urban and suburban population constitutes the following proportion of the total population:

TABLE 14—PERCENTAGE WHICH URBAN AND SUBURBAN POPULATION IS OF TOTAL POPULATION IN 132 COUNTIES INCLUDING OR ADJACENT TO LARGE CITIES

Number of counties	Percentage
9	Identical with cities (100)
22	90 and over
24	50–90
77	Less than 50

Here, in other words, in 42 per cent. of all counties in immediate contact with great cities, the total population is primarily metropolitan. How many counties related to small cities would show something of the same phenomenon has not been calculated, the object of the present data being simply to show the inadequacy of the categories "urban" and "rural" in view of the facts of metropolitan civilization in relation to political areas. It all goes to show the unexpected extent of the suburban trend and its importance among the great aspects of American civilization.

We have now examined summarily the suburban movement in the nation. The obvious moral is that the urban problem, so called, is greatly enlarged by the inclusion of the suburbs, especially since they interpenetrate with rural civilization. In other words, the actual urban problem has much greater magnitude than the bare population of cities implies, whatever definition may be given to the term "city." Some day the census may become scientific enough to measure specifically each of the elements concerned and to combine them into an accurate total. Till then one must be content to pioneer somewhat vaguely in a slightly explored field.

Regional Extent of the Suburban Trend

So much for a generalization based upon the country as a whole. It is not equally true for all sections, as is clear from the following table showing what percentage of the population of metropolitan areas within each section falls outside of the boundaries of the central cities:

Table 15—Percentage of Metropolitan Population Which Falls Outside of Central Cities, by Regions

Region	Percentage
New England	45.0
Middle Atlantic	34.0
Southern	20.0
Western	18.0
North Central	16.5

On this showing the New England cities have relatively the largest suburban populations and the cities of the North Central States the smallest.

There is general correspondence between the suburban trend and the general trend of population, in that regions having heavy urban populations have also large surburban ones. This should of course be the case if the suburbs are really a footnote of urban civilization. The Southern States, however, constitute an exception to this rule. Their urban population is relatively smaller than that of any other section, and their cities are not characteristically crowded. Nevertheless they have a larger percentage of population outside the central cities than are found in the Western or North Central States. To be sure the average size of the Southern city is below that of any other section and the large adjacent population may not be related as intimately to the city as that in sections where cities are larger. As measured in census categories, however, the fact remains and requires explanation. From a superficial study of Southern cities one gets the impression that they strongly incline to segregate their industries in factory villages outside the political limits. There may also be something in the hypothesis developed in another connection that a warm climate makes for suburban development while a cold climate impels people to live snugly together in urban quarters.[9]

Future of the Suburban Movement

The suburban trend has been shown to be of one piece with the trend within the city toward its less crowded areas. There are suburbs within and suburbs without the political city. Recognizing this raises afresh the

[9] Page 114.

question of the meaning of rapid suburban growth for the living conditions of the future. The suburbs within the cities are generally in the way to become urbanized. They continuously tend to follow the central areas in congestion and other characteristics and to become more and more homogeneous with the total structure of the city. May this not also be what will take place outside of the city? Can rapid growth mean anything else? Westminster itself was once merely an outlying parish of London. Does not the present trend inevitably spell overgrowth and the submergence of suburban characteristics in city ones?

Obviously exactly this is happening before one's eyes in the case of all too many suburbs. They are simply getting to be cities. The structures erected to house their additional people follow the city type. Their vacant land tends to be closely occupied. Their street traffic increases. Rising land values make the maintenance of single-family homes increasingly difficult. Rapid growth urbanizes the suburbs. Annexation to the parent city or political integration with other groups of suburbs into new cities are the formal accompaniments of the process.

Growth is thus the undoing of the suburb. Must it not generally be so, and does not the present rapid increase of suburban population simply mean that they are on the way to self-extinction?

Will the Suburban Trend be Maintained?

Of course even at their present rapid rate of increase

it will be a long while before the smaller suburbs become cities. New suburbs are forming out beyond the overgrown ones, and the process of flight from the congested center has no physical limits except the ability of transit facilities to move people back and forth with a reasonable time and cost. Of course this does not guarantee that any particular suburb will be preserved; nor does it guarantee that the trend as a whole will be maintained. There will always be room for suburbs, but will as large or a larger proportion of people be living in them a quarter of a century hence than now? This is the crucial question. Will the people of metropolitan areas in the future have to live under more congested conditions, and will the escape to the suburbs be less practicable and available for a smaller proportion than at present?

No happy outcome can be predicted with any certainty if the expansion of cities continues to be so largely as in the past an uncontrolled process. What the possibilities and prospects are, and how the suburbs preserved and perfected may function in civilizations of to-morrow, is the theme of later chapters. The immediate discussion will content itself by showing that the city does not need to crowd the suburb out.

Future Growth Will Not Make Suburbs Physically Impossible

Even with the most extreme rate of expansion which can be conceived, there is room enough for the suburbs if the available environs of cities are rationally di-

72 THE SUBURBAN TREND

vided. There is even room for a much larger number. To prove the point we may take the most extravagant case possible, that of Greater New York. Its suburbs have been growing faster than the city since 1900, and the curve of mathematical probability indicates that they will do so until about the year 2100, after which the ratio between the two will become stabilized. The present and predicted ratios of population as made for the "Plan for New York and Environs" are shown in the following comparison:

TABLE 16—DISTRIBUTION OF POPULATION IN NEW YORK CITY AND ENVIRONS

Year	Urban		Suburban		Rural Suburbs	
	Number	Percentage	Number	Percentage	Number	Percentage
1920	6,664,000	74.3	1,383,000	15.4	932,000	10.3
2100	19,818,000	57.1	10,748,000	31.0	4,140,000	11.9

Now, in A.D. 2100, when the present suburban area has eleven million inhabitants and includes more than twice as large a proportion of the total metropolitan population as it does at present, it will still have but half the density of the present urban area.[10]

Assuming that many people will still prefer to live in luxurious multiple-family dwellings near the heart of the city, and certainly not assuming to abolish the great centralizing forces and motives which crowd cities,

[10] Pearl and Reid, "Predicted Growth of the Population of New York and Its Environs," Plan of New York and Its Environs, (1923), pp. 18–24.

MEASURING THE SUBURBAN TREND

it is obvious that much space might be left for relatively roomy communities in 2100 even in the present area. At that time the present rural suburbs will have considerably fewer people to the square mile than the present suburbs have now. Consequently if transportation can be technically improved and the cost reduced there will be opportunity for very uncongested living conditions for 4,200,000 people prophesied for that area at that time. In brief if in 175 years from now Greater New York has a total of nearly thirty-five million people it might still have a larger proportion of them than at present living under suburban conditions if rational planning and control were used.

The future of the suburbs is thus partially in the hands of the present. The trends which we experience may largely overwhelm and submerge them but will not necessarily do so if reason and social intelligence have a fair show.

CHAPTER III

THE MAJOR SUBURBAN TYPES

SUBURBS so manifestly differ from one another that even the most generalized account of their character, such as was undertaken in the first chapter, could not ignore the fact. At one extreme, for example, we found the resort and amusement suburbs given over exclusively to the pleasure of the people of the near-by city. No work goes on within them except as connected with the recreation of others.

At the other extreme is such a manufacturing suburb as Harrison, New Jersey, with a total population of some 15,000, but with 13,000 wage-earners, most of whom come in from the outside to their daily toil. The area of this suburb is primarily devoted to industries having large space requirements. Consequently it has little room for people. It is almost exclusively a place for work in contrast with play or even with rest.

Other exceptions noted were, for example, the near-by agricultural suburb, a survival of the past now practically surrounded by urban life; the old and self-contained community resistant to city influence; and the county-seat. All these illustrate the variety of the phenomena comprehended within the suburban trend and challenge to a farther study and explanation of the

THE MAJOR SUBURBAN TYPES 75

distinguishable types. Even though only a part of the city can be decentralized, and all the suburbs combined are not as varied as the city, nevertheless the suburban fragments represent a wide range of interesting variations.

How Suburbs Differ

The factors which prove most significant in differentiating the suburbs from the city were size, congestion, and distance. None of these, however, serves as a significant basis for the comparison of suburb with suburb. Of course suburbs are larger or smaller, more congested or less congested, farther or nearer; but there is little presumption that groups of suburbs will be alike in fundamental respects because they are alike in these respects.

Equal Size Does Not Characterize Similar Types

We have seen that the suburbs scale down in size from the parent city. The large suburb of New York is larger than the large suburb of St. Louis. Its characteristics are developed with reference to its own metropolis. Consequently if one takes it out of its setting and compares it with another suburb merely of the same population, he has no reason to suppose that he will find anything necessarily alike. It is true that the largest suburbs are themselves generally cities with city density of population and that the smaller ones are on the whole less crowded and generally less connected with the city.

Nevertheless groups of suburbs of approximately equal populations do not closely resemble one another. For example, some are residential to an extreme degree, others almost exclusively industrial. All sorts of other variations run through groups of suburbs with equal populations. Thus, one suburb may get a high degree of social advantage and belong to a conspicuously desirable environment without having a large population, because its people use the resources of the city more completely. They may live a simple life at home but a very varied one in their total relationship. Another suburb of equal size composed of another type of people may be totally different. In other words, suburbs have alternatives because of the proximity of cities. They may develop a full round of facilities and activities within themselves or they may depend upon the metropolis. This tends to equalize advantages as between big and little and to make differences in size of population in the suburbs less significant on the whole than similar differences between independent towns.

Degree of Congestion Does Not Distinguish Types

Suburbs scale down from their parent cities in degree of congestion as well as in size. While as a group they are less densely populated than the parent cities and the residential suburbs are less crowded than the industrial ones, it is not possible to find a homogeneous group by putting together suburbs with approximately the same degree of congestion. The larger and generally more crowded cities have so many more suburbs than

THE MAJOR SUBURBAN TYPES 77

the smaller ones that when all suburbs of a like degree of congestion are put together these dominate the total and distort the average.

In general the residential suburbs of the large cities have about the same degree of congestion as the small cities. Thus the median of excess of families over dwellings for all cities of from 10,000 to 25,000 population is 22.6 per cent., while that of twelve high-grade residential suburbs of Boston, New York, Chicago, and San Francisco is exactly the same. The degree of congestion therefore cannot be used directly as a basis for distinguishing types of suburbs. At most it points to the conclusion that the suburbs of large cities and of small cities are on the whole rather different social phenomena, though with respect to their parent cities they are all equally suburban.

Distance Does Not Distinguish Types

Even when distance is translated into terms of accessibility, it does not result in like suburbs. If one should take all the suburbs half an hour distant from the center of the city, all the suburbs one hour distant, etc., he would not get homogeneous groups. As already indicated, some are residential, others industrial. It is important to note that an industrial community may retain essential economic dependence upon the city at a distance beyond that which workers can ordinarily afford to cover in their daily commutation. If this is the case without sacrifice of other economic relations, it can still be called a true suburb. For even though the majority of workers in industrial suburbs do not commute to and from the city, some part of its working population does commute. The father, for example, may work in the local factory while younger members of the family find other kinds of work in the city. These commuters are frequently a small fraction of the working population, but they are the fraction which turns the scales economically speaking. To be able to get other kinds of work for more members of the family than the industrial suburb itself can afford is a supplemental advantage of a most vital sort, and one of profound importance to people living near the economic margin. This can be found only in the city. Industrial suburbs are thus bound within substantially the same distance limits as the residential ones; yet the two types are not at all alike internally. This will prove the crucial point in the later discussion of suburban economics. It is cited here to show why suburbs at equal distance from the city are not necessarily at all alike.

Unequal Capacity of City Elements for Decentralization

But if neither size, congestion, nor distance from the city distinguishes significant varieties of suburbs, what does?

The answer has already been anticipated: significant variation is caused by the character of the particular elements of the city which are decentralized in a given suburb. It has already been assumed as obvious that the many elements which go to make up a great city would show unequal capacity for decentralization. Of those which can be moved to the suburbs, some go to one place, others to another. Thus different types are created.

The range of possible variation from this source will be suggested if one considers some actual examples of aspects of social life showing unequal capacity for decentralization.

Examples of Unequal Decentralization

The home and its processes of domestic consumption characteristic of the family as a group can be more completely separated from the city than can recreation. About 20 per cent. of Montclair, New Jersey, commuters say that they find their major recreational activities in New York. Fifty-three per cent. of the memberships of the men of Webster Groves, Missouri, in social clubs, are in St. Louis.

Explanations for such facts easily occur to one. The suburbs cannot compete with the city in its recreational appeal; say, in the quantity of its theaters and concerts. Again, social clubs have a business side. They exist partly because profitable contacts are made, consultations held, "deals" consummated better in the social atmosphere. Such experiences cannot be entirely decentralized.

To measure the decentralization of the home is to discover that the suburban process does not treat men and women alike. One systematically goes and comes to and from work; the other stays at home and goes occasionally. In discussing the unequal decentralization of different functions a sex differentiation needs constantly to be made. Thus returning to the topic of recreation, while 53 per cent. of the memberships of Webster Groves men in social clubs were in St. Louis, only 24 per cent. of the memberships of women in social clubs were in St. Louis. In brief the suburb decentralizes women, unless they are gainfully employed, more completely than it does men.

Education, Recreation, and Religion

Under our system of public support, education, in its elementary phase, is compelled to decentralize along with population. But there is no possible substitute for the great city universities. Municipal higher education in the Central West is increasingly dependent upon commutation of students. The University of Pittsburg has seven to eight thousand students without a dormitory, drawn in large numbers from the surrounding suburbs. The very striking difference between the "subway university"—as New York has come to call it—and that which centralizes student life on and around a campus is having increasing recognition in educational policy.

The cases of recreation and of education show that functions which are separately performed for the different age- and sex-groups cannot be equally decentralized. The suburb is not so independent of the city with respect to its youth as with respect to its children. It cannot create a complete response to the detailed needs of every

THE MAJOR SUBURBAN TYPES 81

class at every time, competing with or duplicating the city's provision.

Religion, on the contrary, is almost completely decentralized. Indeed, having churches of their own is one of the marks of the true suburbs. While communities just beyond the limits of small cities may not have them, and while the majority of church-members in well-marked suburbs even of cities of 100,000 and upward have been found in city churches, yet the rule is that religious connections follow the home. Thus Webster Groves, the largest residential suburb of St. Louis, is only nine miles from the center of the city. An almost complete religious survey of its population found only 6 per cent. of church adherents connected with St. Louis churches.

UNEQUAL INDUSTRIAL DECENTRALIZATION

On the side of production it has already been noted that certain industries require more ground space than others do. They deal with large and heavy materials or else require ample room for storage and operation, as in the case of railway freight-yards. The manufacture of steel is essentially a one-story industry, its space requirements being chiefly lateral.

Other illustrations are industries existing in the immediate vicinity of mines and handling crude material. Analogous conditions accompany the production of oil, as exemplified in the environs of Los Angeles and Tulsa. Such industries tend to produce numerous suburbs. The characteristic industries of New York City on the contrary—typified by the ready-made garment trade—are economical of ground space and are carried on in many-storied lofts. This greatest manufacturing center of the nation is a city of few smoke-stacks. The factory has "gone up" as well as the home and travels by elevator.

The range of contrast in the use of space by industry is shown in the following comparison of the amount used by different types.[1]

Type of city and industry	Average square feet of ground area per worker
Manhattan Island loft industries	30
Massachusetts textile and shoe cities	40
Suburbs with varied industries	1,500
Suburbs with heavy industries	4,000

Now, while physical and economic necessity distributes the extremely heavy and the extremely light industries, sending one to the suburbs and piling one up in the city, the operation of these forces is uncertain and vacillating with respect to industries of the mediating type. Investigation discloses a vast amount of misplacement of industry which is both inefficient and expensive, and individual initiative has often resulted in foolish and disorderly location. Many could well move to the suburbs but for a sort of gregarious impulse which herds industries of a common type into traditional districts.

[1] Ford, "Regional and Metropolitan Planning," "Proceedings of Fifteenth National Conference on City Planning," p. 15.

THE MAJOR SUBURBAN TYPES 83

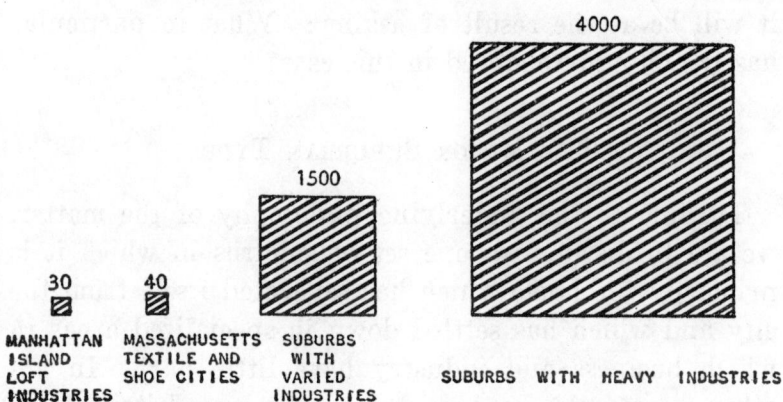

VARYING SPACE REQUIREMENTS OF INDUSTRIES

Comparison of average square feet of ground-area per worker in types of urban and suburban industry.

Neither the economic nor the psychological forces governing the actual location of industries are fully understood. Some are so bound to shipping facilities that they cannot move far from the waterfront; others have become excessively mobile by reason of motor-truck transportation. City planners are just now engaged in surveying the requirements of the different types of industry to determine which can and which cannot be decentralized and under what circumstances.

The industrial suburbs necessarily reflect those economic activities which are capable of suburbanization, and their inhabitants are primarily people engaged in these particular industries.

The above illustrations serve to show in how many realms of activity and interest the city reserves many of its functions and only surrenders parts of them to the suburbs. On this basis, if suburbs are to be classified, it will be as the result of asking: What in particular has the city surrendered in this case?

The Major Suburban Types

Turning to the underlying philosophy of the matter, we are to distinguish one set of suburbs in which it is primarily the home which has separated itself from the city and which has settled down in specialized areas in which business and industry have little part. In another set of suburbs, industry has separated itself from the city and taken over suburban communities for its more or less exclusive and dominating use. Why should such differences exist? It is this question which we must answer before we can understand how by separate roads the two types achieve both suburban character and partial independence of the city.

The Decentralization of Consumption

The basic distinction of economic science is that between production and consumption; that is to say, between the creation of wealth and its expenditure. The residential suburb represents the decentralization of consumption. Man creates wealth in the central city and spends it in the suburbs. He makes his living in town but lives at home in an intentionally contrasting environment. He leaves his work in the city but takes wife and children and moves out to the country, going back and forth daily in order to keep both aspects of life going.

THE MAJOR SUBURBAN TYPES 85

Part of the pay which he receives for his work in the city he immediately pays out there in return for services or goods, but the goods which he buys are chiefly consumed at home, and in the suburb are his major expenditures—for rent and taxes, for most of his food, for doctor and dentist, for automobile, church and club, for charity, self-improvement and self-indulgence. There could hardly be a greater error than to think of the residential suburbs as mere dormitories. They are rather the realms of consumption as over against production, of play in contrast with work, of leisure in exchange for business. Only incidentally are they places to sleep.

Of course some work is done in the residential suburbs, but it is primarily in the service of rest, recreation, and refreshment for others. The gainfully employed breadwinner goes to the city, but the work of the homemaker, as we have already seen, is decentralized along with the home; and round it gather the types of business immediately related to consumption.

Indeed, more domestic work takes place in the residential suburb than in the city. It moves the woman from the apartment-house with its centralized heating-plant, its elevator, laundry, incinerator, and janitor service, and with no premises outside of the house, to the single or double house with its independent equipment for each family and its grounds to look after. More work is necessary to make the process of consumption efficient and agreeable and to maintain esthetic standards under these circumstances. Nevertheless in the largest sense it is the mark of the residential suburb to have left productive work in the city and to have solved the problem of the worker by a daily movement from home in the morning to the shop, factory, or office and back again at night.

The Decentralization of Production

The "going up" to the city is a result of the competition for space for goods and for room to carry on processes related to their production and distribution, as well as for space for homes and for independent human action. Urban congestion as experienced by populations is largely due to the reception, transportation, handling and processing, storage and reshipment of material things. The sidewalks are blocked by barrels of produce and bales of goods, and the streets are crowded with trucks.

In the industrial suburb these things are decentralized, together with the manufacturing plants and facilities which go with them. The factory becomes suburban as well as the home. Production moves out as consumption has already done. Both halves of the city reëstablish themselves in the country in a roomier environment. The industrial suburb is more independent of the parent city than is the residential one because the workers work near home as well as live there. Nevertheless, marked relations to the city continue, and subordination is definitely a fact although taking different forms. The city constitutes the major center where the brains, credit facilities, the docks and railroad terminals which are the ultimate factors of transportation, and the primary labor markets all remain.

THE MAJOR SUBURBAN TYPES

Industrial suburbs and residential suburbs thus constitute the major suburban types. For both the city continues the economic center as well as the focus of ideals and imagination.

The Statistical Determination of the Major Types

The census makes it possible to distinguish and study these types statistically because it enumerates industrial wage-earners [2] in all cities of 10,000 population and over. Calculating the ratio between wage-earners and total population, one is able to compare the suburbs which have more wage-earners than the parent cities, those which have an equal proportion and those which have less. The first we will call "industrial," the last "residential," and the second "mixed."

Such a classification follows for fifty-seven suburbs of the following cities: Albany, Boston, Chicago, Jersey City, Los Angeles, New York, Philadelphia, St. Louis, San Francisco, Springfield (Massachusetts). Only 8.3 per cent. of the population of Los Angeles are wage-earners, this city having the smallest proportion of those mentioned, while 15.5 per cent. of the population of Philadelphia are wage-earners, this being the largest proportion. The median is about 12 per cent., falling between Boston and Jersey City.

The actual classification of the ten cities and fifty-seven suburbs according to this method follows:

---

[2] As distinguished from proprietors, salaried officers, and clerks. Fourteenth Census, V. IX, Table 6, by States.

THE SUBURBAN TREND

TABLE 17—PERCENTAGE OF WAGE-EARNERS IN 10 CITIES AND 57 SUBURBS, BY GROUPS

Groups	Number		Percentage of wage-earners	
			Median	Range
Parent cities	10	12.4	8.3 (Los Angeles)–15.5 (Philadelphia)	
Suburbs—				
Mixed	10	11.9	8.2 (Orange, N. J.)–15.8 (Rahway, N. J.)	
Industrial	28	25.5	16.0 (Portchester, N. Y.)–83.0 (Harrison, N. J.)	
Residential	17	2.6	0.4 (Revere, Mass.)–7.8 (Irvington, N. J.)	

It will be noted that the last group, which we thus distinguish statistically as residential suburbs, has substantially only one tenth as many wage-earners as the previous group of industrial suburbs, and between one

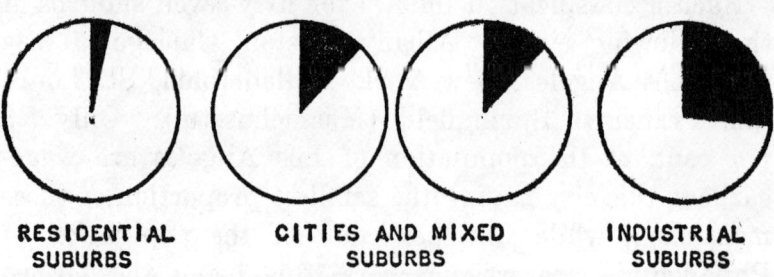

RESIDENTIAL SUBURBS   CITIES AND MIXED SUBURBS   INDUSTRIAL SUBURBS

PERCENTAGE OF INDUSTRIAL WAGE-EARNERS IN TOTAL POPULATION
By parent cities and types of suburbs.

fifth and one sixth as many as the mixed suburbs or the parent cities. The second group, the mixed suburbs, are obviously partly residential and partly industrial just as the parent cities are. They are the least numerous

THE MAJOR SUBURBAN TYPES 89

type and fail to present many of the special characteristics of suburbs.

Considering the range of difference within the types, it will be noted that Harrison, New Jersey, has about five times as high a proportion of working population as Portchester, New York, while Revere, Massachusetts, has only one twentieth as many workers as Irvington, New Jersey. This measures the wide difference within the industrial and residential types respectively. Consequently, while the industrial suburbs as a group have ten times as many workers as the residential suburbs—thus constituting a very definite ground of distinction—the difference between the extreme resort suburb and the exclusively factory suburbs are measured by the hundredfold. In other words room exists for many minor differences within the suburban field.[3]

How the Major Types Achieve Suburban Character

Though the two types are equally suburbs, they achieve suburban character by different paths. This is to be insisted upon in opposition to the frequent assumption that only residential suburbs are suburban. The residential suburb gets its distinction by cutting its daily life into two halves, one of which it spends in the city and the other at home. The fact of distance, coupled with the slighter congestion of living-conditions and

[3] Taylor, "Satellite Cities," defines itself as a "study of industrial suburbs." It is rather a study of their extreme developments, not representative of the type as above defined.

specialization upon the activities and interests involved in consumption, easily differentiates such suburbs. From these points of departure they work out their special social patterns and type of community consciousness.

The industrial suburb, on the contrary (with distance from the city and some reduction of city congestion as its conditions), acquires suburban quality by reducing the number of its connections with the city on all sides of its activities exactly as a more distant community might do. But it does not go away so far in miles nor get along with so small a number of relations. Economic analysis will still find it intimately related to the city's central transportation facilities with which it may be connected by water or belt railway. Moreover, it is, as we have already seen, vitally dependent upon the city as a central labor market, and the minority of the workers who do commute frequently represent a link in the economic chain without which its whole structure would be impossible.

The mixed type of suburb might be supposed to show two streams of suburban tendency flowing side by side toward a common result. As a matter of fact they largely neutralize each other. Not enough people are specializing upon consumption to make such a community a characteristic suburb by reason of the fact. Nevertheless, the commuting population serves to prevent its development of independence through the alternative method of the cutting away of city relationships. The mixed suburbs are therefore generally in effect merely other cities within the metropolitan zone; or else they are communities in transition which must ultimately

THE MAJOR SUBURBAN TYPES

find equilibrium either by one method or the other. This is not a true type and has no distinct rationale.

Relative Rapidity of Decentralization of Consumption and Production

Which has moved to the suburbs more easily and quickly—the home or industry? In measuring the suburban trend as a whole, this question was not raised, and in discussing its cause we were content to make congestion the chief factor without asking what aspect of the city is first to be affected by it. Something might be inferred by a direct comparison of the rate of growth of the residential and industrial suburbs, but since nearly all suburbs are really mixed and our distinctions a matter of degree only, the results would not be wholly conclusive. Counting manufacturing establishments and number of wage-earners, it is clear that the suburbs as a group have outstripped the city to a much greater extent in industry than in population. In the suburbs of the thirteen largest cities wage-earners increased 98 per cent. between 1899 and 1909, while the number increased but 41 per cent. in the parent cities.[4] The recent census does not report the facts in comparable form; but students of industrial decentralization calculate that the larger cities have relatively lost ground, the suburbs held their own, and the smaller independent cities gained most of all in the last decade.[5]

[4] Thirteenth Census, Vol. X, Table 6.
[5] Piquet, "Is the Big City Doomed as an Industrial Center?" "Industrial Management," Vol. LXVIII, No. 3 (September, 1924), p. 139.

We have hitherto assumed that the worker's home decentralizes with the factory. In general this is true. The discrepancy, however, between the rate of suburban growth in population and in industries undoubtedly means that, in a good many cases, the factory has shifted to the country to escape congestion, but has left the workers largely to live in crowded urban quarters. Graham Romeyn Taylor found that less than one third of the workers employed in two Cincinnati industrial suburbs lived there, the rest being scattered all over Cincinnati and even in Kentucky.[6] Household servants commute to suburban kitchens, and day laborers even commute to remoter suburban farms. The factory merely leads the way. Even after it has suburbanized, the problem of housing for the workers is not solved and the difficulty of meeting the costs of suburban living still shuts up many of the poor in tenements and slums. Before considering these problems, however, it is necessary to complete the description of suburban variations.

[6] "Satellite Cities," p. 92.

CHAPTER IV

OTHER VARIETIES OF SUBURBS

IN arranging the statistical measurement of difference between the two major types, one came upon extreme and striking cases at either end of the series. These stand out as subtypes requiring separate recognition. We have already contrasted the resort town which decentralizes, not domestic consumption in general, but only that part which is spent in intentional recreation and the active pursuit of pleasure; and, on the other hand, the industrial suburb which is so full of factories that it has little room even for working people. Such extremes are not adequately expressed under the type-distinctions "residential" and "industrial."

In contrast with the previously discussed differences which do not involve uniform consequences and do not regularly make a specific difference in the social life and experience of the suburban community, we now come to those differences which, while not so fundamental as those between residential and industrial suburbs, do nevertheless directly tend to create separate subtypes. One ground of difference is obviously the original composition and the wealth of suburbs, another is their history and social fortunes. Under these headings minor differences group themselves.

Demographic and Economic Variations: Rich Suburbs and Poor Suburbs

Within the boundaries of the city the social complexion of its more prosperous districts is in most glaring contrast with that of its poverty-stricken ones. The same contrasts occur along the margins of the city and out into the suburbs. Rich and poor suburbs constitute for practical purposes different kinds.

It follows from the ordinary distribution of human fortunes that the residential suburbs are richer than the industrial ones. Extreme cases occur in which their average wealth as measured in real property is two or even three times that of the parent city and much more beyond the average place of the same size.[1] Housing costs in the better residential suburbs catering to the upper middle class are so high as to exclude all but about ten per cent. of the population of the urban area. Nevertheless, both major types of suburbs occur on all economic levels. Somewhat rarely an industrial suburb gathering skilled laborers in selected industries, develops a surprisingly high average of community wealth. Plainfield, New Jersey, is such a community. In a ranking of twenty-two New Jersey towns and cities according to the percentage of pupils from high school going to college, this is the only industrial suburb standing in the

[1] Statement based upon an estimate of the true per-capita value of real estate in 1922 for Illinois cities, by the tax commissioner of the Chicago and North Western Railway.

OTHER VARIETIES OF SUBURBS 95

upper third. All the others standing toward the top of the list are residential suburbs.

Most suburbs, either residential or industrial, are inhabited by people of the middle class on the economic scale. This is because there are relatively few rich people and because, as we shall later see, the suburb is not generally available for the very poor. There are, however, many residential suburbs of the better-paid industrial classes, but they are usually closer to cities, especially to minor cities within the suburban zone. The industrial worker cannot ordinarily commute so far as the salaried man. Consequently his residential suburb must lie nearer his work.

The presence of such residential suburbs makes the daily movement to and from work complicated. It does not run wholly in the same direction. There are many outbound commuters, as well as others who move across the prevailing pathway of commutation from the suburbs to the parent city. These create cross-currents of transportation. Only so, however, are the industrial classes generally provided with residential suburbs. They must have working-men's residential suburbs adjacent to industrial suburbs or to cities.

Besides the very poor industrial suburbs where foreign immigrants in industry live on a characteristically low level in the shadow of the factory, many purely residential suburbs exist on exceedingly unsatisfactory economic planes. Thus the projection of the Delaware River Bridge between Philadelphia and Camden started hordes of poorly paid workers to building mushroom suburbs in the country beyond. Many of them were cheap, planless, vulgar, and inconvenient to the last degree. Some indeed started in temporary summer bungalow communities and adapted their style of architecture and standards to year-round living. Without civic coherence or community consciousness, suburbs of this sort present many of the aspects of the frontier mining-camp. Scores of them exist along the edges of the Los Angeles oil-fields, their sordidness redeemed only by the outdoor climate and the somewhat esthetic tradition of the California bungalow. Nearly every great city since the war shows similar phenomena. There has been a veritable suburban hegira of the very poor in an effort to escape high rents. Much of this movement lies in the semisuburban zone. How great opportunity for such urban pioneering even within city limits is apparent when one recollects that one third of the incorporated area of St. Louis is unimproved, without sidewalks or sewers, and that Chicago has even to-day more street frontage without buildings facing it than with them. Genuinely frontier life along the margins of cities is thus a grim reality, subject to many shortcomings in spite of the undoubted relief which it affords from central congestion.

There are also numerous examples of downright suburban slums typified by the squatter community of shanty-boatmen in St. Louis, the "tin-can colony" hidden away in the pine thickets in the outskirts of Springfield, Massachusetts. Similar pauper or degenerate suburban types survive here along the margins of most great cities.

OTHER VARIETIES OF SUBURBS

The rich suburb, the middle-class suburb, and the poor suburb, with their minor variants, furnish then a set of typical distinctions of genuine importance for social analysis.

A second very profound series of differences between suburbs reflects the varying population elements which compose them. These differences may be racial or may concern the balance between the various age- and sex-groups or between the occupations through which people gain their livelihood.

Foreign and Negro Suburbs

Considering first racial composition, one comes upon the striking discovery that the heaviest concentrations of foreign-born populations in the United States are not urban but suburban. Also that no Northern city has massed so large a proportion of negro population as some of the Northern suburbs.

The relation between industry and the presence of these alien groups of population is well understood. It is in the industrial suburb, therefore, that we must look for these extreme concentrations of alien population. A limited sampling of the industrial suburbs seems to show that as a group they have about the same percentage of foreign-born as have the parent cities. No great city, however, has so high a number of foreigners as East Chicago, Indiana, or Passaic, Garfield, and Perth Amboy, New Jersey. No Northern city has relatively so many negroes as the residential suburbs of Englewood, East Orange, and Montclair, New Jersey, and Evanston,

98 THE SUBURBAN TREND

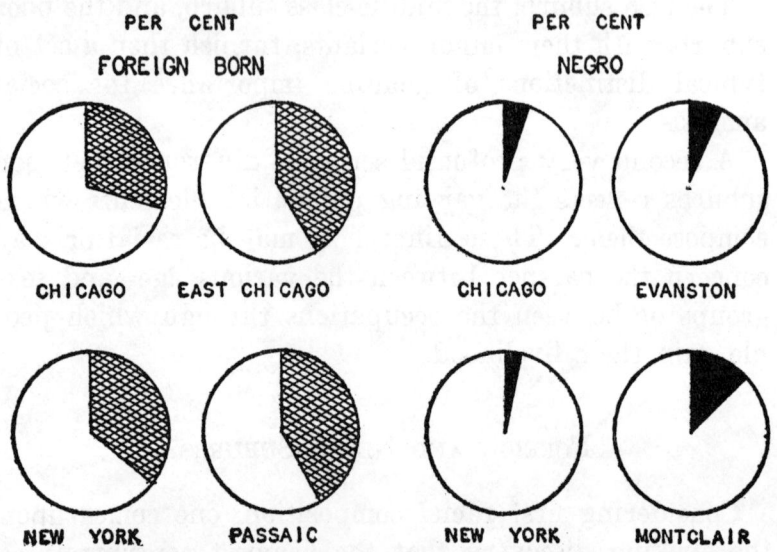

EXCESS OVER PARENT CITY OF FOREIGN-BORN POPULATION IN EXCEPTIONAL INDUSTRIAL SUBURBS AND OF NEGROES IN EXCEPTIONAL RESIDENTIAL SUBURBS OF CHICAGO AND NEW YORK

Illinois, where the negro colonies represent primarily domestic service groups.

On the other hand, there are distinctly industrial suburbs actually with fewer foreigners than the average residential suburbs of the cities have. Examples are Hammond, Indiana, and Plainfield, New Jersey. These strikingly American suburbs may, as already noted, stand on a high economic level.

The foreign industrial suburb, the residential suburb with a subsidiary alien colony, and the exclusively American industrial suburb are important variants having the value of subtypes.

OTHER VARIETIES OF SUBURBS

Children's Suburbs and Old People's Suburbs

Suburbs also differ significantly with respect to the relative proportion of their age-groups. As compared with the rural population, the city has a surplus of youth and of vigorous young manhood and womanhood. It draws the virile and adventurous in their most eager and strenuous years. It is most conspicuously deficient in children and aged people, of whom the farm and country village have a corresponding excess.

There are certain statistical traces of the tendency of the suburbs to revert to a more rural type of distribution of population by age-groups than the city proper has. For example, the New York suburbs of all sizes have relatively more children than the city has. The same thing is true of the San Francisco suburbs. But the difference is not great enough to be impressive, and the use of averages conceals the fact that it is not uniformly true and that in an important group of cities it is not true at all. Los Angeles has more children than its more important suburbs; Chicago, Boston, and New York have more children than many of their suburbs. One must look more closely, therefore, into the different types of suburbs already discovered.

Deficiency in children compared with the city is most marked in the case of residential suburbs dominated by American populations. One may assume that these populations have gone to the suburbs for the sake of such children as they have; but they have not gone there to have large families. The foreign populations of the cities, who most need space and country life for their teeming families, do not get them, while the American family, which is already smaller, does. Brookline and Newton have fewer children than Boston; Evanston and Oak Park than Chicago; Montclair and East Orange than New York. Such suburbs exist, not for children but for fortunate children!

In contrast with the residential suburbs, the industrial suburbs frequently, though not always, show an excess of children compared with cities. This is most characteristic of those with heavy foreign population. East Chicago, Hamtranck, and Perth Amboy are "full of boys and girls playing in the streets thereof." They show the suburban foreigner partially winning the room for life and play which childhood so greatly needs, and

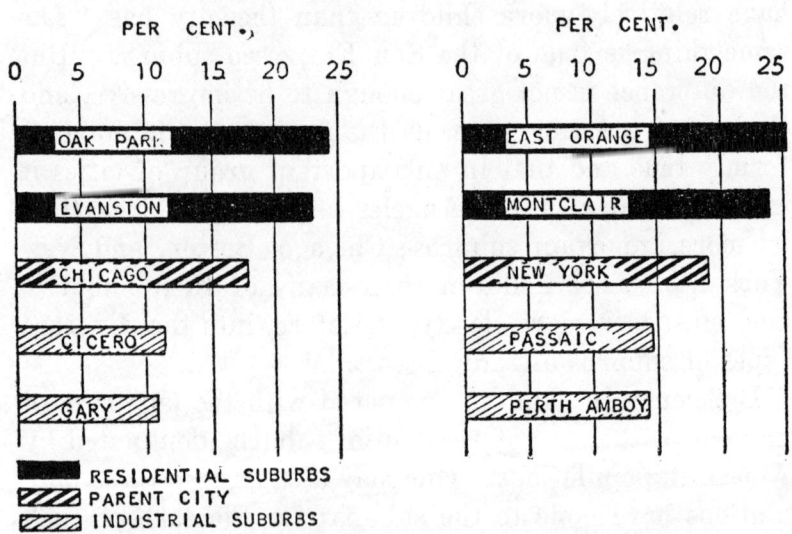

PERCENTAGE OF POPULATION WHICH IS 45 YEARS OF AGE AND OVER IN CHICAGO AND NEW YORK AND IN EXCEPTIONAL RESIDENTIAL AND INDUSTRIAL SUBURBS

OTHER VARIETIES OF SUBURBS 101

then having plenty of children to enjoy them, as the American suburb does not.[2]

In striking contrast with the children's suburbs, the six high-class residential suburbs mentioned above are all old people's suburbs. They have a notably larger percentage of population of sixty-five years of age and upward than have their parent cities, or than has the average of the suburbs. Thus, while only about 27 per cent. of a normal city population of working age is beyond forty-five years old, approximately 60 per cent. of the commuters of Montclair, New Jersey, according to a recent survey, are beyond this age. Montclair is a suburb of the successful professional and business man who has become well established, but shows an excess also of elderly retired people. The young family cannot afford to live in such a place.

Pasadena and Long Beach are the most notorious of the strictly old people's suburbs—in this respect going far beyond Los Angeles, which, in turn, has filled up with more than a normal share of retired people from the farms of the Middle West. One may guess the resultant conservatism of towns of this sort and moralize accordingly.

---

[2] While the above contrast between American and foreign population is generally a true one, it is not true, even for the native American population separately considered, that the suburbs as a group have a higher proportion of children than the city. The reason, of course, is that the majority of city populations are poor whether the stock is native or foreign, and the poor have the large families. If there were statistics enabling one to compare American families on the same economic level in city and suburbs, the latter would probably show a greater proportion of children.

WORKERS' SUBURBS AND BOSSES' SUBURBS

Variations within the residential type of suburb based on occupations reflect obvious economic differences but require separate recognition.

There are residential suburbs of artisans and mechanics, of clerks or so-called "white-collar workers," as well as of factory workers as previously noted. In sharp contrast with these are suburbs dominated by the professional and managerial classes. Still others are in almost exclusive possession of the unoccupied rich.

Nearly all suburbs show occupational selection of one sort or another. Thus Webster Groves, Missouri, has proportionately one half more people engaged in commerce and trade than has the parent city of St. Louis, and three times as many professional men, while only about the same proportion are engaged in transportation and public service. Only one half as many are in industrial pursuits, and one sixth as many in domestic service. In other words, here is primarily a business and professional man's suburb.

Montclair, New Jersey, on the other hand, presents an extreme case of selection in that its population is very largely of the managerial class. Of 529 commuters recently canvassed, three fifths were found to be employed in some executive capacity. Less than 5 per cent. were professional men.

Within the group of industrial suburbs another important occupational difference is found; namely, that between those dominated by industries employing many women and those employing chiefly men. Thus, while

OTHER VARIETIES OF SUBURBS

only one third of the workers of Albany are women, and one eighth of those in Schenectady, the collar factories of Troy have attracted women workers to an extent of three fifths of the city's total. The social atmosphere of the three adjoining cities varies accordingly.

Where populations of different occupational strata are mixed in the same suburb they are largely sifted out by the hour of going to and coming from work. The industrial workers take the earliest trains, the clerical workers next, and the managerial the latest. This reduces the social contacts of the various groups and carries still farther into practice the principle of occupational selection.

HISTORICAL AND SOCIAL VARIATIONS: SUBURBS WITH AND WITHOUT PREVIOUS COMMUNITY TRADITION

Many suburbs are the mere overflow of cities upon what was previously farm land or open country. Others are built upon foundations occupied by old towns or villages. The influence of previous community tradition is a very potent differentiating factor.

Sometimes the earlier social order has impressive traditions, an effective machinery of social life, strong institutions and personalities. Unless and until utterly overwhelmed by the weight of masses of new population, such forces conspire to give rich and peculiar flavor to the suburban blend. Suburbs which are mere city extensions must, on the other hand, literally start from the ground up and develop their own characters as they go along.

Numerous special elements are to be recognized which enable the social tradition of older communities to withstand the influence of new populations and to restamp its image upon the growing suburb.

One of the most frequent of these is historic prestige. West Springfield, Massachusetts, for example, has never quite forgotten that up to the time of the Revolutionary War it was a larger and more prosperous community than Springfield. Similarly the long memory of many a New England town defends its venerable institutions and helps to perpetuate a type of life which it believes to be more worthy than that of the upstart city which now overshadows it. Such towns largely maintain their own characters even after becoming suburbs in the economic sense.

Again, communities whose earlier populations were on the whole wealthier than the average incoming suburbanite frequently frown him into an inferiority complex which enables them to impress the old social pattern upon him. Among the humors of a suburban Young Men's Christian Association building campaign near New York was this: Those in charge of the project were offered a large initial subscription from a man who had lived in the community only ten years! They dared not accept it because, in order to get community following for their project, their initial gift had to come from one of the old families, even though for a considerably smaller amount. The old element had become a small minority, but its social leadership was unbroken.

Even without special social or economic defenses, certain stocks of people appear to be more stubbornly re-

OTHER VARIETIES OF SUBURBS 105

sistant in meeting the inundating flow of new-comers. Some of the old Dutch communities around New York, and the Quaker communities around Philadelphia, illustrate such intractability. The latter early showed special genius for suburban life. Their temper enabled them to differentiate strongly between home and neighborhood life on the one hand and business on the other. The latter they conducted in the city, while cherishing the former in outlying home communities still unique in atmosphere and spirit.

Additional strength is lent to any of these types of resistance by protecting physical barriers. Thus, as already noted, the low line of the First Mountain constitutes a division between the more urbanized and less urbanized suburbs in New Jersey. As is well known, the psychological effect of even a slight barrier is considerable. One can easily step over a hedge, but one does not do so. Similarly, a very little shelter from the overshadowing city, coupled with the deflection of direct population movements by physical barriers, gives the suburbs a sense and attitude of greater independence.

When the study of the psychology of suburbs is reached, one of its points of crucial significance and greatest interest will be found to be the transitional phase through which old and obdurate communities gradually yield to the suburbanizing influence of the city and take on new character. Even so, strangely persistent elements from the past often survive, harking back to the older stratum of community tradition for their inspiration and strongly influencing the situation from which they are supposedly obliterated.

Successful and Unsuccessful Suburbs

The city is not always successful in the effort to create suburbs. Some of its outgoings are abortive. The city's expansion on the whole has been largely accidental. This is not to forget that somebody cut up a farm and offered people lots for sale. Often, however, this was purely a speculative venture. Sometimes a suburb was the result, sometimes not. Generally there was little prevision and no such control of resources as to guarantee results. The original tendencies of city growth have proved to be extremely freakish, often changing as new elements entered into the situation and sometimes apparently from mere social whim. Consequently there has been a very high percentage of suburban failure or partial failure, reflecting the small degree of social intelligence hitherto employed and the incalculable character of some of the factors at work.

Later home-seekers and investors also have guessed wrong almost as often as they have guessed right. Chance has left them stranded in many an unsuccessful suburb.

Oftener than not the stranded suburb started in by imagining itself an integral part of the city itself in the not distant future. Sometimes it built houses on narrow lots designed to fit into solid rows of city structures. At any rate it did not anticipate that suburban status would continue. It was essentially a speculative venture, not an attempt to develop a distinct and semi-independent community. Nearly all cities, but especially those which have suffered depreciations following

OTHER VARIETIES OF SUBURBS 107

boom periods, show such a fringe of unwilling suburbs where the city started to expand but failed. Tacoma, for example, is favored with a superabundance of such suburbs. Gradually the saner of them accept the suburban rôle and come to develop a social life on the basis of the facts. Many, however, continue to justify the picture of "Lonesomehurst" familiar in caricature. Realty values have not maintained themselves; promised public utilities have not come. Life remains hard and inconvenient, involving pioneer privations within sight of the city's bright lights. This is a distinct suburban variety sufficiently frequent to be recognized as a subtype.

The suburb which is succeeding better than its expectations is no less frequent. It did not foresee and does not merit the success which comes from a rapid influx of population. It is a spill-over from the unparalleled growth of cities. The opening of new lines of transit often operates like the breaking of a dam. The result is nothing short of an inundation with such feverish and helter-skelter community building as has already been illustrated beyond the Camden end of the Delaware River Bridge. Such suburbs must ultimately reach equilibrium on some level or other, getting such transit facilities as their size and demands justify, such improvements as they can pay for, and such character as the years may evolve. Meanwhile the new and rapidly growing suburb which has not found itself—sometimes on a relatively high economic plane—stands out as an amazing, perplexing, and sometimes inspiring spectacle, an important by-product of urban growth.

Suburbs Planned and Unplanned

The only stabilizing resources which territory not politically incorporated has with which to meet such a sudden influx of population, are the traditional methods of subdividing land and dedicating highways to public uses, and state legislation intended for rural people. Beyond these scanty limitations, the spill-over of the city is often essentially an uncontrolled process. Such planning as enters into it is on such a fragmentary scale, and its several parts are so unrelated, as not to characterize the total results. Consequently, few new suburbs are the result of definite physical planning or of social design.

Where suburban growth imposes itself upon old communities, there is the steadying influence of the past which has already been explored. Inasmuch, however, as most of these old communities were themselves largely unplanned, and at least not planned as extensive suburbs, the results often show little trace of intelligent design.

In contrast with the general planlessness of suburban growth, a small but rapidly increasing number of planned suburbs are to be recognized.

These range from communistic would-be Utopias to fenced-off islands of physical and social exclusiveness where the roads even are not dedicated to the public and coming and going is at the sufferance of the proprietors. Planned suburbs fall chiefly, however, into two groups: first, those planned primarily to secure better

OTHER VARIETIES OF SUBURBS

living-conditions for industrial workers; and, second, intelligent real-estate developments undertaken primarily for the sake of profits.

Later consideration will be given to the deliberate attempt to create suburbs. For the present it is sufficient to note that the primary responsibility in the creation of suburbs planned for human well-being has fallen in America to manufacturing corporations. They have expected indirect and ultimate economic returns from improved stability and character of labor, their primary object, however, being the creation of proper living-quarters for their workers. By far the most extensive group of examples is the series of projects undertaken by the United States Housing Corporation in connection with the World War industries. Many of these were left incomplete or have since been partially abandoned. Great impetus, however, was given to the idea of suburban industrial housing and its technical conditions were more completely mastered than ever before.

Current examples of corporations actively promoting suburban housing schemes are the American Woolen Company in several New England cities and the Standard Oil Company in New Jersey.[3] Most industrial suburbs, however, are still quite unplanned as communities, their improved quality depending upon the gradual elevation of standards of living and some slight educa-

[3] For a more extended list and description of projects, see Magnusson, "Employers' Housing in the United States," U. S. Bureau of Labor Statistics, "Monthly Review," November, 1917, pp. 869–894.

tion of popular imagination and taste, together with better legal requirements.

Of semiphilanthropic demonstrations of the possibilities of a modern residential suburb, the most outstanding example in the United States is Forest Hills, Long Island, founded and developed by the Russell Sage Foundation. Very high-grade suburbs covering extensively planned areas are now, however, springing up about most American cities under strictly commercial impulse. They spread at intervals from the plains of Long Island to the heights overlooking San Francisco Bay. An extensive site is secured. Physical and engineering problems necessary to transform it into a seat of community life are carefully thought out in advance. Prospective public facilities are planned for. The structure of the community and its central agencies and institutions are foreseen and controlled. The type of houses and their relation to the land, to the streets, and to one another is determined. Enough actual creation of buildings is assured to fix the type and set the pace. Parks, playgrounds, and open spaces are laid out and made available from the beginning. As such a community comes into actual beginning it gradually takes charge of its own destinies. Local government is required to enforce the restrictions fixed by the first planners and founders. The original pattern tends to dominate adjacent farther development. Sometimes groups of real-estate interests with similar ideals and standards, operating in contiguous territory, contrive to cover rather large areas with a network of planned sub-

OTHER VARIETIES OF SUBURBS

urbs which grow into a broad zone about a city. Sometimes a single development company, working from a center, develops successive sectors of territory with reference to the creation of a balanced community of well-to-do and like-minded people as in Bronxville, New York.

When a suburban community erects itself piecemeal upon the foundations of an old but sound and substantial village or small city, planning is usually effected by legal means. Community tradition enters into the public engineering processes, building codes and the creation of public facilities and finally culminates in zoning ordinances. Forty per cent. of the urban population of the United States is now declared by the United States Department of Commerce to be living under zoning restrictions which fix the uses to which land may be put in given areas. Such zoning is particularly frequent in the suburbs. Nevertheless by far the greater area even of the "good" residential suburbs of the United States have reached their present state of development without definite plan. They are the result of good tradition and the gradual development of public tastes and standards.

While thus many generally satisfactory results have been reached without technical planning, and while suburban planning is rapidly increasing, it still remains true that hundreds of thousands of people rush annually into suburban life without social forethought or reasonable means of controlling the future, and not infrequently with almost criminal misdirection of effort and investment.

WITH AND WITHOUT INTERNAL CENTRALIZATION

A very important variation in the social structure of suburbs is based upon their physical structures. Some are physically unified by the presence of a single center which is the chief focus of movement, the gateway for entrance and exit, as well as the site of most of the internal business. Community interests cluster around it. The possession of such a center naturally tends to integrate a community. It makes for such unification as the nature of the population and of suburban life permits.

Other suburbs are mere series of detached neighborhoods strung along the line of transportation and immediately tributary only to their railroad stations. Webster Grove, Missouri, for example, is served by two railroads and has a total of seven different railroad stations for its 9000 people, besides minor centers for trolley traffic. Montclair is similarly served by two railroads, one of which has five stations. The so-called center of such a town has a very subordinate significance for the majority of its inhabitants. Not only is the parent city the real focus of their life, but large numbers of people never patronize the stores at the "center" of their own community, make no use of its central institutions, and literally may never go to it for months at a time. In other words, the alleged center is not a center for them, and the alleged community is only a shadow of a real community. Such a situation makes for social decentralization. The legal fiction which makes such people inhabitants of a common municipal corporation is, from the standpoint of social significance, a scrap of paper.

Specialized and Non-Specialized Suburbs

While, as we have seen, virtually all suburbs reflect the principle of specialization, either economic or social, only a minority are so definitely specialized as to be characterized or named by some one function which goes on within them. Of course a suburb built about a single strong industry inevitably bears the label of that industry. Other suburbs, however, are built about certain interests or institutions not primarily economic in character. Thus there are educational suburbs attaching themselves to schools. There are the minor political capitals developed around the activities of government and administration. There are suburbs surrounding asylums or protective institutions. There are resorts and recreational suburbs. All these reflect a specific phase of specialization, from which they largely take their character and from which they get their reputations. The center of the school suburb is its faculty and the parents of pupils. The staff, attendants, and guards of an institution create a community about it. Political office-holders, executives, and clerks form the nucleus of the political suburb. The employees of recreational facilities make up the core of such communities. Around these gather the businesses and professional classes which serve their needs, and—since few suburbs are of any pure type—these are added to by a fringe of commuters or even by a few minor industries. Thus have grown up a series of specialized suburbs reflecting some original central interest not economic in character. Evanston and Forest Park are familiar educational suburbs of Chicago. New York has decentralized most of its asylums, around which suburbs have grown. It has its children's village, its Sing Sing, its Kings Park. The contrast between Mineola, the county-seat of Nassau County, and the surrounding commuting suburbs has already been noted. From Boston Harbor to Venice, California, the resort suburbs constitute a distinct and famous group.

More General Grounds of Suburban Variation

In so immense a country as the United States with so wide a range of cities still more general grounds of difference between suburbs are to be anticipated. Thus the suburb in the South does not perform exactly the same functions as that of the North.

Climate and Suburbs

We have already noted the unexpected degree of suburban development surrounding the uncrowded cities of the South. It is perhaps too much to argue explicitly that a warm climate makes for the decentralization of cities. This hypothesis, however, is strongly reinforced by the example of Southern California. In the Los Angeles suburbs particularly, a distinct type is to be recognized based upon climate. Already this metropolis of Southern California has proportionately more automobiles in its streets than any other American city.

OTHER VARIETIES OF SUBURBS 115

Obviously ease of transit by any method is greatly facilitated by an equable climate, and transit has been hitherto the soul of suburban existence. It is not too much to say that suburban life in Southern California has reached a development relatively greater than anywhere else in the United States. Thus the worker in the newly opened oil-fields does not in the main settle in congested industrial towns, but, by grace of his flivver, scatters out into many cheap bungalow suburbs. The farmer, on the other hand, who is characteristically shy of town institutions, finds close social connection with the town not only possible but congenial. But the farmer's changed attitude undoubtedly reflects his change of circumstances. He no longer lives upon an isolated farmstead, but upon a small acreage near town, where he enjoys all urban facilities and has many and near neighbors and frequently a town business besides. The ultimate secret of the far-flung suburban area, in which both the industrial worker and the farmer keep close connection with the city without the surrender of spacious conditions, is climate. It permits and encourages a broader basis of civilization in suburban life than ever before. This unique relationship between the city and its distant environs explains and partly justifies the apparent intention of Los Angeles to annex most of the population of the southern half of its State.

Suburbs of Smaller Cities

Except for types based upon climatic conditions, the largest cities have developed virtually all the varieties of suburbs which this chapter has described. The smaller cities naturally have to content themselves with fewer sorts, primarily because they are themselves simpler and less varied. Frequently small cities are virtually without true suburban population.

We have already had occasion to ask whether such suburbs as these smaller cities have are actually suburban in character. Omitting smaller cities which are themselves suburbs or which fall into urban clusters not related to one another as suburbs and center (as, for example, Davenport, Iowa, Moline and Rock Island, Illinois), the following variations appear worthy of note:[4]

(1) Apparently more often than in the case of large cities, communities adjoining smaller cities are virtually merely other parts of the same city. They are under a different political jurisdiction and may perhaps be separated by physical barriers or by somewhat different types of population and occupation. But they present no contrast in the degree of congestion of population and are not more distant from the center or distinct in their community life than many areas included in the political city. They do not function as suburbs in the sense in which they are defined in the first chapter. They are rather marginal areas of urban communities without definite functional distinctions.

(2) The most representative industrial suburbs of the

[4] The following generalization is based upon a limited and non-statistical examination of the seventy-six cities of from 50,000 to 100,000 population. Their incorporated suburbs have been listed and the general character of their surrounding populations considered. No body of statistics, however, exists covering this field.

OTHER VARIETIES OF SUBURBS

small city is the mill village or small industrial community surrounding a single industry. Such suburbs radiate in all directions beyond the boundaries of the minor manufacturing cities of New England. They are the outstanding type in the suburban development of the industrial South. Thus, Spartanburg, South Carolina, a city of one-family houses, in the main but one story high, housing some 20,000 people on minimum-sized lots, has more than a dozen dependent villages surrounding near-by cotton-mills. The ratio of dwellings to families gives Spartanburg little more congestion than a country town. The people in the mill villages also occupy one-story single-family houses on small lots. There is consequently virtually no contrast in the degree of congestion. These villages are, however, almost without independent business and are strongly dependent upon the city for recreation and many institutional services. They are the characteristic suburbs of the Piedmont section.

Only occasionally do smaller Southern cities present an example of a genuine suburb like West Tampa. Here a foreign population has developed a full round of separate institutions and a highly organized community life.

Similarly, the minor Northern cities built upon the coal-fields have developed their own type of industrial suburbs.

(3) The favorite residential suburb of the smaller cities of New England and the Northeast is some fine old country village with a long tradition now brought within the sphere of city influence and appropriated by

city people. Good examples are Fairfield, with respect to Bridgeport, and Watertown, with respect to Waterbury. Small cities in all regions also send out their own new suburban offshoots, frequently reflecting various economic levels. Thus Montgomery, Alabama, has three suburbs, one distinctly of industrial workers, one of middle-class people, and one of the unusually well-to-do.

Returning to the question whether suburbs have the same significance for their cities that the suburbs of larger cities have, it is obvious that they have not the same value in relieving the pressure of great central congestion. The small cities do not have such pressure. Their one or two tall buildings are Towers of Babel—monuments to urban pride rather than the legitimate consequences of high land value. Their suburban people, as has been shown, do not have characteristically larger house lots, fewer families to the acre, or more cubic feet of space per dwelling than is to be found in most of the area of such a parent city. Often, indeed, housing congestion is actually greater in the outlying mill village. In other words, the character of the environment is not greatly changed either for work or for home life. Such phenomena reflect the simple physical expansion of cities rather than their definite differentiation into center and suburbs such as has taken place in the larger metropolis. It is a mere overflow of urban life not under pressure. There is, on the contrary, something eruptive about the true suburb, of relief from tension, a strong propulsion in the search for space and freedom. The suburbs of the smaller cities are therefore

OTHER VARIETIES OF SUBURBS 119

largely suburbs in the making rather than true suburbs. Such a spreading out of population may be very desirable for individual families and is a safeguard against possible harmful congestion in the future. It has, however, little in common with the travail of already congested cities to find breathing-space for their people or with the tremendous compulsion under which they are continuously reassorting their elements in response to the competition for space.

While, therefore, the suburbs of smaller cities properly fall within the general suburban trend and constitute an important element in the total movement, their variety is less interesting. Both logically and numerically they are the lesser aspect of our theme.

SUMMARY OF TYPES OF SUBURBS

The long series of differences between suburban communities which has now been listed and commented upon does not directly serve to fix a set of types. The industrial suburb may be either foreign or American. In either case its dominant population may be either young or old, its origins ancient or recent, its development planned or unplanned, its physical structure centralized or scattered. Any tendency seeking to become established by reason of any one of these factors may be neutralized by others. It is only when a number of factors looking somewhat in a common direction coincide in the same suburb that anything consistent enough to be called a type appears. Thus industrial suburbs are apt to have many foreigners. If they are small, newly created, and centralized about a single industry, if they have no previous community tradition to steady them and are so isolated that foreign traditions get unchallenged sway, a very definite type of the poor industrial suburb eventuates.

Similarly a community of American commuters of more than average wealth is apt to be composed of people of more than average age. It may be built either upon the foundations of an old community or upon new foundations; it may or may not have a physical center around which the new forces rally. The tendency of its factors to checkmate one another may leave a rather incoherent and colorless result in which accidental propinquity and common dependence upon the city is the main bond between populations. On the other hand, if a successful and well-to-do suburb of American population is based upon the long-established ways of a slowly evolving community with an acknowledged center and a unifying tradition the elements of the situation tend to reinforce each other and to develop a consistent type.

Nearly all the larger suburbs include such a mingling of elements as make them essentially cross-sections of the entire range of city life. While, therefore, the suburban movement as a whole consists in a series of siftings out of factors of urban life which can be decentralized and in giving each a fairly coherent grouping of forces and a broad place in which to weave its pattern of community life under its own name, the attempt fairly to characterize even the simpler cases thus appears to be difficult if not impossible.

OTHER VARIETIES OF SUBURBS

Popular Categories

Our study accordingly must confess its inability to furnish a satisfying list of the types of suburbs which surround American cities. The rough categories, "poor industrial suburb," "decentralized residential suburb," "well-marked suburban residential community," and "mixed suburb," will have to serve until very much more intimate and comparative social studies of individual cases enable us to do better. The resort suburb, the school suburb, the exclusive suburb of the very rich, the suburban mill-town, also furnish self-defining characteristics sufficient for practical use. But our analysis at least satisfies the major purpose of this chapter, which is to awaken a realization of the wide variations which lie beneath the necessary shorthand of generalization. If, therefore, we continue to talk about the suburbs as a group we shall also continue to remember the wealth of concrete variety which the term embraces.

Validity of Basic Generalizations

This confession does not mean that our generalizations are not valid and valuable. The basic distinction between the decentralization of consumption and of production is unchallenged. The suburbs as a group do represent selection. Not all industries and not all people are fit subjects for suburbanizing. The city is a crude and unsorted aggregation of all sorts of men and processes gathered into an accidental collection. The suburb is a natural process of sifting and of the more or less efficient disposal of the specific elements of urban life in separate places. It is a series of areas devoted to partial and limited segments of the broad interests and activities necessary to civilization. It is a set of specializations with a geographical basis.

What makes the big city bad is the omnibus character of its contents. It is a jumble and a confusion, incoherent and therefore inefficient. The smaller size and more select quality of the elements entering into the suburb make it more promising to take hold of the problem of the city at that point. Our analysis has proved the thesis of the opening chapter: The suburbs are simpler, more homogeneous, more rational, and consequently more manageable. Pulling a larger fraction of the city out into them is equivalent to unscrambling a mess of complications and serves to divide urban social difficulties up into masses of such proportion that mankind can perhaps handle them. The suburbs at least give it a better chance to try.

CHAPTER V

THE COST OF SUBURBAN LIVING

THERE are two main reasons why more people do not live in the suburbs: first, because they do not wish to live away from the city, and, second, because they cannot afford to. The first is a psychological reason which is assumed throughout the book; the second is an economic one.

It is the economic factor with which this chapter deals.

Non-Comparability of City and Suburbs

A major difficulty of the subject is that the things which it desires to compare are not really commensurate. City and suburbs each have fundamentally important advantages which the other lacks. The city, on its part, has to practise real old-fashioned economy in the sense of doing without. The thing primarily economized is, of course, space, particularly space for the housing of human beings.

A concrete illustration of this economizing is found in the tendency of apartment construction in New York City compared with the actual provision of housing space for 22,000 families (chiefly in suburban areas) by the United States Housing Corporation during the war. The New York tendency is strongly toward small apartments as shown in the following comparison between 1912 and 1924:[1]

TABLE 18—PERCENTAGE DISTRIBUTION OF NUMBER OF ROOMS PER APARTMENT CONSTRUCTED IN 1912 AND 1924

Number of rooms	Percentage distribution	
	1912	1924
3	20	42
4	44	38
5	24	12
6	5	4
All other	7	4

This table shows clearly the persistent tendency of the New York family to cut down its housing space from four to three and from five to four rooms in an attempt to meet rising rents, 80 per cent. of the new constructions of 1924 being of four-room apartments or less.

The United States Housing Corporation, on the contrary, housed 85 per cent. of its workers in one-family houses, most of them detached structures, and gave nearly half of the families six rooms, as shown in the following table:[2]

Number of Rooms	Percentage
3	5
4	20
5	22
6	47
7	3
8	3

[1] From chart shown in exhibit of data from the "Plan of New York and Environs," 1924.
[2] Report of U. S. Housing Corporation, Vol II, p. 387.

THE COST OF SUBURBAN LIVING

In contrast with present New York tendencies the Housing Corporation built 75 per cent. of its houses with a larger number of rooms than 80 per cent. of the New York construction in 1924 provided, and gave only 25

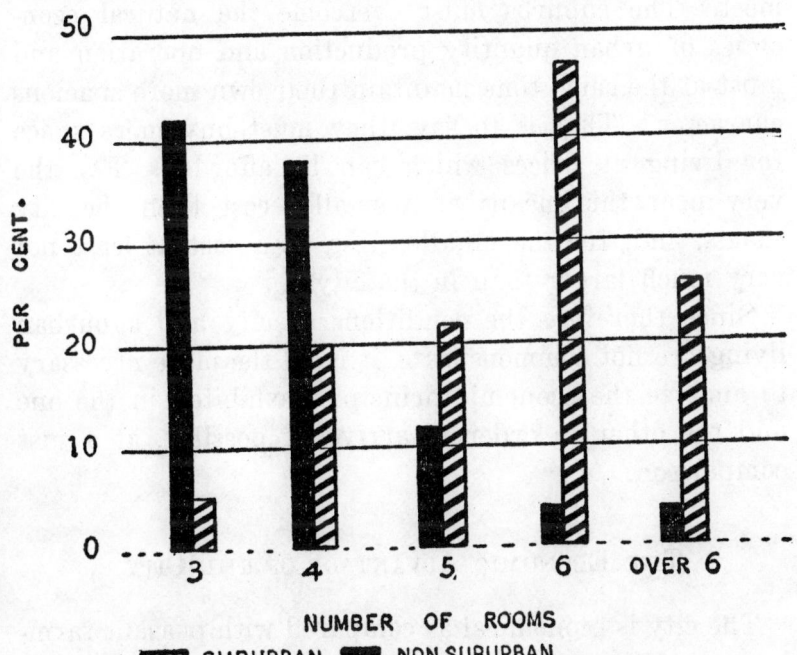

PERCENTAGE DISTRIBUTION OF NUMBER OF ROOMS PER FAMILY IN NEW YORK CITY APARTMENTS

Constructed in 1924 and in houses, chiefly suburban, erected by the United States Housing Corporation during the World War.

per cent. the number of rooms which 80 per cent. of the inhabitants of the new New York apartments will have to get along with. No wonder the theme of the civic hymn of the metropolis is "The Sidewalks of New York" and not its homes.

The difference between city and suburb in the matter of cost is not therefore one of reërecting identical living conditions in another setting, but of providing better living conditions at a cost which people can afford to meet. The suburbs must overcome the natural economies of urban quantity production and operation and must at the same time maintain their own more spacious character. That is to say, they must buy more space for living at prices which can be afforded. For the very poor this means at a smaller cost than the city exacts, and, for the middle class, at a cost at least not very much larger than in the city.

Since therefore the conditions of city and suburban living are not commensurate, it is all the more necessary to analyze the economic principles exhibited in the one and the other in order to arrive, if possible, at a just comparison.

The Economic Advantage of the City

The city is economical as compared with peasant farming and the cottage industries which preceded it. There were great savings in labor and time when the workman was brought to the factory and given a machine tool to work with; when both were placed on natural trade routes and near the great markets; when goods were produced in the immediate vicinity of immense masses of consumers who in turn constituted a vast labor supply. The fact of these savings has virtually required an ever-increasing proportion of the manufacture of

THE COST OF SUBURBAN LIVING 127

goods to be located in cities. A greater percentage of the industrial wage-earners of the United States were in cities of 10,000 and over in 1919 than in 1899, the rate of gain being greatest in the largest cities.[3] Certainly there is no trend as yet toward general decentralization.

ECONOMICS OF CITY VS. SUBURBS

A good part of the city's advantage over the remote country-side applies also to the suburbs. Cities are ecomical; suburbs are costly. This is true partly because cities economize space, partly because many of their methods and conditions are inherently less expensive. They enjoy savings incident to large-scale production, and to quantity operation of housing and public facilities; also in the merchandising of goods in large quantities. They perform their functions near at hand, while the suburbs are distant. The disadvantage of distance can be largely overcome by the rapid transit facilities of modern civilization, but it costs money to do so. Cities crowd people and businesses close together in an effort to save time, and in large measure they do save it. The elements in cities which do not decentralize readily, or not at all, are largely prevented by the greater cost of suburban living. This is especially the fate of the poor. Suburban life is less available for them than for other classes, a circumstance

[3] Abstracts of the Census of Manufacturing, 1914 (p. 284) and 1919 (p. 289).

which led certain sociologists to define the suburbs as characteristically the habitat of the well-to-do.[4]

The matter may be most quickly understood by an examination one by one of the factors of cost differently involved in city or in suburban living respectively. The question is: If the city and the suburbs each furnished equal quantities of goods, facilities, and advantages, with no difference in quality involved, in which would living cost the most? The five factors primarily involved are land, housing, taxes, cost of transportation, and economic security through opportunity of employment. On four out of five of these counts the city has the natural advantage.[5]

Land, to be sure, is cheaper in the suburbs where there is less demand and less competition for it; but—other things being equal, except space—housing, taxes, and transportation tend to be cheaper in the city, and economic security is greater there.

Housing is cheaper because to build one house upon

[4] Lindeman, "The Community," p. 46.

[5] The above list is longer than that usually given, which makes land, housing and transportation the essential factors and stops there. It excludes food, clothing, recreation, and expenditures for health and higher ideals—such as education and religion—as not being essentially affected one way or the other by suburban living. Professor James Ford (in Nolen's "City Planning," p. 334 f.) thinks that expenditures for health, vegetables, clothing, recreation, and drink are smaller in the suburbs. The first ought to be true to some extent, but there are no proofs of it. The second is to be doubted. The inclusion of the other items sounds suspiciously like a formula for getting along without what one wants, which is precisely the reason why so many people are not willing to live in the suburbs.

THE COST OF SUBURBAN LIVING

another saves a foundation, and to build one against another saves a wall, every time the process is completed. There are similar economies in operation and upkeep. Taxes are cheaper because the unit cost of providing equal public utilities is less where there are more to share the cost. Transportation is cheaper because distances are shorter and there are more people to support transportation facilities. Economic security is greater because a wide variety of functions is what makes the city, and this affords wide opportunities of work.

Of course in practice these natural advantages of the city are greatly diminished by a multitude of modifying and neutralizing factors. The forces involved do not all work in the same direction nor with equal power. The actual costs of living are the outcome of many causes. We must trace some of these neutralizing factors and try to estimate their total force in modifying the city's natural advantage.

The City's Handicap in Land Partly Overcome

By a strange reversal of the natural tendency, the handicap of the city in the matter of the high cost of land is in some measure neutralized both for the poorer classes of people and for the weaker businesses and industries.

The city is a place of colossal and incredible land values. In the greatest cities they constitute the controlling factor in the total cost of completed structures. Thus on Manhattan Island land constitutes 60 per cent.

of the average total value of improved property, in contrast with 39 per cent. in Brooklyn and 20 per cent. or less in suburbs. It dwindles down from this to farmland values which would make the cost of the average rural house-lot some twenty-five to fifty dollars.

This is a heavy handicap to overcome; but the city is also the place of spectacular contrasts and changes in land values. A corner lot is very often worth more than twice as much as the "inside" lot next to it. A block's distance from a strategic point can make an almost unimaginable difference in values. Within a half-mile radius prices may easily fluctuate a hundredfold. Finally there is much land in cities of virtually no value whatever.

The most conspicuous areas of this sort are just outside the central business and industrial sections. The encroachment of industry and business have made them undesirable for human habitation, but they are not yet required for other use, and one does not know whether or when they will be. Industry and business always ruin a larger area than they can use. The suburban trend itself works havoc with values in such areas by providing an outlet for the more ambitious people who wish to escape from the proximity of factories and stores. The consequence is the "blighted areas" in which land for which there is no present demand is covered with old structures.

In these structures the poorest of the city's people find habitation. Their presence farther depreciates the surrounding property from a residential standpoint,

THE COST OF SUBURBAN LIVING 131

and the almost endless process is thus set up which has put 100,000 negroes in Chicago's most fashionable district of a quarter of a century ago, has given the finest mansions of old St. Louis over to Russian Jews and rural emigrants from the Ozarks, and put a "furnished rooms to let" sign in the old Rockefeller homestead in Cleveland.

Now, the suburbs can nowhere compete with the cheapness of urban housing under such conditions or, if they can it is only by furnishing living conditions still less desirable. Obviously this is living below any normal or decent human standards, but from the standpoint of bidding for population by cheap housing the city has this advantage in spite of its very high average land values. Its weakness has become its strength. Probably the hardest suburban problem is to meet the competition of these abnormal low costs of giving the poorer people a place to live in the city.

The City's Advantage in Housing

Apart from the socially disastrous use of worn-out housing, the city has a natural advantage in the construction of new dwellings in the economy of multi-family housing. This may be measured by the percentage of rent which is absorbed by taxes for single-family houses as compared with apartments. An investigation of the Boston Real Estate Exchange in 1924 showed apartments in that city paying only half as much of their rental income for taxes as single family houses did, two- and four-family houses falling between the two extremes. The experience of the United States Housing Corporation proved afresh that the single-family house is by a large percentage the most expensive type.

In spite of important offsets, which a subsequent paragraph will concede, the city's advantage in housing continues. The main proof of it is that city apartments and tenements are being built in very large quantities, while one-family houses are not being built except for people of more than average prosperity. A special "Report on the Building Situation" of the National Industrial Conference Board in 1924 summarizes the case in the epigram, "Small Houses—Small Profits."

In view, however, of the greatly reduced space for living which this "cheaper" city housing affords, it is better to regard this item as not really comparable as between the city and the suburb. Cost comparisons relate to such different quantities of the same thing that they do not really mean the same thing.

The City's Advantage in Taxes

Taking American cities as a whole, taxes as measured by the proportion of income from property which they absorb, are highest in those of from 25,000 to 100,000 population, one third of which are suburbs. The street and sidewalk in front of the middle-class suburban home would amply suffice for fifty families in New York, or for twenty-five families in the neighboring middle-sized city of Paterson. It is obvious that communities which

THE COST OF SUBURBAN LIVING 133

put the cost of such extensive public facilities upon the shoulders of few people must levy high taxes to meet them.

This is particularly true of the newer small city which is suddenly confronted with a demand for up-to-date facilities and is trying to pay for them all at once. Very clear evidence of this condition appears in the census bulletin entitled "Financial Statistics of Cities, 1922." The following trends appear: The smaller the city, the larger percentage of its costs of government go for "outlays," defined as "the acquisition and construction of more or less permanent properties and public improvements." The rate of expenditure for this item increases progressively as the size of the city decreases. It is 26.7 per cent. for cities of 500,000 population and over, and 30.3 per cent. for those of from 30,000 to 50,000 population.[6]

Again, the smaller the city, the larger the proportion of its costs devoted to general departments of government which have to go to schools and highways.[7]

Finally, the smaller cities have the greater excess of governmental costs over revenue receipts, though the discrepancy on this point is not great. This means, however, that more of the money which they spend has to be borrowed.[8]

Consequently, the larger city can generally offer equivalent facilities and public functions at a smaller per capita cost than the adjoining suburb. Its advantage in

[6] "Financial Statistics of Cities," 1922, p. 189.
[7] *Ibid.*, p. 210.
[8] *Ibid.*, p. 177.

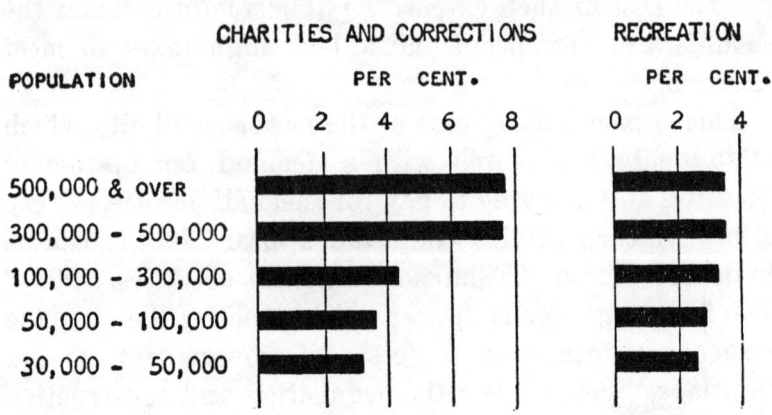
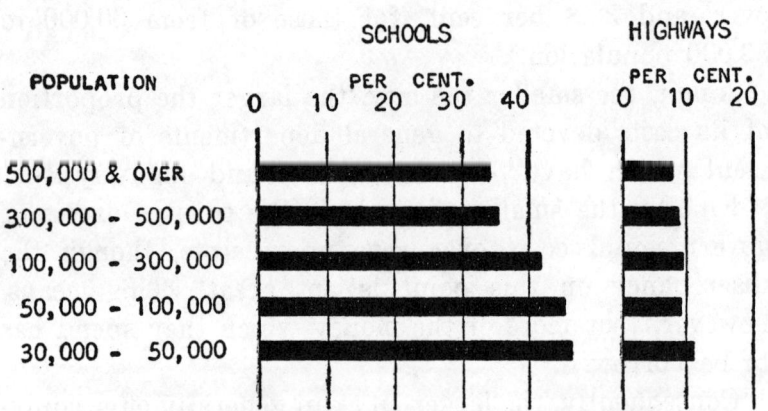

PERCENTAGE OF GENERAL MUNICIPAL EXPENDITURES GOING TO SPECIFIED DEPARTMENTS OF GOVERNMENT BY SIZE OF CITIES

Increase with size of city (above); decrease (below).

THE COST OF SUBURBAN LIVING 135

this respect is only partly neutralized by the factors above mentioned. The average per capita tax of fourteen larger residential suburbs of the nine cities used in previous calculations is $49, while that of the parent cities is only $44.[9]

The City's Advantages in Transportation

Obviously the cost of moving people and goods within the smaller area of the city is less than that of bringing them in equal quantities from the distant suburbs. Distance, as before remarked, can be overcome by modern facilities, but only at a price.

The additional cost of the long haul is virtually prohibitive to the very poor. The city's advantage in cheaper transportation is decisive and probably permanent.

The City's Additional Advantage: Greater Opportunity for Employment

When the city worker says that he cannot afford to live in the suburb he is not thinking exclusively of what it would cost him in cash. There is the very important additional consideration of economic security. This the city furnishes by affording wide opportunities of work.

Such opportunities the worker needs because it frequently takes the labor of more than one member of

[9] "Financial Statistics of Cities," 1922. Calculated from Table 14.

the family to support it. Suburbs might furnish work for one, but only the city can furnish it for two or three in the industries or business which each prefers. American youth do not follow the callings of their fathers. The father may work in a factory, the daughter in an office, the son in a garage. Even the mother may go her own economic way, of necessity if not from choice. At this point the city's lead over the smaller suburbs is unquestionable.

Then there is the question of the future. Danger of unemployment forever haunts the worker. He may have a job to-day but lack it to-morrow. If he is out of work the city furnishes wider choice of re-employment.

Industry, on its part, is largely dependent upon an accessible labor supply, and some industries, particularly those of a seasonal nature, think that they need a large labor surplus. Workers who live at home cannot be carried off into remote suburbs by separate industries. They can only be found in the city where transportation lines converge. Consequently industry can frequently better afford to pay the high cost of city land than to take its chance on a scant labor supply in the suburbs.

The Narrow Margin of Suburban Economic Opportunity: The Turn of the Tide

These advantages operate strongly in favor of the city up to a certain point. Beyond this point they steadily diminish until a margin of possibility is created for the suburbs. The factor which turns the tide is congestion. Cities become so crowded that they can-

THE COST OF SUBURBAN LIVING 137

not use their advantages exactly as an army jammed into a narrow space cannot manœuver systematically and becomes a mob.

Thus, city land values, always a heavy offset to other economies, frequently pyramid to unbelievable heights.

Next, for example, city conditions require dearer building construction. The city's economizing in multi-family dwellings is sharply subject to the law of diminishing returns on this score. City building has to be more expensive structurally to sustain the weight of adding story after story. Legal requirements are more severe in the interests of sanitation and safety from fire. Economic considerations also make it more costly because all elements of expense must be balanced by corresponding income: one cannot afford to put low-cost housing on high-cost land.

Increased Cost of Government in Cities

In the matter of taxation, it is obvious that cities face mounting costs in the effort to meet new problems of their own creation. They could furnish more economically what the suburbs have by way of public facilities, but they cannot do with what the suburbs have. The penalty of congestion is relatively higher taxes for health, charity, and crime, and for recreational facilities.[10]

Again, cities require more expensive types of facilities—wider streets (which they frequently do not get), heavier pavements, larger sewers, etc.

[10] "Financial Statistics of Cities," 1922, p. 210.

Finally, cities are over-large units of administration, and this partly offsets the natural economies of large-scale service. Their governments are notoriously bad, and taxes may not go as far as in more intelligently managed smaller places.

Transit Inefficient and Slow

Turning to transportation, it is notorious that the city's transit facilities are frequently slow and crowded so that it often takes the suburbanite no longer to get from his house to his work than it does the city-dweller. The suburbanite also travels in greater comfort than does the strap-hanger on the street-car. In not a few cities transit facilities have come close to breaking down, and, considering the wear and tear of travel within their borders, urban advantage at this point is often wholly neutralized.

Even the wide labor market which the city affords sometimes becomes over-organized and costly to such a degree that a narrower but more contented working population, more closely identified with a particular industry, becomes more profitable.

In the larger and more congested cities all these factors conspire to give the suburbs an economic chance; a chance, that is to say, to furnish the additional living space which is their essential advantage at not impossible costs.

The utmost which the most extreme modification of city advantage gives to the suburbs is, however, a narrow margin of opportunity. They must not ask or ex-

THE COST OF SUBURBAN LIVING 139

pect too much. It is important, therefore, to measure this margin very precisely.

THE CITY'S SACRIFICE: THE SUBURB'S SUPERIORITY

One needs to emphasize afresh the city's extreme sacrifice of space by reason of which alone its offer of cheaper rents is possible. Only by so doing can one appreciate the seemingly modest anticipations of the suburbs. Reverting to the experience of the United States Housing Corporation, he finds that, of fifty thousand families provided for, 43 per cent. were housed in detached homes, 18 per cent. in semi-detached, and 23 per cent. in row houses, leaving 16 per cent. to be housed in other types of buildings including apartments and dormitories. One fifth were in four-room houses, another fifth in five-room houses, and nearly one half in six-room houses. The recommended density was six or seven families per acre, including streets, with a maximum allowed of twelve families per gross acre. A lower density was declared to be "seldom economical or necessary for proper living."

The above may be regarded as a reasonable American standard for suburban industrial housing. Compare it with recent zoning restrictions of the industrial city of Paterson. This city plans to house the bulk of its population in habitations accommodating six or twelve families on a fifty-foot lot, or at the rate of from 55 to 110 families per acre. This provision of space is in immense contrast with the towering tenements of the greater cities; yet the average housing of the industrial workers of the Housing Corporation communities would furnish approximately ten times the room enjoyed by the least densely housed tenement-dweller in Paterson.

This fairly states the contrast for the working classes. With respect to the middle classes the characteristic fifty-foot suburban lot of the residential suburbs would have to serve twenty to twenty-five, or even forty families in residential apartments in the greater cities. In moving into such an apartment the suburbanite would expect to sacrifice at least two thirds of his gross living space, including cellar and attic, and nearly half of the space of the more constantly used rooms.

Drawing the contrast between the residential suburbs and even the "model" industrial ones, one notes that suburbs using 50- to 100-foot lots are consuming from one and one half to three times the space per family regarded as essential for satisfactory suburban living for the industrial classes. This is luxury in the use of space.

Of course the much larger space occupancy of the suburbs has to be paid for; consequently the net result is in danger of going against the suburban dweller, even when he lives on much cheaper land and when he takes careful account of the factor of the city's diminishing advantage, and profits thereby.

Living on the Street

It is also to be remembered that the consequence of city congestion is not entirely proportionate to the

THE COST OF SUBURBAN LIVING 141

spacial differences as mathematically stated. Humanity is not actually compressible to any such extent. As we have seen, the life of the poor simply flows out of their crowded habitations to occupy the streets, sidewalks, and public places. The middle classes spend much of their time in restaurants and amusement places. Life ceases to be lived at home. The family has to adjust itself to changed circumstances. Unquestionably it does so at very serious loss. Yet somehow the adjustment is made, and nothing which the suburb has to offer seems worth its costs to the more adaptable city-dweller.

The more serious factor, however, is what may be called the unequal compressibility of the different age-groups. While unmarried youth, childless couples, and the aged may fit easily into narrow quarters which they can supplement by the use of public places, the city is no place for children.

Theirs is the great necessity which largely creates suburbs in spite of their frequently greater cost. The question therefore is, not whether suburban living is literally cheaper, but whether it is within the options open to the poor and middle-class populations for the sake of childhood and a sane and more wholesome life for all. This is the next point for direct consideration.

What the Suburb Must Do to Meet Its Naturally Higher Costs

This problem may be faced either directly, as in the case of the residential suburb, or indirectly as in the case of the industrial one. The question in the first instance is: Can the home afford to suburbanize? The question in the second instance is: Can the factory afford to move to the country, thereby carrying with it other homes (which might not be able to afford the cost independently) to form new industrial suburbs?

This is virtually to say that the problem of suburban cost must be solved in different ways for the poorer industrial workers and for the middle class, it is being assumed that the rich can already take their choice as between city and country.

From the standpoint of the standard of living of the poor in cities it is obvious that the economic problem of suburban living is to reduce the cost to the veriest minimum. No mere change of the theater of life can in itself increase income. Practically speaking, the question is whether, by the severest cutting down of cost, the poor can afford cottage homes surrounded by green grass as a substitute for tenement-houses, sidewalks, and pavements.

For middle-class purses the question is that of substituting one set of advantages for others not precisely equivalent ones. This class enjoys an economic margin on the basis of which choices may be made. The decision as between city and suburb thus becomes partly a matter of determining the values of what is surrendered as over against those of what is gained, and it is impossible entirely to disentangle the cost factor. Practically speaking, the question is then whether a middle-class family which wants to live in the suburbs can afford to do so.

THE COST OF SUBURBAN LIVING 143

SUBURBAN LAND VALUES

With respect to land, the question is that of using the suburban advantage of cheaper land without abusing it.

Of course surburban land, in attractive surroundings carrying with it social prestige, can never be cheap. Cheap land lies in inaccessible places. There is only one way of making it accessible, and that is to get enough other people to live near-by in order to support rapid transit facilities. But this inevitably raises land values. The decision to build a Hudson River bridge would, it is said, increase suburban land values in the area affected by an amount equal to its entire cost, overnight.

Land values increase with population. Double the population, and one doubles its price. The exactitude of this statement has been challenged, but the principle is clear. New calculation for the New York suburban area substantiates the fact that residential land values increase directly as population and inversely as taxes. The ratio of increase undoubtedly differs for land devoted to other uses than residential and for land of different physical types.

The poor can meet the increased cost of suburban land only by going far out, and thus adding transportation cost and undue length of time to the work day, by scattering out in thin settlements along the lines of existing transportation facilities, or by occupying the unfashionable and frequently unhealthy margins of established communities. In other words, they have to do in the suburbs exactly what they had to do within the city if they desire to escape the immediate central congestion; namely, live on the margins or on land so undesirable that more fortunate people have passed it by, such as swampy or undrained land or areas which have seen better days or have been passed over by the whims of fashion.

There is also a great and virtually incalculable inequality of the diffusion of increased land values about strategic or focal points. We have seen what vast difference in value a block's distance makes in the city. All the factors above mentioned and other obscure ones conspire to make equal distances from centers of work or of transportation very unequal in their effect upon land values, and thus to leave many opportunities within reach of the poor man's purse.

On the whole, however, the only terms on which the poor can probably hope to occupy suburban land permanently is by economizing it. They must, in other words, make a compromise between the intensive use of land inevitable in the city and the luxurious use of the residential suburbs. We have already noted the standards of the United States Housing Corporation, which placed eight or ten working-men's families on an acre, with a possible maximum of twelve families. This latter is the standard set by the British Labor party in its post-war political platform. This whittling down of suburban space seriously challenges the conception of the suburb as popularly held and inevitably surrenders many of the advantages of land contacts which a later chapter will attempt to appraise. For the present, however, the best thinking of the world does not see

THE COST OF SUBURBAN LIVING 145

any more generous economic solution. The suburban poor must seek out cheaper land and economize even on that.

The middle class, with their ampler economic leeway, can afford to subordinate the land factor, since suburban land constitutes a relatively small proportion of the cost of the average suburban home. The home owner has the farther backing of appreciating land values. He may maintain himself on land which he could not otherwise afford to own on account of the fact that the increase of population is making it more and more valuable every year. But even so, the trend in growing suburbs is always to smaller average lots as relentless rise in land values proceeds.

With respect to land for industry, the greater cheapness of suburban sites is a most important advantage for those which require large space for their processes or which produce bulky products of low value relative to its bulk.

Housing

The suburbs can overcome the city's advantage with respect to economic housing by using cheaper construction. This is not inappropriate and does not constitute a lowering of the standards of living in view of the greater safety and privacy of the detached home. Its fire risks are less, and it is freer from the over-close contact with neighbors. Putting the matter in another way, the suburbs can utilize the type of housing which has been evolved by the American country-side and village, adapting and improving it to its own purposes. The city, on the contrary, has devised and must use a special type.

Cheaper construction, however, cannot solve the problem entirely. In connection with the compromise in the use of land proposed for the industrial suburb, there must undoubtedly also be a partial use of multi-family dwellings. Housing two or even four families in semi-detached houses does not detract from the hygienic and social advantage of suburban living nearly so much as from its esthetic qualities and its pride. Neighborhoods in which such houses are properly proportioned to single-family houses may still remain at least five times as roomy as the average tenement district in the small city. Here some lawn and play space in the home yard, together with shrubbery and a bit of garden, are still possible.

There is no immediate human possibility that more than this can generally be made available for the poor. To a considerable extent they will have to occupy multi-family dwellings, and even these are not a commercially profitable investment under present suburban conditions. Roger Babson has recently pointed out that at least 75 per cent. of the new houses built in the United States within the past two years are within financial reach of only 10 per cent. of the families. This does not make the case for the suburban housing of the poor very promising unless strenuous social measures are taken to advance it.

There is of course the alternative of substandard housing of which illustrations have already been given.

THE COST OF SUBURBAN LIVING 147

Many cheap suburbs are building the type of habitation which humankind should not attempt to occupy. The exchange of tenement for such houses under suburban conditions is of doubtful value. Virtual slums for servants and for common labor are shamefully present on the outskirts of some of the wealthiest suburbs. In other words, the residential suburb for the poor is generally a poor thing. The man just moving up in the economic scale may profitably build a skeleton house which he will soon abandon. Ultimately, however, it will go into the hands of the permanently impoverished and constitute a sore spot in community life. Owing to climatic conditions of advantage, the cheap bungalow of the Pacific Coast does not entirely fall within this unfortunate category. It remains, however, that the real suburb of the poor must be the industrial suburb which must be large enough to afford variety of employment but spacious enough to permit the hygienic and some of the esthetic values of suburban life.

For the middle class the question of housing is essentially one of social standards. If the house is to be pleasant and to reflect the accepted manner of living of the group to which the family belongs, it cannot be cheap. More and more the luxuries of yesterday are taken for granted for the very conveniences of to-day. It is the cost of what some are pleased to call "complete living" as reflected in the habitation, as well as the essential luxury of the single-family dwelling within metropolitan areas, which works to the economic disadvantage of the middle-class man. He cannot have the housing he wants without paying roundly for it. Each family has to decide for itself whether the gains are worth the cost, and the decision rarely rests upon strictly economic grounds.

Taxation

Before considering whether the suburbs can do anything to meet the economic handicap of high taxes, one must consider what suburban taxes stand for. Tradition will answer, "safety, education, and charity." It requires radical restatement in the case of the American city. The cost of protection of property and life as expressed in the police, fire, and health departments is a very minor factor in the modern cost of city government. Education takes from one fifth to one fourth of the taxes, but over one half of them have to go for the maintenance of highways, for public service facilities, and for the creation of new permanent improvements or the payment of debt contracted therefor. The rising American standards of public facilities bear with unusual heaviness upon the suburbs, which naturally imitate the near-by cities and demand expenditures not dreamed of in independent communities of the same size.

In the careful cost-accounting of the United States Housing Corporation, even the most economical provision of facilities for industrial workers in suburban environments represented a cost of $400 per family on improvements outside the house lot, or more than twice the original value of the lot.

THE COST OF SUBURBAN LIVING 149

In no possible way can suburbs reduce taxes except by adopting policies of public economy. The luxuries must be subordinated to the necessities. In the practice of the United States Housing Corporation the water system, sidewalks, sewers, and lighting facilities were regarded as necessities, but paved streets, curbs, and gutters were deferred, and large permanent economies were effected in the use of eighteen or twenty-foot streets where traffic would be permanently light.

Of course, in the smaller and cruder suburbs economies go much farther than this, scaling down from communities which have the same external appearance as their neighbors but are without gas and with private cesspools to those which go frankly without sidewalks and compel each house to find its own water-supply. This solution of the problem of taxes by the acceptance of simpler community facilities works generally for communities up to a population of 25,000. A recent nation-wide investigation by the National Association of Real Estate Boards of the proportion of rent absorbed by taxes in American cities showed that it is lowest in those below this size. The explanation is that many of them are in the frontier stage of relationship to their physical site and to the problem of collective living. They have merely perched upon the land which they occupy, whereas the larger cities have had to dig themselves in. Rural standards of convenience and comfort have only been slightly departed from. The farmer scratches the surface of the earth but does not attempt radically to modify its contours. Before a city can reach permanent equilibrium, however, it has to remodel much of the original topography in creating the grades for its permanent highways and installing its various public facilities. Measured in terms of rent, taxes, as we have previously seen, are highest in cities of from 25,000 to 100,000 population, one third of which are suburban. The ultimate reason is doubtless because these cities are in transition from the perching to the permanent stage. They are undergoing the vast expenditures necessary to secure the full round of standard civic conveniences in a day in which the demand for every up-to-date luxury is rapidly mounting.

The problem of suburban life from the standpoint of taxation is largely that of a preservation of a type of relatively inexpensive suburb which is content to make a reasonable compromise between rural standards and the over-exacting demand of the modern city which the relatively smaller populations of suburban places should not expect to meet in full. Exactly as in the case of the individual family, so with the community, the question of doing without luxuries must be faced.

To some extent the suburbs can meet the high cost of facilities by coöperating with other political units, or they may hire some of their public services from places large enough to constitute efficient units for the operation of such facilities. Not every suburb can possibly afford an independent water-supply. The creation, therefore, of special districts in which groups of municipalities can unite in meeting such fundamental problems economically is one of the outstanding political phases of the suburban movement.

All told, however, if the poor are to have suburban

THE COST OF SUBURBAN LIVING 151

life, they must live in communities which go without many of the facilities which they have in the city, while the middle class must make legitimate compromises if they are not to be asked to pay out in taxes more than they can afford.

This solution is frankly adopted by the industries. They habitually attempt to maintain the advantage of cheaper land by finding out and locating in non-improved sections, frequently outside of corporation limits, where the taxes are low.

Transportation

The average wage of the industrial worker will not permit him to pay the cost of long-distance commutation. Nor can he afford to add the time necessary to his already long work day. It is proverbially stated that half an hour's time and a seven-cent fare constitute the practical maximum for the majority of such workers. A second fare is roughly equivalent to adding 10 per cent. to rent. Part of the advantage of suburban residence for the worker is often sought in the possession of sufficient land to furnish a garden. The difficulty with this idea is that land which is economically possible for gardening can generally be found only at great distances. The time which ought to be used in gardening is spent in going back and forth. It also means that the time in which the suburbanite hopes to enjoy with his family is correspondingly reduced. The claims of the work day, therefore, practically set rather narrow limits upon the possible distance of the home from the factory. The time is at least as important a factor as cost.

Generally, therefore, the working-man's suburb must be within the city limits or else in strictly industrial suburbs or in residential suburbs adjacent to them. As has repeatedly been indicated, only decentralization of industry makes suburban life generally possible for the poor. Daily commutation, in the sense that the middle-class residential suburbs know it, is beyond his reach.

Urban Transit Requirements

The technical problem of moving middle-class workers back and forth between their city work and their suburban homes is beyond the purpose of this discussion. Some of its factors may, however, be noted.

Transit requirements may be analyzed into means of meeting the needs of definite elements of the commuting population at the time and by the routes which they are compelled to travel. First, there is the movement of workers from their homes to the city; second, the later movement of the business and clerical workers; third, the movement within the city and within the work hours as required by industry and business; fourth, the movement of suburban shoppers after the domestic home work of the day is done; and, finally, that of recreation-seekers at night. The peak of the morning movement falls between eight and nine o'clock, during which hours about 10 per cent. of the total daily traffic is expected. There is a still higher peak at evening, constituting some 14 per cent. of the day's traffic, be-

THE COST OF SUBURBAN LIVING 153

cause the returning movements of workers and shoppers partly coincide.

Transit facilities must supply each of the component parts of these movements along the routes of daily travel of each. The simple formula of: walk to the trolley, ride to the city, walk to the office, gets indefinitely complicated in the case of the larger cities. Populations are increasingly served by motor-bus routes which deliver them at railroad stations. After the railroad trip comes one by ferry or subway, still followed frequently by a street-car trip, a walk to store, factory, or office, and finally a trip of very appreciable distance by elevator. The time necessary for each of these stages and the time lost in transfer from one to another counts up excessively, and the technical adjustment necessary to coördinate all into a constantly fluctuating but ever-flowing circulation of people and goods, day after day and year after year, constitutes a problem very imperfectly solved for most metropolitan communities.

The Cost of Commutation

The cost of average rail commutation probably adds from one sixth to one fifth to the nominal rent of the middle-class suburban dweller. As with the industrial worker he can find cheap land and housing only by going out to such a distance that the cost of transportation and the length of the work day entails great sacrifice upon strength and the enjoyment of family life.

The actual economic waste of this process in time and human energy is hard to calculate. On the one hand it is sometimes seriously proposed to finance billion-dollar transit improvements on the theory of adding the fifteen minutes saved thereby to the length of everybody's productive work day. On the other hand, there is the possibility that the time spent in transportation should be credited to relaxation and sociability. At least a process which consumes one eight to one sixth of the waking hours of suburban people cannot go on without involving very serious economic and social results.

Highway and Automobile

The outstanding factor in the transportation situation is, however, the return of the highway to primary importance for suburban traffic through the use of the automobile. Thus, even for New York City, the new city planning studies declare that highways are more important than all other systems of communication between the parts of the metropolitan districts. The autobus is rapidly supplementing where it is not supplanting trolley systems; and in smaller cities the use of the private automobile radically adds to the possibilities of economic suburban transportation. A group of working-men jointly using a depreciated flivver in going to and coming from work frequently have both convenient and profitable industrial transportation. The greater flexibility of the automobile, not dependent upon fixed routes, promotes the diffusion of increased land values and tends to prevent their extreme concentra-

THE COST OF SUBURBAN LIVING 155

tion around points of congestion created by rail and trolley transportation.

CRUCIAL SIGNIFICANCE OF TRANSPORTATION

The poor, as we have seen, cannot decentralize their homes independently of the movement of industry to the suburbs, and in the decentralization of industry the problem of transportation is of primary importance.

Two major processes are involved, the first being the delivery of goods to the immediate consumer. Here proximity must largely govern. Goods produced for city consumption should be manufactured as near the consumer as possible. A recent study of the food manufacturing industries [11] shows this trend as, for example, in the case of bakeries. The situation is, however, not without many inconsistencies, food products being frequently produced upon land higher in value than that adjoining the very people who are the ultimate consumers.

Goods, on the other hand, which are intended for the world market must be produced within easy reach of the basic distributing facilities such as harbors and the major railroad terminals. Inasmuch as the deep-water fringe of harbors is so limited, virtually all of it becomes surrounded by congested urban developments. Railroad belt-lines, however, and, increasingly, motor-trucks somewhat tend to equalize the accessibility of suburban

[11] "Plan of New York and Its Environs—Economic Series," Monograph No. 3 (1924).

factories to the great transit terminals. The cost, however, is at best a serious charge on the more distant factory.

Transportation an Impossible Solution

Neither for men nor for goods is improved transportation the major or ultimate solution of the problem of decentralization. The practicable limit of economic transit facilities is already more than reached in many communities. The real unraveling of the situation is such decentralization as will prevent the necessity of much of the present movement. Transit improvement so-called is at present largely a means of carrying more people and goods from one place where they ought not to be to another. What is needed is a logical arrangement of metropolitan districts so that the goods which are consumed may be produced near the consumer and the home of the worker located near his work. All the space necessary is to be found within the present range of metropolitan life. How it may be done is the theme of a subsequent chapter.

Opportunity of Employment

Here the suburban handicap is extreme and no solution is in sight except the radical one of the essential reconstruction of cities as just suggested. A wide opportunity of employment means economic security, and this the residential suburbs, as at present constituted, are less able within themselves to guarantee than any other form of civilization.

THE COST OF SUBURBAN LIVING

In contrast with the suburb the independent town has ordinarily a dependent rural area. The work which it performs is needed primarily in the service of the people of that area and only secondarily in the service of the townspeople themselves. Very frequently for towns of average trade development located in rural sections of average density, the population of the community outside of the town is greater than that inside and its wealth many times larger.

The suburbs characteristically do not have dependent areas for which they perform service, while on the other hand the city performs frequently the major part of the service for their own population. Consequently, work within the suburb is reduced to a minimum, determined not merely by the failure of production to be decentralized, but by the lack of contributory territory.

Indeed, frequent grouping of cities in clusters rather than in single urban units is the only thing which has made much of the suburban life of the industrial classes possible. These are large self-contained and overgrown suburbs which are really satellite or companion cities. They afford space for suburban life around them and at the same time offer a wide range of opportunity for employment as the necessarily more distant suburbs of a single central city cannot do.

SUMMARY OF SUBURBAN ECONOMICS

Summarizing what the suburbs can do to meet their severe economic costs, the following points should be emphasized:

With respect to land, they must compromise between the over-intensive use of the city and its extravagant use in the wealthier suburbs. An acre, or a half an acre, to a family is an idle dream. As suburban population increases it will have to sacrifice the time necessary to go out far enough to find cheap land, or else sacrifice elsewhere in its standard of living.

With respect to housing, the suburbs will have to use cheaper material and house part of their population in multi-family houses.

With respect to taxes, they must accept a standard of public expenditure for utilities which compromises between the crude and inconvenient life of the rural sections and the extravagant standards of mechanical efficiency and the public luxuries of the larger cities. To a limited extent they can economize on taxes by combining with other municipalities to provide service which they cannot economically handle alone.

With respect to transportation, the masses of suburban population must stick closer to the larger industrial suburbs and keep within the single-fare distance. The use of the private automobile, partly credited to recreation and health, is an increasingly possible resource in many cities. The middle-class suburbanite who can afford to pay for a long haul must credit the time spent with adding to his personal efficiency and put it so far as possible to social advantage.

With respect to work, the majority of industrial workers are limited by this factor also to proximity to the larger industrial suburbs where a variety of employment may be found.

THE COST OF SUBURBAN LIVING 159

For the individual family, the crux of the situation lies very frequently in the social requirements which it acknowledges and the compromises with them which it is willing to make. Thus the suburbanite has to operate his house as a detached domestic unit. The service of engineer, janitor, elevator-man, and the like which the more fortunate city dwellers enjoy and collectively pay for—and which add from one fifth to one fourth to the cost of their nominal rent—must in the suburbs be performed by unpaid family labor or by private servants. Someone must shovel away the snow for each suburban family in winter and mow the individual lawn in summer. If the family is willing to perform for itself the full equivalent of the labor part of these services it can frequently bring the cost of suburban living within its financial ability. If all must be performed by hired labor the cost is proportionately greater than for the same service collectively secured in the city.

This is the immediate factor which frequently turns the scales as between possible and impossible suburban life. A more remote economic consideration is of course that of health, to which the work of the private home may contribute not inconsiderably. Ultimately, however, this merges with social considerations such as family integrity and privacy, closer neighborhood ties, and richer human fellowship.

From the standpoint of industry, suburban economics involve the working out of an equation in which the cheaper land and generally smaller corporation taxes of the suburb offset greater distance from the primary transportation facilities such as docks and railroad terminals and the lack of a wide labor market.

Can the Suburb Meet Its Costs?

Certainly not all elements of the city's life can ever afford to decentralize. Far more, however, than at present, it ought to do so, on the grounds of broad social and human advantage. This makes it important to use any possible economic loophole for an escape from the city. The possibilities are by no means yet exhausted. There is a margin of available suburban advantage even from the economic standpoint.

The inconclusive character of much argument on the subject is due to the fact already indicated that the experiences involved are not directly comparable. A not inconsiderable fraction of the human contracts of city men and suburbanites is taken up with endless debate as to the respective advantages of the two versions of metropolitan life. Many of the disputants have tried both sorts, and all have thought much about them both. The inexhaustible nature of their debate and its intriguing quality are of course due to the fact that ultimately there are different values which different minds ascribe to the respective advantages and disadvantages. For the things compared are not physical equivalents, and the two types of life do not permit identical procedures.

The only conclusive argument is that of the facts. There is, as we have shown, an actual suburban trend greater than that toward living in more congested

THE COST OF SUBURBAN LIVING

urban environments. If, therefore, costs of suburban life are greater, they are at least costs which can be borne for the sake of peculiar suburban advantages.

HOME OWNERSHIP

Perhaps the most encouraging evidence of suburban economic possibilities is in the realm of home ownership. For even though the cities may house more economically in large structures, only the small detached dwelling has in the past been within the reach of the private resources of the average man.[12] Consequently, only in the suburbs has the average single family been able to enjoy a home of its own.

The extent of suburban advantage in this respect is made clear by a little dip into the home-ownership data of the Fourteenth Census.[13] Using the standard classification of this discussion, the average home ownership has been found for a group of twenty-two parent cities and their various types of suburbs. The results appear in the following comparison:

TABLE 19—HOME OWNERSHIP IN CITIES AND SUBURBS

Cities and types of suburbs	Percentage of homes owned
22 parent cities	22.5
23 industrial suburbs	32.6
8 mixed suburbs	34.3
30 residential suburbs	40.5

[12] The growth of coöperative ownership of city apartments, a relatively new phenomenon in America, may result differently for the future.

[13] Population, Vol. II, pp. 1289 ff.

A heartening aspect of this showing is that even in the industrial suburbs 50 per cent. more people have been able to acquire their own homes than in the parent cities, while the proportion in the residential suburbs is nearly twice that of the cities.

This does not at all prove that home ownership is cheaper than renting. What is proved is that it is economically possible and that its acknowledged values in social stability and civic responsibility can be gained in the suburbs as they cannot in the cities.

What Class Profits Most in the Suburbs?

We have so constantly had to distinguish economic phenomena in the terms of the several income classes that it is natural to ask at the end which is most benefited economically by suburban living. The answer is undoubtedly the upper middle class of suburbanites.

The advantage to this class arises in an interesting anomaly of city rental values based ultimately upon psychological factors. As has often been noted, a great gulf is fixed between first- and second-class city accommodations. The up-to-the-minute apartment-house equipped with all luxuries, the last word in elaborate service, with all imaginable conveniences installed from radio to incinerator, boasting of its branch postoffice, its nursery, and its dancing-floor, costs in rent more than twice as much, and in the largest cities very much more than twice as much, as wholly comfortable and hygienic living quarters of equal size but less fashionable and up to date. It is this wide margin between first-class

## THE COST OF SUBURBAN LIVING

and second-class city living that is the opportunity of the upper middle class in the suburbs. The man who would hesitate to label himself as second class by the choice of his city apartment yet who cannot quite afford to go first class can here find a happy compromise where he can live according to his standards and still save money. For this rather limited class, as probably for no other in the social scale, the suburbs hold out actual economic advantages, the ultimate grounds of which, however, lie fully as much in the vagaries of urban social habits as in true economic considerations.

This final illustration simply uncovers again the twin roots of the problem. The question is never merely whether suburban life is financially more profitable. The real question is whether it is better, for whom it is better, and whether and how it can be had at costs which he can afford.

CHAPTER VI

SUBURBAN SOCIETY AND INSTITUTIONS

SUBORDINATE to cities, performing but half of the normal functions of communities, with much of their populations living in them only half of the time, what sort of a social structure and life can suburbs, especially residential suburbs, have?

Any answer which one can make must be subject to the fact that the suburban situation on the whole is one of transition. Nearly all suburbs are either being made or being unmade.

One is tempted to conclude that they are not abiding phases of the city and that they can have no character which is not described in terms of change.

On the other hand, one cherishes the hope that the suburbs are perhaps to be the salvation of the city, that in them it is to reach self-discovery on new levels and sense fresh possibilities which may affect its whole fabric now and still more largely in the future. He will therefore desire to believe that suburbs have their own permanent character and genius, that they add alternatives to the manner of urban living and give the city a second chance. It was further presumed in the first chapter that a unique social structure would be reared upon peculiar suburban foundations; that consequently suburbs were to be defined not primarily in terms of their physical separateness from the city, or of their spacial contrasts, but in terms of distinctive organization and consciousness.

The time has now come to discover whether this insight is justified. Have the suburbs a distinctive society and set of institutions, and is their character coherent and tenable as one of the permanent expressions of the civilization?

THE SUBURBAN FAMILY

Has the suburban family any special and distinctive character? We have already discovered that the natural and prevalent assumption that, since the family is decentralized in the suburbs, they will naturally show large numbers of children compared with cities, is not statistically true.[1] We may well, therefore, begin our reconsideration of the matter with a concrete case: namely, that of Webster Groves, Missouri, a residential suburb of St. Louis, with a population of about 10,000 composed almost exclusively of American born, with very few negroes.

Analyzing the population in terms of family relationships, one finds the following distribution:

Relationship	Percentage distribution
Fathers	22.5
Mothers	23.0
Adult children	7.8
Minor children	37.9
Other relatives	5.6
Roomers	1.3
Servants	1.9

[1] Page 99.

Of the members of the approximately 1300 families of this distinctively residential suburb, fathers and mothers constitute 45 per cent., the slight excess of mothers over fathers reflecting the fact that a few homes are presided over by widows or divorced women. Minor children in Webster Groves are slightly more numerous than generally in the American-born population of the United States. Adult children, relatives, roomers, and servants constituting the remoter members of the family, equal about 17 per cent. of the total. There are few resident servants, probably because the majority come to work by the day from near-by communities.

There are few roomers, but about one third as many adult children as there are families.

Marital Condition

Additional data shows that 63 per cent. of the male inhabitants of 15 years of age and upward are married, which is just about normal for the American residential suburb, but that 64 per cent. of women of the same age are married, which is exactly the right average for the American rural population, but is over 10 per cent. high for the residential suburb.[2]

If the case of Webster Groves is to be regarded as representative, how does the social complexion of the

[2] The data for Webster Groves in this chapter is based upon the civic survey made in 1922 by Miss Bessie McClenahan of the Missouri School of Social Economy coöperating with the St. Louis Religious and Social Survey under the auspices of the St. Louis Church Federation and the Institute of Social and Religious Research.

family differ from that found in cities or in independent communities of similar size with itself, and what is the meaning of its peculiarities?

Webster Groves is a typical suburb in that it has no larger proportion of children than the city has. This we explained on the theory that, while populations of the American stock may have more children in the suburbs than they would have elsewhere, they do not have so many as the foreign or poor American population of the adjacent city. The essential character of the residential suburb as a place of homes is, however, strongly reflected in Webster Groves in the high percentage of married men and women. More than 10 per cent. more men are married than among native-born males of St. Louis, or of ten parent cities whose suburbs have been studied. But, as we have noted, the equally high percentage of married women in Webster Groves is not characteristic of American population in residential suburbs. They are usually places of many married men and few married women. That they are the peculiar habitat of homes the American woman at least refuses to substantiate.

This anomaly is so interesting that we may perhaps risk introducing a somewhat complicated table into our text in order to make the facts plain, particularly since no similar calculation seems ever to have been made:[3]

[3] This table is based upon data for the same ten cities and suburbs used in calculations in previous chapters, except that they are necessarily limited to places of 25,000 population and over, because the census does not furnish information on marital conditions in smaller places.

TABLE 20—PERCENTAGE OF MARRIED POPULATION FIFTEEN YEARS OF AGE AND OVER IN PLACES OF 25,000 POPULATION AND OVER, BY SEX AND NATIVITY, AND BY CITIES AND TYPES OF SUBURBS

Percentage

	Cities	Suburbs		
Male		Mixed	Industrial	Residential
Native born of native parentage				
Median	53.0	57.0	54.4	63.2
Mode	53.0	57.0	53.4	64.8
Range	43.8—61.1	51.2—66.8	43.3—62.5	53.4—67.2
Foreign born				
Median	68.0	73.8	72.1	74.9
Mode	66.3	73.8	72.0	73.0
Range	51.2—73.1	62.6—76.4	61.2—77.1	69.4—80.3
Female				
Native born of native parentage				
Median	52.0	58.9	51.8	52.9
Mode	52.0	58.0	53.8	52.6
Range	41.6—55.1	45.5—63.8	42.4—61.5	42.7—59.0
Foreign born				
Median	66.0	72.5	72.7	59.6
Mode	61.6	none	70.9	59.5
Range	60.6—70.5	65.8—75.0	56.6—80.7	34.4—75.8

VARIATIONS BY STOCK AND PARENTAGE

The significant facts which this table reveals are the following:

(1) For males of native stock marriage is least frequent

in cities and industrial suburbs. Here the young single men constitute a large percentage of the workers. Marriage is more frequent for American men in the mixed suburbs and very much more frequent in the residential ones.

(2) The proportion of married males of native birth is above the city average even in these residential suburbs where they are fewest. Hunting down these exceptional cases, one locates them in close-in suburbs like Mount Vernon and New Rochelle, New York, and Revere, Massachussetts, where the characteristics of the city have spread out beyond their usual reach. The variation in the percentage of married men is greater for residential and mixed suburb than for industrial suburbs, showing the extreme specialization particularly of the former type in behalf of the home. Nowhere in city or country are there so many married American men as here.

(3) Males of foreign parentage are more generally married than those of the native stock. For them also the ratio of marriage is greater in the residential and mixed suburbs than in the cities and industrial suburbs, though the variation between the types is much less pronounced than with the native born. Some of the industrial suburbs indeed have few married men because their industries are filled up with an excess of single immigrant males—a fact to which the census calls explicit attention. For the foreign-born men, however, the residential suburb is the place of the home beyond any other type of community.

(4) For females of native stock the average ratio of

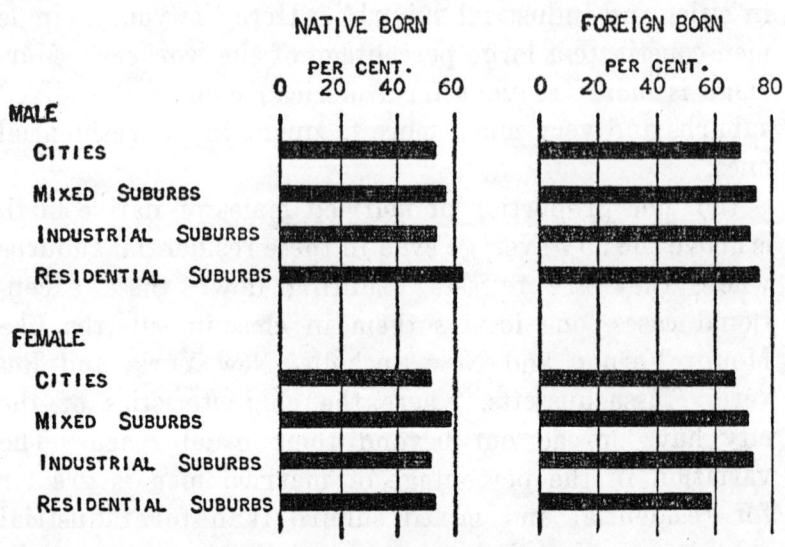

PERCENTAGE OF MARRIED POPULATION 15 YEARS OF AGE AND OVER

In cities of 100,000 population and over and in representative suburbs by types.

marriage is not very different between city and suburbs or between suburbs of the different types. The variation, however, is greater in all types of suburbs. That is to say, in some suburbs of all types there is a higher rate of marriage and in others a very low rate. Thus certain industrial suburbs have many working girls. Here one finds the deficiency in marriage among women, which brings down the average to such a point that statistics fail to show any particular affinity between suburban womanhood and home life.

Even at best the percentage of married American

women in residential suburbs is much lower than that of married men.

(5) For females of foreign birth the chief phenomenon to be noted is the great excess of unmarried ones in residential suburbs. These clearly reflect the presence of the household servant class. There is also a wide variation within the industrial suburbs, revealing the fact of women's industrial employment and consequent avoidance of marriage in some of them.

Variations by Sex and Age

Summarizing the matter as between the two sexes, one finds much wider variations in the case of the female. For men as a group the suburb is a place of marriage, but for women not always so.

This discrepancy has been explained for the foreign-born woman on the grounds of employment either in household service or in industry. Only 34 per cent. of the foreign women of Brookline, Massachusetts, are married, while the average for the American cities is 68 per cent., and for residential suburbs, 60 per cent.

With respect to the unmarried American woman in the residential suburbs, the factor of employment also doubtless holds the key. It is, however, not employment in domestic service or in industry so much as in clerical and other business positions. Deferred marriage without employment also doubtless figures in the wealthier suburbs. One must see the combinations of these factors behind the great excess of unmarried women in such conspicuous cases as those of Brookline, Massachusetts, Berkeley and Pasedena, California, Evanston, Illinois, Mount Vernon, New York, and Montclair, New Jersey, all residential communities of a high type.

Whether employed or not, these excessive numbers of unmarried women are largely living at home, since the suburbs are notably without living accommodations for detached people. (Note in confirmation the very small number of roomers in Webster Groves, Missouri.

The same thing holds true in some measure for men whose marriage is deferred and helps to explain the large element of relatives and adult children in the suburban community. These, for example, constitute 20 per cent. of the commuting population of Montclair.

A relatively small, but still significant, factor in the group of older adolescents and adults living at home, is the commuting school population. The suburb, of course, cannot ordinarily furnish higher education, but the city does. Consequently the suburban family does not have to send its children away from home to go to college or university. This is an additional advantage in keeping the family intact.

The difference between men and women in this respect required farther comment. The adult unmarried male tends strongly to detach himself from the family in order to lead an independent bachelor life in the city, while the woman, more conservative and more hedged by convention, more often remains under the parental roof.

Summary of Suburban Domestic Peculiarities

The peculiarities of the suburban family then are these: There are many families compared with the number of men; and the family tends to keep its adult children under its roof because marriage is deferred. It succeeds in the case of its women, but fails in the case of its men; hence the perplexing phenomenon of a surplus of unmarried women—in this particular, Webster Groves, as we have seen, being an exception.

The suburbs thus justify the reputation for domesticity with which the hardened urbanite is accustomed to reproach them. Home ownership is the outer sign and the home atmosphere and spirit the peculiar inner grace which they contribute to the metropolitan complex.

Of course the lingering in the home of the grown-up children, employed in the city and economically independent, is a diluting influence. Their major interests are in the city. This is the all-pervasive fact which the home, as well as all other suburban institutions, has to face. Even within its walls the gulf is always implicitly present, if it does not actually yawn, between the commuting and the non-commuting population. This great division of suburban society is the next point which demands our attention.

Commuting and Non-Commuting Elements of Suburban Population

Who are the commuters and the non-commuters and what is the function of each in suburban society? We have already noted occupational variations as an obvious basis of differentiation in suburbs, but no set of objective studies exists on the basis of which one might answer this question for a large number of cases. The example of Webster Groves, Missouri, however, may again serve to show the nature and variety of the differentiations possible. In this suburb the commuting population is almost exactly one fifth of the employed population, which probably means that it is a considerably smaller fraction of the total. This closely approximates the average for suburbs distant enough to depend chiefly upon train service for transportation. The median percentage of commuters in the total population for twenty-six Long Island suburbs within twenty-five miles of New York is found to be 16, the percentage in more than half of the cases falling between 14 and 18, and the highest percentage being 26. Small suburbs, depending on adjoining large communities for most of their economic services, frequently show much larger proportions of commuters than this; but they are not typical. The commuting population, however, as we shall soon see, is much more influential than the bare weight of its numbers would suggest.

Occupational Contrasts Among Commuters

Distributing the commuting population of Webster Groves according to occupation reveals a very wide range of difference as shown in the following comparison:

SUBURBAN SOCIETY

Occupations of gainfully employed persons	Percentage of each who are commuters
Transportation	43.5
Trade and industry	43.5
Public service	38.8
Professional	29.4
Skilled labor	15.2
Clerical occupations	14.6
Unskilled labor	10.5
Housewives	1.0
Domestic servants	0.0

While in the nature of the case no two communities could be exactly alike in the occupational distribution of their commuters, it is instructive to carry the comparison still farther to see what it exhibits. In this case the population engaged in transportation is relatively small, and the very large ratio of commuters within it may be due to an ability to command free transportation.

The main body of business commuters which constitutes the background of Webster Groves, are employed in trade and industry in St. Louis. Of professional men, doctors and dentists are most closely identified with the suburban community, few commuters being found among them. A somewhat larger proportion of lawyers and clergymen live in Webster Groves who work elsewhere, while many teachers and most of the architects and engineers commute. Relatively few clerks and skilled laborers (among the latter of whom machinists and electricians predominate) live in Webster Groves but work in the city. Such a residential suburb is naturally not a suitable place for these classes in numbers beyond those needed to do the work of the community itself. This is still more true of unskilled labor. There are no barbers, laundrymen, or domestic servants commuting out of Webster Groves. Obviously this group could not possibly live there unless employed.

As between the sexes, women constitute only 7.7 per cent. of the commuters, whereas they number 15 per cent. in Montclair, New Jersey. Of the total employed population, 23.6 per cent. of the men commute, and 5.1 per cent. of the women.

The case of Webster Groves is probably typical in the following aspects: It shows the great bulk of commuting population belonging to a few classes of occupations. The non-commuting population, on the contrary, represents the full range of occupations, but limited in most of them to such numbers as can find employment in the community itself. In no occupation, however, is there actually a larger percentage of workers who commute than who live and work in Webster Groves.

The Commuter's Prestige

Why, then, the fact that when commuting reaches anything like typical proportions the commuter almost invariably enjoys superior prestige and that his group seems to dominate the suburban community?

First, though no statistics exist to prove it directly, the commuters probably have greater average wealth as individuals. Primarily, however, their influence is

SUBURBAN SOCIETY

based upon their daily connection with the city and its vast overshadowing enterprises. As the active links between the home-staying majority and the metropolis, they tend to monopolize the imagination and to control the social situation.

This almost invariably appears from the complexion of the local suburban newspaper. The "society column" almost exclusively concerns the doings of commuters; its current news, on the contrary, being strikingly lacking in community-wide interests. Some statistical evidence of the same tendency is found in a recent limited study of leadership of character-building agencies in suburban counties. The agencies enumerated are definitely organized so that their work covers the suburban and rural areas, but excludes the city. In other words, it concerns both commuting and non-commuting populations. Under such conditions what proportion of the leadership will be drawn from each? The answer of the actual practice of the agencies is shown in the following comparison:

TABLE 21—NUMBER OF COMMUTERS AND NON-COMMUTERS ON COUNTY COMMITTEES OF CERTAIN CHARACTER-BUILDING AGENCIES

Agency	Membership of county committee	
	Commuters	*Non-commuters*
North Bergen County, N. J., Boy Scout Council	18	10
Bergen County, N. J., Young Men's Christian Association	14	6
Camden County, N. J., Young Men's Christian Association	21	0

To these may be added:

	Scout-masters
Camden County, N. J., Boy Scout Council	14	3

Here, although the commuter is a distinct minority in the population, one finds three and one half times as many commuters as non-commuters engaged in the leadership of well-known types of work projected on a county-wide basis. The Westchester County, New York, Young Men's Christian Association, on the contrary, reports that its county committee is divided half and half between commuters and non-commuters. It adds, however, that these proportions were achieved only after years of deliberate effort to bring the non-commuting element to the front.

Without such definite efforts the two elements rarely contrive to integrate just as the "bosses" and the workers rarely get together in industrial suburbs. The suburban community consequently lacks unity in the sense that independent communities of equal size habitually have it. With all its preponderating influence in wider relationships, the commuting minority is nevertheless not widely influential within its own community because it is so little of an organic whole. Its influence does not radiate along natural lines of power fixed by a favorable community structure as it would under normal conditions.

We must examine further phases of this lack of community unity and note the actual types of community organization resulting from the presence of two diverse elements in suburban population.

SUBURBAN COMMUNITY RELATIONSHIPS

The frequent lack of a physical center for the suburban community has already been noted. Thus the commuters of Montclair, New Jersey, recently classified themselves by neighborhood as follows:

Railroad centers	Number of commuters reporting
Old. center (2 railroad stations)	195
North End (3 railroad stations)	139
Watchung section (at geographical center)	102
South End	79

Now, in very large degree, these fairly distinct geographical groups are furnished with separate commercial and social institutions, as well as separate transit centers. The old center of the town functions somewhat generally as a community rallying-point for the non-commuting population and as a minor recreation center for all, but is only incidental in the lives of the larger group of commuters. Of course this means that the city is the real functional center of the commuter's existence. The community to which he primarily feels allegiance is the metropolitan community. His home suburb is primarily his neighborhood. In decentralizing the side of his life which represents consumption, he has nevertheless kept the city for many of his choicest experiences even in this realm. The climaxes of his satisfaction generally occur there, and the city is the theater of his most active expressions of personality.

Suburban Handicap in Natural Leadership

An additional cause of the failure of the suburban community to integrate socially is the failure of those sources which generally furnish leadership to the independent community. As noted in the discussion of its economics, the suburb is limited behind and before. The city cuts into its functions for its own people, and on the other hand it has no independent rural area to serve. This reduces not only the opportunities of work for its people, but similarly affects all of its other functions. Thus, the business classes are the recognized leaders of the little town. They are not so in the suburb, first, because the commuter will not follow their leadership and, second, because there are relatively so few of them. The suburban section in which the author lives numbers five or six thousand people. It has one bank, a movie house, a group of small stores, four churches, a ward school, and a woman's club. If it were an independent community, say a county-seat, of similar size in the Middle West it would have five or six banks, a variety of amusement enterprises, its own high school, one or more hotels, more than ten churches, from thirty-five to forty other social organizations functioning for more than narrow groups, besides three or four times as much local business. To cap it all, it would have the trade of three or four thousand farm people. In such

SUBURBAN SOCIETY 181

a community the ascendancy of the business classes would be unquestioned. Their sheer deficiency of numbers holds them back from leadership in the suburbs.

SOCIAL STATUS OF THE BUSINESS CLASS

Added to this is the fact that the greater prestige of the commuter makes the status of tradespeople in the suburbs less desirable than in the independent community. Business consequently gravitates into alien hands. Beginning with the news-stand and the fruit shop, all sorts of retail stores have, even in the wealthier suburbs, come to be controlled by the foreign born. Frequently they have pitiably small stocks of goods and little permanence. Add to this the prevalence of the chain-store managed and even operated by people living at a distance.

These tendencies still further rob the suburb of its natural leadership.

DIVIDED LOYALTIES OF THE PROFESSIONAL GROUP

The professional classes, which habitually reinforce the business element in the independent town, just as characteristically desert it in the suburbs. Although not themselves commuters, they hasten to ally themselves with the broader fellowships of the metropolitan area. For example, it is hard to get a New Jersey suburban clergyman of the first order of ability to be active in local religious responsibilities beyond his own parish because he has more rewarding entrée in New York City circles. The educator no less promptly joins the schoolmasters' club in the metropolis. The leaders, supposed to be fully identified with the suburb where they exercise their professions, have therefore only a minimum of community significance.

When a distinguished retired banker recently shocked the nation by a speech upon political corruption before the Ossining Rotary Club, the metropolitan press professed to find amusement in the fact that Ossining has a Rotary Club. That every self-respecting independent town of similar size would have one goes without saying. This is because the independent town is normally a community with a complete range of functions largely centralized and under a dominant natural leadership—all of which the suburb characteristically is not.

SUBURBAN DEFICIENCY IN SOCIAL INSTITUTIONS

The outstanding result of the Webster Groves survey was the discovery of striking social deficiencies compared with ordinary places of the same size. Though the choicest of the residential suburbs of St. Louis, it nevertheless had no public library, no park or playground, no community center or any substitute for one like a Young Men's or a Young Women's Christian Association. It had very acute problems of sewerage and sanitation, and the development of its public improvements was distinctly ragged. These were in part the marks of rapid growth which institutions have not been able to keep up with. In part, however, they are the general and almost inherent marks of the suburb, which habitually does not

SUBURBAN SOCIETY

create a full round of social institutions because it has those of the city to fall back on and because the affections and loyalties of so many of its people are so divided.

Statistical proof of this tendency is found in a comparison of the number of social institutions in fifty-nine suburbs compared with 261 other incorporated communities in forty-nine counties widely distributed throughout the United States.[4]

On an identical list of nineteen typical institutions, only one tenth of the non-suburban communities were found to have less than five, while one sixth of the suburban communities had less than five. These were primarily communities of less than five hundred population. In these the suburban lag was considerable. The lag persisted with the successive size groups, as revealed by the following comparison:

Population	Average Number of Social Agencies	
	Non-Suburban	Suburban
Less than 500	7	5
500– 1,000	12	8
1,000– 2,500	13	13
2,500– 5,000	25	23
5,000–10,000	37	31

These average tendencies occurred in spite of the fact that a small group of the suburbs investigated tended to be very much over-developed institutionally. This is quite ample statistical justification for the prediction that, both by reason of the lack of a dependent rural area

[4] From a forthcoming study of "Rural Religious and Social Agencies," made by the author for the Institute of Social and Religious Research, 1924.

and because of their own dependence upon the city, the suburbs as a group would show institutional deficiency.[5]

While the broad tendency as measured by the number of social institutions, is thus confirmed, no such generally striking suburban shortcomings are revealed as was suggested by the examples of Upper Montclair, New Jersey, and Webster Groves, Missouri. This is partly because these two cases are actually extreme, but also because of the contents of the list of nineteen items on the basis of which the above communities were compared. It was a list intended to reflect the entire range of social organizations found in independent communities. Accordingly it combined the little and the big, the relatively trivial and the significant. The general deficiency of the suburb as thus revealed is therefore quite consistent with the fact that in some kinds of social organization it shows a great excess. This brings us to our next important generalization.

Preponderance of Minor Group-Organizations in the Suburbs

We have been primarily considering community-wide social factors as expressed in major institutions. In this

[5] The majority of the suburbs included in this study are below the population-size for which the census reports the number of wage-earners. Consequently it was not possible to classify them exactly as residential and industrial. The field-work of the study, however, found many examples of institutional deficiency in suburban factory towns. These undoubtedly contribute heavily to the above showing.

SUBURBAN SOCIETY

scale the suburbs have been found wanting as compared with the independent town. In the field of narrow and relatively unimportant social organizations, however—that which concerns small and transient groups—the suburbs, on the contrary, have a preponderance. They are the place par excellence of multitudinous incidental contacts, and consequently of comparatively trivial and temporary forms of association. In Webster Groves, an aggregate membership of 17,219 persons was found in 221 social organizations, apart from church membership and school enrollment. In other words, every man, woman, and child in a population of less than 10,000 was entitled to a membership in 1.7 organizations.

For a second example, consider the suburban schoolboy in Montclair, New Jersey. In a recent survey [6] he reported his membership in group organizations as follows:

TABLE 22—AGGREGATE NUMBER OF MONTCLAIR GRAMMAR AND HIGH SCHOOL BOYS BELONGING TO DESIGNATED ORGANIZATIONS

Organization	Number of boys belonging		
	Grammar school	Junior high school	Senior high school
Scouts and Rangers	15	133	88
School clubs	161	0	0
Athletic clubs	42	79	58
Boys' clubs (semi-spontaneous and temporary	125	103	26

[6] By a committee of the Montclair Young Men's Christian Association, 1924.

	Number of boys belonging		
Organization	Grammar school	Junior high school	Senior high school
Boys' organizations in church and Y. M. C. A.	12	90	98
Other	0	37	69
Total membership	542	422	339
Boys belonging to no organization	149	179	50

The data do not indicate how many boys belong to more than one organization; but from any standpoint this very high percentage of belongings in comparison with the number of boys not belonging to any organization is most impressive. Contrast it, for example, with the discovery that in thirty-three counties constituting a cross-section of rural America as occupied by the character-building agencies for youth, the combined work of five such agencies (namely, Young Men's Christian Association, Boy Scouts, Young Women's Christian Association, Girl Scouts, and Camp Fire Girls) reaches less than 10 per cent. of the total youth population in the most favored age (fourteen and fifteen years), and less than 5 per cent. in the next most favored age (sixteen and seventeen).[7]

The advantage of the suburbs in this particular field

---

[7] Data from a forthcoming study of "Rural Religious and Social Agencies" made by the author for the Institute of Social and Religious Research, 1924.

SUBURBAN SOCIETY 187

is thus nothing short of immense. The case aptly illustrates the suburban bent for minor organizations which has doubtless overshot the mark and reached extraordinary over-development.

Why Has the Suburb So Many Minor Organizations?

The representative character of our examples will be more credible if we examine the reasons why the facts might be as alleged.

The suburbs represent the triumph of accessibility over proximity. That they succeed at all is due to the fact that means have been achieved for getting about rapidly and freely within metropolitan areas. This has added enormously to the number of incidental social contacts and given great flexibility to social relationships. Social organization reflects this condition. Lacking strong and permanent community ties, the suburban social instincts spend themselves on incidental levels. The gradually increased number of contacts is reflected in numerous groupings of people according to secondary or temporary interests. Put with this the fact that the suburbanite is not without his minor ties based upon proximity, so that those which accessibility yields are something added to the total by which his time and his loyalties are divided.

Let us begin with a statement of social relationships as based on proximity and gradually build up a total picture of typical suburban social groupings.

The Neighborhood

The inherent selective forces which create suburbs see to it on the whole that immediate suburban neighbors are mutually socially acceptable. Accordingly the Villager, which is the original human nature in us and is closely akin to our inner selves, gets released in the suburbs as he rarely does in the city. The old-fashioned kindly curiosity and the deep-seated lust for friendly gossip re-assert themselves. The block, the little zone of back-door borrowing, the sphere of immediate neighborly kindnesses in sickness and in health become a natural unit of group life. Suburban hedges are full of natural gaps where neighborhood comings and goings have broken through. When growth of population is too rapid or when the incoming neighbors are of a little different type from the older inhabitants these neighborhood processes are slowed up. Yet on the whole they prevail. This assertion of innate friendliness, in an environment which partly invites, it is in most grateful and creditable contrast to the perhaps necessary anonymousness of the city. On the side of the moral forces it scores heavily for the suburbs, and adds to the happiness of existence.

Now, instead of finding in the contracted neighborhood the seeds of organic growth, instead of expanding one's social ties in ever-widening circles tending to embrace the whole community, the next step of the suburbanite is to utilize another fragmentary relationship, and still another, until virtually his entire social energies are exhausted in a series of group relationships which fall into no unified pattern and do not generally intersphere.

The Transit Group

Next in importance to the neighborhood is the transit group. Spending so considerable a fraction of his waking hours in going and coming, the suburbanite naturally creates a somewhat systematic social life upon the process of commutation itself. Railroad station grounds here tend to expand into elaborate plazas, which are the real civic centers of the suburbanite. The station platform is his true Main Street. Thus the gathering of scores of passenger-laden automobiles for the more popular trains, with the contacts incidental to waiting for and boarding the trains themselves, are the chief social events of the day. No other set of habitual experiences so nearly embrace the entire local community.

The station platform is the political forum of the suburb. Here views and issues are discussed, electioneering done, and political publicity distributed. It is the civic rallying-point, all the approaches of which are besieged on "tag day" in behalf of the hospital or the children's home. It is the secondary market where advertising loves to concentrate its appeal. Take the "Eight-seventeen" or any of its earlier or later sisters or cousins; its scenes are of profound social or psychological import. The veteran conductor greets his passengers with the benevolent air of the small-town merchant toward his patrons, or almost the air of the pastor to his flock. Along with the oldest commuter, he is a recognized institution. (One railroad entering New York has named an engine for its oldest commuter. Another discovers him by periodic advertising and puts his picture in the papers!) Most of the social contacts of the transit group are naturally casual; many, however, are systematic. There is always the same group playing cards in the smoking-car. Most of the civic and religious committee work of the suburb, and much of its business, is conducted en route. A county Young Men's Christian Association secretary tells one that he can never find his committee members except on the way to Chicago. In less serious spheres, groups of friends habitually travel together, continue political discussion, discuss sports, and exchange market tips. Courtship is one of the chief pursuits of the commuting trains—and no social phenomenon is more interesting.

Of more individualistic pursuits, there is the ubiquitous newspaper, which, however, as often as not, is the excuse for conversation. The business man plans his day; the student gets his lessons. A very interesting fact is the considerable frequency of the daily reading of devotional books. Other types of meditation get their clue from the esthetic satisfaction of the landscape, the sage brown of the marshes, or the blue of the evening hills.

The morning train is generally a psychological stimulus of some sort, the evening train a sedative. As already noted, the hour at which the commuter takes his train

SUBURBAN SOCIETY

separates the economic sheep from the goats and distinguishes between the long work-day and the short one. Three hundred and eighty-nine Montclair, New Jersey, commuters reported their hour of reaching home at night as follows:

Hour	Number
5—6	80
6—7	281
7—8	21
After 8	7

This distribution reflects the well-to-do suburb with its social stratifications. One can almost change his community by changing the hour of the train which he takes to town.

Thus upon the unique experience of commutation the suburbanite develops an interesting though fragmentary form of social life lived by no other type of mankind.

THE WORK GROUP

When the suburbanite reaches the city he falls in with another social group based on proximity; namely, that of his fellow-workers on the job. This involves contacts of greater regularity and longer duration, which often hold a high degree of social interest for him. They, however, carry him beyond the suburban field. It is necessary nevertheless, to note this fact in order to see that membership in one proximity group after another tends finally to use up nearly all the suburbanite's social energies and greatly to reduce his demand for wider relationships.

Lodges in the suburbs appear to have significance as common interest groups. In the comparison of fifty-nine suburbs with 202 non-suburbs they were discovered to be the only type of standard social agency common to small communities whose frequency was not affected by the proximity of cities. Particularly in the smallest suburbs—those of 2500 population and less—the lodge seems to be the special type of small group into which the suburban people tend to divide. Here they are even more frequent relatively than in the country town.

Accessibility Groups

This multiplicity of proximity groups sets suburban social movements within narrower grooves; but they do not exhaust the number of groups to which he belongs. The very meaning of the suburb is the substitution of accessibility for proximity as the principle of practical existence. Consequently, armed with urban facilities of transit, the suburbanite's social nature causes him to range widely in search of people of common interests. He does not have to content himself with people he does not care for as in the little town, because plenty of other people are within reach. Consequently he spends most of the time which proximity groups do not incidentally absorb, in seeking out common-interest groups and organizing them from widely scattered memberships on a larger or smaller scale. As an observant suburbanite puts it, "The place to meet one's fellow-townsmen is in a New York club."

It falls out in the end that not much social impulse is left for the suburban community as such. The deficiency is largely due to the preponderance at home of minor group-organizations and the substitution everywhere of association based on common interests for that based on geographical proximity.

CHAPTER VII

SUBURBAN SOCIETY AND INSTITUTIONS
(Continued)

Major Social Institutions Based on Suburban Specialization

WE have seen how the residential suburb decentralizes the functions of economic consumption. It segregates women and children in homes as spenders of wealth while sending men away to the city to produce it. It also specializes in recreation. One would only expect that major social institutions would arise to reflect such specialization, and they do. Highly developed women's clubs and athletic and golf clubs are the unique suburban additions to the ordinary category of major institutions.

These two types of organization are apt to have larger memberships than any other in residential suburbs. Having the suburb so much to themselves during the daytime, it is not to be supposed that aggressive and self-conscious women will not do anything with it. Suburban womanhood, one remembers, is often highly educated and possesses great executive ability. Accordingly one often finds women's clubs of spectac-

SUBURBAN SOCIETY

ular size, with palatial buildings, sometimes representing federation or other forms of complex organization. Their interests are all-sided with strong tendency to stress civic responsibility, and in their seriousness and competence of administration they often go far beyond the traditional dilettante character of the average women's club in places of like size.

RECREATIONAL ORGANIZATIONS

The gravitation of large-scale organization for recreation in the suburbs is partly due to the high cost of land necessary to carry on the major sports. It falls in, however, with suburban character and the trend of suburban specialization, and thus easily becomes one of the important bases of social integration. Athletic clubs with extensive grounds and buildings are conspicuous factors of suburban life, often taking the place which such organizations as the Young Men's Christian Association fill in other communities. Golf-clubs have come to absorb very large acreages of suburban land. In Westchester County, New York, for example, thirty-eight such organizations command 5230 acres—far more space than is occupied by all the improved public parks outside of cities. A recent well-considered comment upon the lapse of the Montclair, New Jersey, Club after a long and distinguished career, pointed out the seeming impossibility nowadays of rallying suburban people in cultural or other so-called highbrow interests. In contrast with the failure of organizations of this type, the recreational clubs are increasing by leaps and bounds, their waiting-lists seeming to grow longer as their charges grow higher. Of course the explanation is that the suburbs cannot compete with the city as a cultural center, while the amateur sports must decentralize in order to find room. Furthermore, the development of great recreational organizations is congenial to the inherent instinct of the suburb for sundering its work and its play. Here, for the first time on the North American continent, sport begins to be taken as seriously as it is in the Old World.

Charities

Still another type of social agency which suburban peculiarities have thrown into an importance beyond its usual place in the community is the local philanthropic institution. A recent comparative study of expenditures for philanthropic purposes in American cities revealed that the highest rate of cost was in such wealthy suburbs as Morristown and Montclair, New Jersey. In 144 reports of per capita gifts through Community Chests in 1923 and 1924, eleven out of twelve reports for residential suburbs fell in the upper quarter of the list. Their median per capita amount was two thirds higher than the median of this list as a whole.[1] The explanation is by no means that such communities have the most acute demands. It is rather another symptom of suburban over-organization. Specifically in this case, one fears, the impulse is to find an outlet for the activity of able and well-to-do people rather than to serve the

[1] Bulletin 82, American Association for Community Organizations, National Bureau of Information, Inc. Executive Secretary.

actual needs of the poor. Women with considerable money and little to do are frequently responsible for the over-organization of philanthropic agencies.

Congestion and Competition of Social Agencies

In the sphere both of major and minor social organizations, stimulus and probably over-stimulus is largely to be credited to the influence of the city. Many of the recreational clubs are a direct response to city demand, and they are sometimes largely under city control. As in the matter of facilities and physical improvements, the suburb is tempted to feel that it must have everything which the city has. Promotional exploitation from city sources naturally falls first upon the suburb. A very large proportion of the alleged "rural" work of certain national social agencies start there and gets little further. Of five well-known character-building agencies for youth, 55 per cent. of the organizations in smaller and non-incorporated communities were found to be in suburbs. This constitutes the actually larger fraction of their supposed work for the farmer!
The result of this tendency of the suburbs to start everything there is, is inevitably the duplication and competition of agencies. As demonstrated by the study of a large sample territory throughout the nation, two or more character-building agencies of the type above mentioned had been organized in 60 per cent. of the suburban places occupied by any of these agencies. In one third of these cases relationships were definitely competitive, appealing to the same boy or girl groups and making

necessarily conflicting appeals for community favor and support. Such situations are more frequent in suburbs than in independent communities of equal size and are found particularly acute in suburbs of about 2500 population.

Summarizing the matter, one concludes that the suburbs are undoubtedly over-organized in the realm of minor social organizations. Their actual relationships are so numerous and the example and exhortation of the dominating city so strong that they have overdone the matter. Webster Groves does not need 212 separate organized groups for less than 10,000 people, especially while the community is deficient in some of the standard and essential social institutions.

Suburban Fortunes of the Standard Social Institutions

Just how does subordination to the city and the over-organization of minor groups of suburban population modify the rôle of the standard social agencies, such as government, school, and church?

Government

Political responsibility, which sits all too lightly on the shoulders of the average American, is doubly vague for the suburban because his social life is so little centralized and his community so undetermined.

A surprising number of suburbs get along without even the minimum of political organization customary for closely built-up communities. A multitude of non-incorporated "places" exist within rural territory around the cities. In size they are much beyond the places which habitually incorporate when they are independent, because motive for the assertion of political identity fails. Government, in other words, is an expression of community self-consciousness and coöperation which the suburbs frequently lack.

The most populous rural townships of America are in the vicinity of New York City. Nowhere else has the disinclination of the people of the locality to get together under the usual forms of civic organization been so extreme. In a few cases very compact communities have even organized their inhabitants as joint-stock companies for the purpose of carrying on the ordinary functions of government instead of resorting to the machinery of the incorporated municipality.

Trend to Larger Units of Government

Part of this disinclination is the feeling of the uselessness of organizing politically what is confessedly a temporary and unstable situation. These bits of a vast and evolving metropolitan community do not feel that their separate acceptance of political responsibility is either logical or reasonable. Hence there are important movements for the political integration of large suburban areas. Alameda County, California, for example, recently attempted to become one unit of government. The same thing is being agitated for Westchester and Nassau Counties, New York, and Bergen County, New

Jersey. Recent efforts to consolidate the northern municipalities of Hudson County, New Jersey, into what would have made the fourth city of the State in point of population, were only partly successful but point to an undoubted trend.

The economy of larger units than the average suburb for the operation of public facilities has led to many joint municipal projects involving the frequent creation of special district authorities of which the Boston Metropolitan District Commission is most notable. These are the possible ground work of more extensive political integrations.[2]

The ultimate solution of the political problem of metropolitan areas is undoubtedly the inclusion of the whole area under some form of unified government with the recognition of different zones in which different degrees of local independence shall be maintained. Suburban communities will then be federated with the city and with one another. There will be areas with common facilities and administration in larger matters with the careful preservation of individual community identity where social structure is really definite and community consciousness strong.[3] The suburb will be a daughter in her mother's house, but mistress in her own.

[2] Urban school districts are already frequently larger than the political city.

[3] This ought not to mean the perpetuation of political units which have no genuine social identity. Thus, the "City Plan of East Orange" (New Jersey), after showing that the community is continuous with several other Oranges so that no logical line

The School

With industry largely absent and business reduced to a minimum, education is the outstanding community activity of the residential suburbs. Naturally under these circumstances the school is magnified. A much larger proportion of the regular tax bill goes to education than in the parent cities; more of it than in the average independent community of similar size, and more than in the industrial suburbs. Even the industrial suburbs are strikingly beyond the parent cities on this point.[4]

Suburban school systems have been particularly fertile in experiments. The tendency to imitate the city and to provide all sorts of facilities works in this realm also, perhaps advantageously.

The main distinction of the suburban school system in the residential suburbs is, however, the greater relative importance of the high school. To be sure, not so high a proportion of smaller suburbs have high schools as can be drawn between them in structural design, somewhat naïvely adds, "Each municipality very properly aims to preserve its individuality," (page 25). The question is, "Has it any?" and the answer frequently is, "None, except in the most arbitrary sense."

Of course neighborhoods within such municipalities may have very genuine individuality, while the municipality as a whole has none.

[4] Calculations made for twelve parent cities, thirty-eight independent cities, fifteen industrial suburbs of from 30,000 to 50,000 population, and sixteen residential suburbs of similar size from "Financial Statistics of Cities," 1922, Table 8.

of independent places, because they are near enough to borrow education from neighboring places. The high school, however, bulks large, relative to the elementary school. In Webster Groves, for example, the high school enrolment is 17.4 per cent. of the elementary, whereas it is only 13 per cent. in the parent city of St. Louis. Again, much larger numbers of high school pupils graduate in residential suburbs. The percentage is from 50 to 60 in the New Jersey residential suburbs, as against 30 to 40 per cent. in the cities and industrial suburbs. Still again, a much higher percentage of high school graduates go on to college, the range being from 50 to 80 per cent. in the New Jersey residential suburbs. In brief, suburban public education shows a strong trend to its more advanced form and to expenditure for college preparation at public expense.

Still another characteristic educational phenomenon of the suburb is the private school, in which city people seek to put their children away from urban crowding and distraction during the plastic years. Scores of such schools are found in the environs of the largest cities.

The Library

The residential suburbs, on the contrary, are not good library communities. The attitude of their people is that they want their books at once and do not care to share them with others. The public library is a little too democratic for them, consequently residential suburbs do not ordinarily show a high per capita rate of the circulation of books.

Libraries, however, are one social facility which suburbs in the communities investigated have more often than independent places. This is because a method intended to meet the needs of rural people has worked out to notable advantage in suburban zones. The county library system, with its multitude of small branches, has been notably successful in some of the New Jersey counties. Thus Camden County, adjacent to Philadelphia, and with only three independent libraries outside of the city of Camden, has a county system with 133 stations. Seventy-eight of these are in public schools; fifty-five are for general public use, located in grocery stores, book-shops, garages, and city halls. Custodianship and service is furnished by each community. Book collections of from 50 to 500 volumes are distributed by library truck. Such service has been of inestimable advantage in the new and cheap industrial communities which are rapidly developing in old Quaker farming areas.

The Church

The suburbs do not have so many churches as independent communities of the same size. In the comparison of fifty-nine suburbs with 202 non-suburban places, the lag in the number of churches runs consistently throughout the suburban size groups. The independent town of less than 500 averages two churches; the suburb of this size, one. Average frequency is shown in the following comparison:

TABLE 23—AVERAGE NUMBER OF CHURCHES BY SIZE OF COMMUNITIES, SUBURBAN AND NON-SUBURBAN

Population	Average number of churches	
	Suburban	Non-suburban
Under 500	1	2
500– 1,000	3	5
1,000– 2,500	4	5
2,500– 5,000	7	10
5,000–10,000	10 plus	10 plus

Very little actual religious dependence upon the city was discovered in the cases of suburbs intensively studied. Their deficiency in number of churches, therefore, must be ascribed primarily to their lack of rural con-

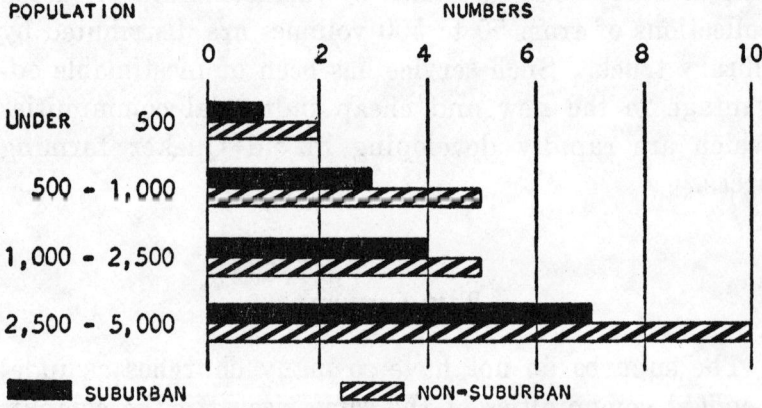

AVERAGE NUMBER OF CHURCHES IN SUBURBAN AND NON-SUBURBAN COMMUNITIES, BY SIZE GROUPS

stituencies which make the actual religious community in the independent town much larger than its nominal size. Suburbs, however, have more churches relative to their population than the city has.

SUBURBAN SOCIETY

No detailed comparative study of suburban churches exists. The following generalization, based on the study of the Protestant churches of the Missouri suburbs of St. Louis, will doubtless hold true in most areas where suburbs have mainly grown from the ground up rather than being founded on the basis of well-established old communities.[5]

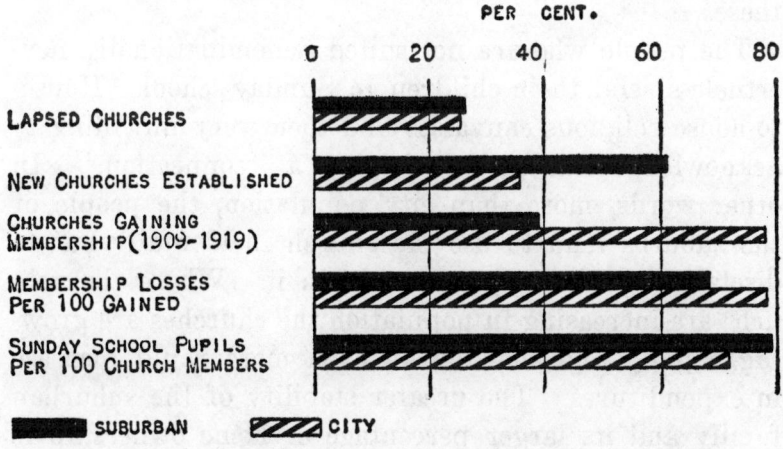

CONTRASTING URBAN AND SUBURBAN CHURCH TENDENCIES, ST. LOUIS, 1899–1919

Suburban churches average smaller in size than city churches. They occupy cheaper land and have cheaper buildings, thus corresponding exactly to the characteristics of suburban residential structures. There is a

[5] Data secured for the author's "St. Louis Church Survey" (Institute of Social and Religious Research, 1924) but not specifically included in the published volume.

narrower range of denominations; hence the constituencies of existing churches are more mixed, and there is a higher proportion of people unchurched because the suburb does not furnish them with the exact church of their preference. There are relatively fewer churches of the "wild denominations"; that is to say, those which reflect religious proclivities of exceptional groups of people. The suburbs are too staid and conventional for these.

The people who are not suited denominationally nevertheless send their children to Sunday-school. House-to-house religious canvasses find them very unwilling to acknowledge this as constituting a "connection." In other words, more than city population, the people of the suburbs tend to use the church incidentally but to disclaim significant partnership in it. Where the suburbs are increasing in population the churches are growing rapidly and showing an even more rapid increase in expenditures. The greater stability of the suburban family and its larger percentage of home ownership is registered in the difference between church losses and gains. While the St. Louis Protestant churches lose, by death, dismissal, and disappearance, 78 for every 100 members gained, its suburban churches lose only 68. On the other hand suburban communities are naturally largely in the experimental phase of development. They have not yet found themselves. They start more new religious enterprises but a larger proportion fail to survive than in the city as well as fail to grow even when they do survive.

Minor Organizations Attached to Major Agencies

The outstanding peculiarity of the suburban church is, however, its great number of subsidiary organizations. In other words, the general tendency of the suburb to a multiplicity of minor organizations has attacked the church also, until it has frequently become less a single institution than a series of loosely connected groups. For example, the seventeen Webster Groves Protestant churches had thirty-two women's societies, nine men's brotherhoods, ten young people's societies, six Boy Scout troops, one Camp Fire Girls group, eight organized Sunday-school classes, eight other children's organizations, and four other adult organizations. This means that every age and sex group tends to be separately provided for. The ratio of subsidiary organizations is much higher than for 1044 city churches recently studied.[6]

This is simply the religious version of the ultra-organization of suburban life.

The total impression of the suburban church which the St. Louis suburbs make is one of rapid institutional expansion in a growing area of select population. While not all suburban churches would show so many excellencies as those of Webster Groves, they would doubtless average well above those of the city in general characteristics. The actual representative city church is a small and inconspicuous affair on a side street. A higher

---

[6] "Types of City Churches"; forthcoming study by the author for the Institute of Social and Religious Research.

proportion of total suburban population belongs to churches, and their conventional place in life is more undisputed.

At the same time the suburban churches are certainly less influential socially than churches in the independent community of the same size. Their constituencies are broken up into so many small social groups that the church infrequently serves them all at once. Their pastors are generally not the oracles that they frequently become in the small town. They compete at great disadvantage with the near-by city pulpits for leadership in original or aggressive religious thought. They find it hard to interpret the whole of life religiously because the group to which they minister knows so little of the major practical interests of the bulk of its membership and because their common community experience is so limited.

Other Social Agencies and Institutions

The comparison of 59 suburbs with 202 communities included a number of other items which throw light upon suburban social characteristics. Naturally the suburbs showed a much higher proportion of labor organizations than the non-suburbs, thus reflecting their proximity to cities and industrial problems. Labor organizations, however, were rarely found in suburbs of less than 2500 population.

Suburbs have fewer commercial clubs than inde-

SUBURBAN SOCIETY

pendent communities of like size. One half of all the non-suburbs had such clubs, but only one third of the suburbs. This reflects the subordinate status of the business classes already reverted to and the trade dependency of the suburban community upon the city.

Curiously, however, there are more commercial clubs in suburbs of less than 500 population, 20 per cent. of all such suburbs having them. This must be charged to the account of the real-estate booster and the impulse to imitate the near-by city. The average place of this size does not feel the need of a commercial club.

The suburbs have fewer newspapers, this reflecting their dependence upon the city press. The deficiency, however, is almost entirely in the smaller places.

No difference between suburbs and non-suburbs appears to exist in the matter of hospitals. Only 10 per cent. of either have hospitals, the suburbs depending upon the cities and the rural towns doing without.

Of recreational institutions the moving-picture establishment proves to be equally ubiquitous. This reflects the recreational decentralization of the suburbs with respect to this type of small-scale diversion. There is a slightly higher proportion of suburban pool-halls, the excess being located in the small places. Here again is a form of recreation which is highly decentralized. On the contrary, the suburbs have relatively fewer musical organizations. The town band is the characteristic expression of civic feeling, but this feeling the suburbs lack; consequently their shortage in bands. This deficiency runs throughout all the size groups.

Objective Measurement of Suburban Advantage

One may assert a preference for the city or the suburbs as a matter of taste. He may demonstrate the large advantage of the latter in terms of more ample living space. Greater suburban home ownership has also been proved, though one was not able to say that this was an advantage from the narrower economic viewpoint. The presence or absence of social institutions is of less consequence to suburbs than to independent communities because any deficiency may be supplemented by the nearby city. They do not pretend to be whole communities and consequently can be neither praised nor blamed because they are not. Are the suburbs, therefore, all in all better than the city or worse?

There are obvious social criteria, the measurement of whose prevalence in or absence from the suburb, if we had it, would go far toward determining objectively the answer to be made. Actual evidence, however, is exceedingly scanty. Little all told has been done toward developing a science of sociometry, and that little has not been specifically directed to evaluation of the suburbs. Certain objective comparisons, however, of the more congested and the roomier districts in the city throw some light upon the problem. For example the "St. Louis Church Survey" drew cross-sectional lines from the center of the city toward its circumference. Along the axes of the outward movement of American population every added mile showed demonstrable and measurable gains in pleasantness of surroundings, safety of health, and moral protection. The comparison was made on the basis of eleven criteria. Thus, "On four decisive criteria of social health the case rate of the least desirable districts exceeds that of the best in the following ratios: infant mortality, four times as frequent; deaths from tuberculosis, eight times as frequent; juvenile delinquency, twelve times as frequent; illiteracy, twenty-two times as frequent. They have almost twice as many families per dwelling, and home ownership is only one-thirteenth as frequent." [7]

The third of the districts ranking highest in the social scale on the combined weight of these criteria included all seven districts touching the boundaries of the city away from the river, three other districts immediately adjacent to them, and *no others*. In other words, the more thinly populated and suburb-like areas within the city had a clear and demonstrable social advantage.

This advantage was strikingly evidenced in the case of Italian and negro colonies living in uncrowded quarters on the outskirts of the community. Improvement was shown in nearly all of the social deficiencies which characterized them in the down-town tenements. Doubtless those who had moved to the outlying sections were select representatives of their respective groups, helping to create the advantages of a select environment as well as enjoying them.

Webster Groves was located beyond the city limits and consequently could not be included statistically in the comparison. It lay, however, in the direct line of increasing social advantage, and undoubtedly suffered fewer of the objective social evils and enjoyed more of

[7] Page 48.

the corresponding advantage than any part of the city itself. This illustrates a method which might be used to determine the actual degree of advantage in the residential suburbs. They undoubtedly reflect even to a still greater degree than the peripheral areas within the city limits the advantage of select people in a select environment.

Social Quality of Industrial Suburbs

If the cross-section had been carried across the river into the Illinois suburbs of St. Louis a very different conclusion would probably have been reached.[8] A social analysis of Springfield, Massachusetts, using the same criteria, included the outlying industrial portions of that city. Districts lying at the extreme boundaries of the city ranked lower than any territory intervening between them and the center. The actual order of the four districts ranking lowest in the scale of social advantage was central, suburban, central, suburban. The next to the worst district in the city was the roomiest district, one occupied by scant semi-rural population, who suffered from the infection of a "tin-can" colony—a group of suburban defectives and degenerates living in shacks in the wooded outskirts of the city.

No general conclusion is to be drawn from such inadequate data. On general grounds, however, one may guess that the residential suburbs are likely to be socially

[8] See the study of St. Louis industrial suburbs in Taylor, "Satellite Cities," p. 145.

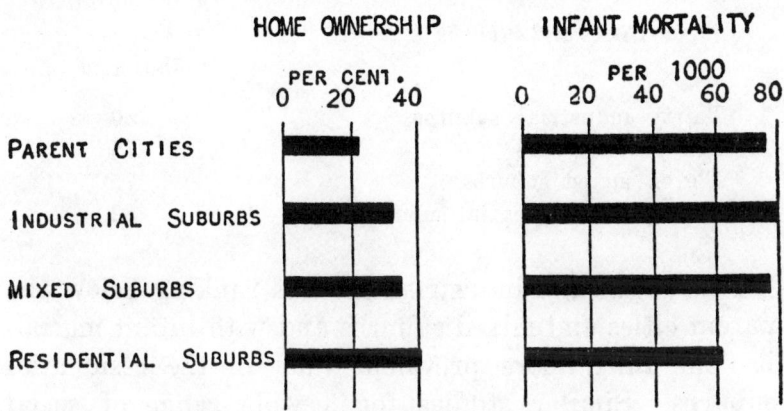

SUBURBAN SUCCESS AND FAILURE
Home ownership compared with infant mortality.

better, while the industrial may be worse than the city average. In other words, the more spacious living conditions of the suburbs may not be able to overcome the weight of adverse selection, as when heavy concentrations of poor and foreign-born workers are thrust into the inferior general conditions of the extreme industrial suburb.

SUBURBS TESTED BY CHILDREN'S LIVES

This diagnosis is confirmed by statistics of infant mortality announced by the American Child Health Association for 1922 and 1923. Averaging both years together gives the following infant mortality rates per thousand for ten parent cities and their major suburban types:

Cities and suburbs	Infant mortality rate per thousand
Thirty industrial suburbs	80
Ten parent cities	75
Eleven mixed suburbs	75
Twenty-five residential suburbs	62

This shows the industrial suburbs ranking below the parent cities and mixed suburbs and with infant mortality one third more prevalent than in the residential suburbs. Similar studies for a wide range of social criteria would tell the story more convincingly and are greatly to be desired.

SUBURBAN DEFICIENCIES

With all their objective advantages, the one-sided life of the residential suburbs cannot be regarded as entirely satisfactory and wholesome. "The community subdivides into little groups of people who like each other. Life is pleasant and relaxed. This is salvation by escape—if it is salvation." Community virtues are not highly developed, and it is questionable whether individual morality can grow strong in any other soil.

While, therefore, one may regard the Elks' Carnival as happily absent from suburban existence, he can hardly help missing Main Street. Loyalty to the home town is not the least of American virtues, and this the suburbs do not breed.

CHAPTER VIII

SUBURBAN SOCIAL DEFICIENCIES

THE deficiencies of the industrial suburb, as it all too frequently exists, are obvious and require only recapitulation. When factories are of first importance rather than people; when hordes of foreign or negro labor are colonized in tenements or shacks; when community growth is undertaken out of these elements and is of the planless, mushroom sort, with subnormal standards of housing, sanitation, and municipal facilities; when the factory which creates the situation gets itself outside of the municipal limits so as to avoid its share in the support of the community through taxation; when the major social institutions are inadequate; when the natural leaders—the industrial "bosses," business and professional classes—dissociate themselves from their own place of residence and find their satisfactions in the city—then inevitably such objective drawbacks as an excessive infant mortality rate appear. The home ownership which is credited to such suburbs may, as Graham Romeyn Taylor shows, be that of a commuting minority rather than of the industrial classes. In the most flagrant cases indeed they go back and forth to and from the country to work but continue to live in city tenements. City planning enthusiasts speak in chastened accents of the unwillingness of the workers to leave the city even for the model factory where housing is within their economic reach. All this is set forth fully in the plentiful literature of the mill-town of which Miss Byington's study of Homestead [1] and Mr. Taylor's "Satellite Cities" are among the classics.

The more subtle problem with which the present chapter deals is the social limitations of those suburbs which possess the largest number of objective advantages. They bring "good" to individual families but lack community loyalty. In other words, their shortcomings are psychological. Our interest is to find out just what is involved in the absence from community life of the Elks' Carnival and in the loss of Main Street.

The Seeping Away of Community Loyalty

The effects of suburban life are not superficial nor incidental. Some of them are extreme and challenging. Thus a suburbanite of some fifteen years' standing supposed that he was set apart from the masses of his fellow-men merely by the external experiences of commuting. Morning and night for all that time he had grasped his hat in New Jersey and run for a train to New York, or vice versa. But he never quite realized what commuting had done to him till, at the end of that

[1] "Homestead: The Households of a Mill Town" (The Pittsburgh Survey), Russell Sage Foundation.

SUBURBAN SOCIAL DEFICIENCIES 217

time, he met his first group of fellow-Jerseymen who exhibited state consciousness and pride even in the most conventional way. They were actually rah-rahing for New Jersey, which is chiefly the back yard of two metropolitan cities. These cities are far more significant and compelling aspects of civilization than anything the State holds within its own borders, and most of New Jersey's inhabitants belong to one or another of them far more vitally than they do to it. Legally a sovereign unit of the American nation and an integral political community, it consequently presents only a faint pattern underneath the major web of actual social structure. In such a situation the really strong and significant strands are those which bind suburbs to cities; so that one could literally wait fifteen years for the first trickle of state consciousness to pass the threshold of the mind.

Such an inhibition of otherwise normal attitudes and reactions toward the State of one's home and long-time citizenship, and such absorption of even conventional loyalty by the city where one does not live, disclose exceptional forces strangely coloring suburban experience and modifying its social organization. One set of social connections has been loosened almost to the point of entire absence, while another and more complex set has evolved differing from anything which the majority of Americans know. The imperialism of the city over the minds and imaginations of its suburban population is a unique fact. It emancipates them from local ties and gives them an enlarged citizenship and sense of metropolitan relationship.

Possible Abnormalities in the Wake of the Suburban Trend

It is this imperious and disturbing quality of certain suburban characteristics which first suggests doubt as to whether they can be altogether normal. This doubt challenges the implicit assumption of the previous chapters that the suburban trend is advantageous and compels one to consider its grounds.

In this chapter accordingly it is our purpose to trace the more radical effects of suburban living, frankly acknowledging as deficiencies some of its extreme social consequences. This will involve a return to the more important traits of the suburb discovered in the previous topical discussions. Some of them it will be necessary to elaborate; others perhaps will be added. The result should be a somewhat unified and balanced view of the outstanding aspects of suburban existence in which both strength and weakness shall be fairly appraised and remedies for its lacks suggested.

First of all, in the cities and their suburbs we are dealing with an excessively bifocal type of civilization. Society has two centers of activity and interest so different in character and so far apart—in spite of all facilities for keeping them in touch—that it falls into very distinct halves. Social loyalties are divided, and run in opposite directions. Mankind is capable of about so much loyalty; dividing its strands makes them weaker in both directions. No such concentration and singleness of social purpose is possible as when they all ran

SUBURBAN SOCIAL DEFICIENCIES

in one direction and were combined into one strand. Man works in the city with half his will and loves it with half his heart. The other half he reserves for the suburbs: but he cannot focus both halves upon either.[3]

All this is not unlike the dissociation of personality and consequent moral dualism which the psychology of the individual finds so abnormal and injurious. The 300 communities, mostly of small population, which make up Greater New York are not so well integrated socially as an equal number of independent communities of the same size. They lack social development and community consciousness. They are not completely themselves.

We shall now trace suburban social deficiencies in greater detail, classifying them according to the most obvious conditions previously described of which they appear to be consequences.

SOCIAL CONSEQUENCES OF SUBURBAN SEGREGATION OF A SMALL NUMBER OF URBAN FUNCTIONS

The residential suburbs are essentially the decentralization of a very limited selection of the activities and processes which make up a city, into social units of relatively small size but still within reach of the city. The sites of these activities are relatively spacious but the activities themselves are of narrow sorts. Even the

[2] The industrial suburbs partly escape this disadvantage, but are likely to divide along lines of class suspicion and conflict.

industrial suburb, which decentralizes production as well as consumption, leaves behind in the central city many of the most important urban functions. Neither type is an all-sided social unit as the independent town is. Each is concerned with part—and the more characteristic residential suburb with not more than half of human interests.

Some of the less desirable consequence of this condition are the following:

Tendency Toward Divided Personality

The half of life associated with the city is always relatively unsocialized. We know that man builds up a social and moral personality primarily with reference to a particular set of companionships and social demands. He is largely what his fellows expect him to be. The most effective social influences are those of fellows who stand nearest to him and his most vital interests; for example, his wife and children, neighbors and spontaneous friends, his spiritual advisers and teachers. But half of a suburbanite's mind is beyond the reach of these influences. His neighbors do not know how a man behaves in the city; his business associates do not know how he behaves at home. Neither aspect of his existence is normally controlled by his "other selves." This tends to make him two men, each with a distinct set of morals because each has a different set of fellows. The social peculiarity of suburban living thus has psychological and ethical consequences of graver seriousness.

SUBURBAN SOCIAL DEFICIENCIES

A Rugged Social Structure Not Built out of Relaxed Materials

In connection with the decentralization of consumption, as in the residential suburbs (production remaining in the city), suburban life exhibits two major interests, the home and recreation. To these it brings the man in his relaxed, non-achieving moods. It is true that play in the suburbs takes on a seriousness not elsewhere known, that, as we have seen,[3] it erects a group of major institutions; and true also that youth for a brief period has surplus energy enough to play as hard as it works. Nevertheless, the play motive does not command the whole motivity of life. Some of the traits of suburban relaxation are very amiable. One has the gentle gardener, the vivacious bridge fan, the golf enthusiast; but none of these is of the stuff of which the builders of cities are made. Every seasoned suburbanite knows that very definite experience of "let down" between business and home. Undoubtedly this is an essential nervous safety-valve for him, a phase of inner rhythm which, as William James showed, changes the mental clothing and induces a fresh set of attitudes. Nevertheless, it is not the mood in which one heeds the clarion-calls of moral responsibility. When the suburbanite has once slumped down at home it is almost impossible to stir him. It is not good for a boy to know his father habitually in such moods. The town wife and children see their husband and father somewhat as his peers see him, because his work or business is within

[3] Page 195.

the practical range of their vision. What the suburban husband and father regards as most important is often but an echo to his family. The fields of his supreme triumphs and defeats are too remote from them, as they are also from the home circle of friends and neighbors. None of them ever knows the other as a complete man and in his greatest stature.

Suburban Mitigations

One thing alone partly saves the situation: the suburbanite has neighbors. In the city also work may be completely disassociated from whatever it offers of home and recreation. That it is not more generally so we owe to the fact that so much of city social life is along trade or craft lines. The fellowships of the job—organized into clubs, excursions, the social activities of trade-unions, as well as expressed through incidental groups and gangs based on industrial association—tend to keep work and play close together for the masses. But this is not the whole story. The tired man, especially of the more privileged classes, may easily slump down into anonymousness or take his pleasure without responsibility. No near-by person knows or cares; he has no real neighbors of what he calls his home.

In the suburbs, however, the individual is known. His neighbors demand something of him, and he dare not altogether refuse. Moreover, as a house-owner he faces increasing taxes which cry out to him not to forget his civic responsibility. This challenge of the suburbs to fulfil a minimum of social obligation is curiously dem-

SUBURBAN SOCIAL DEFICIENCIES

onstrated by religious surveys. City churches have very large fringes of remote and largely anonymous adherents, numbering, for example, 43 out of every 100 adult adherents to the St. Louis Protestant communions. The proportion of these non-member adherents declines with every added degree of suburbanization. It sinks to 29 per hundred adherents in the most residential district of the city, to 27 per hundred in the nearest suburbs, and to 23 per hundred in Webster Groves. In other words, the suburbs do not easily permit one to remain anonymous or irresponsible. There is something in them which says, "Be a full member or nothing." Part of the distinction is of course social in motive. The suburban "family" church carefully weighs who is socially acceptable and uses considerable urgency to get him into religious relations. It does not tolerate such marginal phases of attachment as the city does.

Compared with the little town, however, where everybody's status is sharply defined, the suburbs are a realm of incomplete social relationships and limited obligations—a refuge for many half-men, and they half-known men asleep most of the time they are there! Suburban society, therefore, is not the sphere of the human spirit at full play nor the habitat of the strongest social loyalties.

SOCIAL CONSEQUENCES OF SUBURBAN SEGREGATION OF SELECT TYPES OF PEOPLE

The results of dividing urban interests and locating the exercise of the two halves in separate places would be extreme even if the people involved represented a full cross-section of the city. But in the suburbs they do not do this. Suburbanites are a series of peculiar types. Not all kinds of productive activities, we found, nor all kinds of economic functions can be decentralized; no more can all kinds of people.

Individualists

From the masses of city population the suburbs select only those who are possessed of certain motives and who can adjust themselves to their peculiar method of living. It is not entirely fair to assume that they are the more family-loving and that they move to the suburbs for the sake of their children. Rather, it is nearer the facts to say that they are the more individualistic, people who cannot stand the normal conditions of cities—just as Natty Bumpo could not stand life within the feeble fringe of pioneer settlement. They are those who cannot fully adjust themselves to the era of urban civilization—just as the fur-trader and trapper could not to an era of agricultural civilization. They are the frontiersmen of cities. Other millions of metropolitan dwellers, not less family-loving, are trying out the problems of domestic life within urban limitations.

Urban Alternatives

They are seriously proposing to make existence not only possible but desirable through urban safeguards and remedies. By building-codes and sanitary inspec-

SUBURBAN SOCIAL DEFICIENCIES

tion, by maternity wards, by eye, teeth, and tonsil clinics, by special schools and summer outings, by parks and play streets where playgrounds are not available, by community organization and the stimulation of neighborhood social possibilities, they hope largely to equalize the conditions of life in city and suburbs.

By high schools better equipped and far more specialized than was the college of yesterday, by continuation schools and civic universities, by the combination of schooling and employment, but beyond all else by the mighty stimulus of the city itself and the spell of its vast and intricate business and industry in which one shares even if he plays but a little part, the city expresses the self-confidence and conviction of its capacity both for enthusiasm and for improvement.

By high development of recreational institutions, by the multiplied opportunities of art, music, and drama, by the splendid pageantry of the city itself by day or by night, the city undoubtedly achieves unique esthetic and spiritual results. One who magnifies the suburban trend must nevertheless give the devil his due. Even the convinced suburbanite, who adopts for himself a contrary hypothesis and makes a different choice, generally recognizes that there are losses as well as gains in living out of the city. Indeed a suburbanite is a man who is following a minority opinion. He is a separatist who believes that he is wiser than the majority. He may be more of an individualist or perhaps more of an adventurer. It is, however, an essentially conservative manner of life for which he is striving. He believes that the way to live in an urban situation is to preserve town forms, the small community, the single-family dwelling, and as much as possible of family privacy. Only the gradual evolution of civilization can prove whether he or the city man has chosen the better part.

Family Form without Family Fact

It was admitted at the outset that the suburbs are essentially a compromise. The preservation of the family, for example, is achieved—with a difference. We have seen that large numbers of adult children and relatives remain in the suburban home because marriage is deferred and work within easy reach. But what with their responsible years and economic independence, their necessary relation to the family is slight. They belong to wide-ranging youth and, with the resources of transportation at command, move here and there where interests take them. They are not in key with actual suburban domesticity as typified in the wife and children, are housemates rather than members of the family, and yield little social allegiance to their place of technical residence. Their spirit tends to infect dependent adolescents of high school age. All told, it is the forms of family solidarity which are preserved, more than its substance—except with the young family for a few brief years.

Economic Eviction of the Socially Fit

Besides being select in their attitude toward the family, the residential suburbs, as we have also seen, are

SUBURBAN SOCIAL DEFICIENCIES

economically select. Largely they have been beyond the reach of the poor. The most extreme and convincing illustrations of this fact is that in very large measure they evict their own children.

The newly married couple, naturally with less income than their parents, frequently find no class of housing in the home suburb which meets their needs. The prevalent standard of living is too exacting for them; consequently until they come to have children requiring play space they take themselves off to a city apartment or a cheaper suburb. A community which habitually banishes its own sons and daughters is scarcely a good community; yet to this extreme the selective character of many suburbs has gone.

Selection often still farther narrows the cycle of life which suburban civilization is able to serve. We have discovered that some suburbs are virtually old people's homes;[4] others, however, tend to evict elderly people exactly as they do young ones. There is no type of suburban housing so suited to the failing powers as the city apartment is, with its elevator, its collectively furnished heat and sanitary provision, its janitor service and absence of chores. People therefore are less often suited for an entire lifetime in the suburbs than in any other type of community. At least the years in which the suburbs meet their needs with maximum efficiency are brief.

This has important bearing upon the ability of the suburbs to maintain their character. They do not win continuous loyalty because they do not merit it. For a few years a family are intensely concerned to preserve

[4] Page 99.

their roominess, their single-family houses, their distinctive features. But if they do not lend themselves to the needs either of one's children or of his own declining years, this motive is soon exchanged for that of selling out at a profit or using the land more intensively as an absentee landlord. All this is in utmost contrast to the stable independent community passing its homes, businesses, and traditions down through generations.

One-Sided Outlook of the New Generation

Being thus actually limited in so many directions, it is not strange to find the new suburban generation exhibiting a very one-sided approach toward life. Thus, several hundred Montclair high school boys recently indicated the callings they expected to follow, as follows:

Occupation	Junior high school	Senior high school
Engineers	146	103
Other professions (law, medicine, journalism, architecture)	97	69
Business	57	60
Skilled labor	46	8
Forestry or farming	5	12
All other	0	8

The last item included two prospective aviators, one army candidate, and two intended ministers of the gospel. The trend is obviously neither militaristic nor religious; but since the professional classes (including engineers) constitute only 3.4 per cent. of the gainfully occupied male population of the nation, the extremely

SUBURBAN SOCIAL DEFICIENCIES 229

selective character of the high-class residential suburb, compared with the all-round community, is again emphasized by this comparison.[5] What sort of preparation for life is this which ignores or underestimates so large a proportion of the interests of the human race. The narrow outlook of the country-side or little town could be scarcely less provincial. Besides, what they ignore is far away; hence they are the more excusable. But what the suburbs ignore is near at hand and part of the same larger community.

The Tendency to Snobbishness

In view of his many exclusions and avoidances, the suburbanite cherishes a characteristic sense of superiority which may be generalized as follows: "I am a city man and then something more. All of the essential advantages of the city over the country I have—its vastness, its interest, its opportunity. But I also command rural advantage. I have my own house and yard, my garden and trees, my air and sunshine, my neighbors when I want them, and my convenient and interesting daily change of environment. To be sure, I must make certain compromises from both sides, but I keep the best of both. Only the very rich who exchange city and country seasonally instead of daily are more fortunate than I." This voices the consciousness of a Peculiar People, a conviction of superiority which is very ready to give its reasons.

[5] Of course the outlook of an industrial suburb composed chiefly of factory hands is equally distorted.

Social Consequences of Residual Relations with the City

A recognition of the commanding and determinative character of his connections with the city dominates the suburbanite's attitude. He recognizes the magnitude of the fundamental metropolitan functions which one cannot conceive of as being decentralized. Briefly, these are wide markets and "Big Business." World variety for the buyer and world demand for the seller can only be expressed in a great city. By the time the physical means and facilities of such markets are provided and the goods for exchange assembled, a city is great. This function cannot be removed from a center.

Again, the transactions, contacts, and personal fellowships and competitions of the men who do world business in trade, manufacturing, credit, and every other line occur here. They include politics, religion, and, increasingly, scholarship and research. Only the great office-building, it has been remarked, can compete with the great retail store for the choicest locations and costliest land of the great city. The city is the theater of the supreme struggle and triumphs of man. This is another expression of its inalienable metropolitan functions.

Residual Relationships in the Realm of Consumption

Supreme excellence in esthetic realms equally belongs to the city. It is the focus of the world's genius, the dominant center of its art and literature. Its galleries, music-halls, and theaters exist for all the world even more than for the people of the urban community itself. Consequently they cannot be decentralized. Consequently when the suburbanite undertakes to decentralize his private consumption—home, recreation, and esthetic satisfactions—he finds the situation demanding that he leave the best behind or else recognize residual relations with the city even in these realms.

In view of these unchallengeable metropolitan superiorities, the suburbanite is likely to locate the climax of his own interests in the urban aspects of his experience. Sometimes, as we have seen, he has never withdrawn it. The incidental associations of the city job often exhaust his social appetite. He does not really decentralize his recreation nor take any considerable fraction of the living man out to the suburban community. This turns his home into a mere dormitory. Thousands of men are commuting for their family's sakes, not for their own. They have only suburbanized the externals of their personal lives, and do not contribute as much as half of their personalities to their ostensible communities.

More frequently, however, it is the choice and the rare elements of personal experience with which the city is identified. There are one's most brilliant, learned, or exclusive relationships as the case may be; the things that count!

Suburban Humility before the City

With respect both to his city work, as we have seen, and also with respect to his supreme city satisfactions, the suburbanite remains anonymous to his home neighborhood. His fellowships there do not touch his most cherished concerns. He in turn feels the inferiority of his suburban self to his city self. His docility and loyalty are apt to be reserved for the urban half of his existence. Proud that his existence has two sides, he is nevertheless humble in his suburban capacity and exalted only when his feet are on the pavements.

Social Consequences of Internal Suburban Relationships

We noted in the last chapter the frequent lack of physical unity in the suburbs and the still more general deficiencies in unified social structure and commanding central institutions. The many fragmentary and casual contacts of the suburbanite have also been recognized.

Transient and Trivial Relationships

The consequence of life upon this plane is a social versatility in sharp contrast with the profounder ties and loyalties of more single-minded communities. To borrow a metaphor from transit facilities which constitute the literal cue to the situation, the suburban mind is not a single track but a whole switch-yard within which social relationships are shunted back and forth without going anywhere in particular.

This characteristic tends to infect all the major interests of life. Few groups of neighbors have so little

SUBURBAN SOCIAL DEFICIENCIES 233

in common. Politically the suburbanite is a man without a country, seldom voting where his major economic interests are. Commuter and non-commuter occupy different camps. Behind this difference in diurnal habit lies the profoundly isolating fact that the community is not economically interdependent.

Lack of Economic Ties

Most communities become socially integrated because they are closely knit economic units. In the independent town one merchant buys from another on principle. It is their mutual interest to create the tradition of trade loyalty to the home town. The professional classes trade with the merchants, and the merchants in turn patronize them. The farmer feeds them all and depends upon them in turn. One's fortunes are intimately dependent upon another. Not so with the suburbs. The major relations of each class are with the city, and one might perish without greatly involving the other.

Now, the social ties in the more limited sense are based upon the deep-lying facts of interdependence. When these are attenuated the result in common sentiment and mutual fraternity also dwindles.[6]

The Side-Tracked Suburbs

Add to this that the suburban community is not united by the possession of a dependent country-side.

[6] The laboring class in the industrial suburb is dependent enough, but the interdependence of the classes is not marked as in the self-contained community.

Nobody directly looks up to it. From neither direction is it in the direct line of the hierarchy of communities. In his poem, "New Hampshire," Robert Frost expatiates on:

> The loud laugh, the big laugh at the little.
> New York (five million) laughs at Manchester,
> Manchester (sixty or seventy thousand) laughs
> At Littleton (four thousand), Littleton
> Laughs at Franconia (seven hundred), and
> Franconia laughs, I fear . . .
> At Easton. What has Easton left to laugh at,
> And like the actress exclaim, "Oh, my God" at?
> There's Bungey; and for Bungey there are towns,
> Whole townships named but without population.

So even Bungey has uninhabited townships to laugh at, and is spiritually unified thereby. The suburbs have no such thing. They are a side issue, looked down on by the city, but not looked up to by anybody. They have no dependent hinterland, the consciousness of which tends to integrate their collective processes; no one to laugh at directly. Thus, with all their sense of superiority in individual fortunes, they are short on downright civic pride and lack of strong sense of community identity. They lack town bands!

Talent Not Locally Utilized

Lack of community unity means lack of capacity to utilize natural leadership. We have noted the numerical inferiority and slight influence of the local business classes who habitually dominate independent communities. In their stead the suburb may have a hundred men of national and international reputation—leaders in finance, technical processes, literature, journalism, religion. All are prophets without honor, because suburban community structure does not permit them to exercise any significant influence at home. The world pays them attention, but not the suburbs. It may perish for social vision while counting as its citizens some of the cleverest minds and finest spirits of its generation!

The Quality of Suburban Social Character

Fiction treating of suburban life notoriously concerns itself with neighborhood and cliques. It deals with domestic episodes and country-club escapades. The impairment of the family even while its forms are preserved, the spendthrift lack of a sense of economic reality because all the processes of making a living are out of sight, the accessibility and allurements of the city—these are its themes. Even in exploiting its foibles and deficiencies, the novel cannot treat the suburb as a complete community because it is not one, nor portray its people as living rounded lives in a single environment. Holding up the mirror of fiction to suburban nature confirms this verdict.

Suburban Virtue Based on External Environment

We are reserving our most deliberate praise of the suburbs for the next chapter. There we shall give somewhat adequate consideration to amiable and advantageous traits which rise from the town and country forms in which suburban life is cast in its minor details. That the suburbanite plants, cultivates, and harvests as the farmer does—though on diminutive scale; that he mows the lawn, tinkers with the automobile, and tends the furnace; that he enjoys his own sunshine and shade, his own birds and children, is unquestionably important and gives his life a wholesome distinction not born of city pavements.

All this, however, is a sort of recovery of Eden without recovering innocence. The suburbanite remains a sophisticated spirit, a city man with some modification. Even in the country he wears the fig-leaves of urban civilization.

Summarizing the Verdict

At best the virtues rising from external environment are personal rather than social. No evaluation of suburban social life can blink the fact that it is extremely one-sided. It may—in a fashion and for a time—save the family; it cannot save the basic community values. There is diffusion of interest, lack of localization, deficiency of natural leaders, all reflecting incoherent social structure and relationships. Wide horizons and versatile responses are no complete substitute for the firm and steady coöperation of men in common interests. The suburbs have more than inconveniences and incidental deprivations; they have defects of character. The attempted compromise between city and country does

SUBURBAN SOCIAL DEFICIENCIES 237

not succeed without large elements of failure. One does not really eat his cake and keep it, too.

Deficiencies Aggravated by Rapid Change

The climax of the suburban problem is that, with such peculiar social weaknesses, the suburbs are generally facing an appalling rapidity of social change. From village to suburb, from suburb to city, they are hurled along by the tidal waves of metropolitan life. If therefore one views them hopefully as sortings out of city problems, so that they may be attacked one at a time and reduced to manageable dimensions, he must at the same breath confess that they are singularly unsuited to attempt any serious problem, however simplified. "Like Noah's weary dove," the suburbanite has fled from urban complications; but he has found no abiding-place for his feet in the bewildering phases of suburban evolution, and has little of the proper temper for the stern struggle, little clarity of social purpose, and small social control.

The Remedy

"Cultivation of the community spirit" in so unpropitious an atmosphere and environment is a slight and largely futile mitigation of the difficulty. Logically the remedy should lie in undoing the essential one-sidedness of the situation. If urban life can be more largely decentralized into self-contained suburbs of considerable size and varied interests, whose fortunes can then be fairly stabilized, they may much more largely bring forth the normal social relationships and consequent incentives. This must be one of the chief concerns of policy in the reconstruction of cities. Even the successful control of the specific objective evils—like infant mortality—is of less final significance than the problem of a normal community outlook and a full equipment of responsive loyalties. This will not preclude the cultivation of such capacity for multiple loyalties as man is capable of. The city may still be the rare climax of many experiences, and the sense of metropolitan citizenship may still be cherished. Yet if the suburb ever becomes "good" it will be the place where the suburbanite really lives in his imagination, daily affection, and purpose; and its social interests will furnish the primary challenges and satisfactions for his essentially unified personality.

CHAPTER IX

THE RURAL SIDE OF THE SUBURBAN TREND

WHEN Senator Magnus Johnson moved to Washington and his wife began house hunting, her announced objective was to find a place "where we can keep a cow." Fresh from the farm, she was obviously unwilling to yield that degree of compromise to the city which the average suburbanite takes for granted. But Mrs. Johnson was not alone in her requirements. Nine hundred and sixty-five cows were being kept in the District of Columbia, and there were 204 farms averaging twenty-one acres in size.[1]

Five counties included in the municipal limits of New York City had 800 farms in 1920 on which people kept over 5700 cows, besides nearly 2000 horses, 2400 swine, over 25,000 chickens, besides a handful of sheep and goats. (In this connection the census counts as a farm any area of more than three acres or of less than three acres if it produces at least two hundred and fifty dollars' worth of agricultural product annually, or if it required the service of at least one person in strictly agricultural pursuits.) In two counties these New York City farms were most frequently as small as from three to nine acres, but ten to nineteen acres

[1] Fourteenth Census, Vol. VI, Part II, pp. 133 and 137.

and twenty to forty-nine acres were more frequent in the other counties, some farms running as large as over 260 acres. In the United States as a whole, there is a total farm population of approximately 53,000 people within the limits of incorporated cities of over 25,000! Though they are not exclusively suburban, it is significant that the number of farms of under three acres has considerably more than doubled in the last twenty years.

The Scope of the Rural Suburbs

These statistics help to define the rural side of what is politically speaking the urban situation. The smaller suburbs go much farther in making and preserving rural contacts. There are many others of Mrs. Johnson's way of thinking, and their requirements are not altogether impossible of realization.

The Basic Rural Experiences

In the last analysis a farm is a joint society of plants, animals, and human beings. The family is the basic human social unit. The farm attaches to it a group of domestic animals whose life and work is economically organized. Some of them work to provide food for other animals as well as for man, and all contribute the waste of their bodies to fertilize the soil for a new cycle of production. Wild vegetation is of course a plant society in the botanical sense. It, also, man organizes economically, proportioning the land to each

RURAL SIDE OF SUBURBAN TREND

crop and giving it its appointed place in his scheme of rotation. By loving it and tending it, he makes a weed into a flower—a flower out of place becoming a weed again, because the farm is an economic society.

Now whatever type of life maintains this essential pattern based upon ultimate land contacts is essentially rural; and, however modified by proximity to the city and the limited amount of land involved, this is true of the roomier suburbs. They afford the basic rural experiences. They require the typical processes. While the motive is less completely economic and not at all so in the purely residential suburbs, there is still a combined society consisting of the human family, the animal group (consisting of household pets and wild birds and mammals), and the plant group represented by the grounds and garden of the commuter's home.

These experiences and processes rewaken and recreate in succeeding generations many of the old habits and reactions the acquirement of which was the essence of man's civilization. The old forms, through which human nature grew to be what it is, survive in miniature, coloring the imagination and giving the mind its bent in spite of the increasing complexity and intense competition of the strictly urban experiences and processes.

Where Do the Suburbs Begin?

A strong case might have been made for drawing the line between city and suburbs at this point. One might argue convincingly that the real suburbs do not begin until land contacts have become strong and definite enough to make their impression upon daily life and thus to have a distinct place in molding the growing mind. This would consign to the urban category our working-man's suburbs with eight or ten families to the acre and only a patch of green grass around the semi-detached house, reserving the term "suburban" for that manner of life in which a family lives upon enough land to make the associated life of human beings, plants, and animals a significant reality. Certainly two very distinct types of life part company at this point. The mere contrast in spaciousness between the working-man's suburb and the city and the possession of room enough to live hygienically is a very different thing from that ownership and control of land on which is set up a distinct economy involving a large number of the processes of the farm home. The rural side of the suburbs thus reveals a clearly definable aspect even before one reaches the point where they give themselves to farming as a business.

We have thought best, on the whole, to regard the entire suburban trend as expressing a mediating type of civilization,—one straddling the line between "urban" and "rural," although essentially a foot-note to urban civilization. It is now high time, however, to consider them in their more radical rural aspects, and to see what suburban life is when land contacts are its major premise.

The Rural Suburbs Described

Our new viewpoint intends to comprehend everything that meets the above specifications and still main-

RURAL SIDE OF SUBURBAN TREND

tains sufficient daily contacts with the city fairly to be called suburban. The lower limit will perhaps be found in the residential suburb where the prevailing house-lot has fifty-foot frontage and upward. Lots of such dimensions are interspersed with still larger villa plots ranging upward to estate size. Every house has a lawn, and most have gardens. Besides public parks and play spaces there is considerable unimproved land including woods and swamps within walking distance. All these are comprehended within the general habitat of the community. Whatever variety of hill and valley nature has furnished lies within the range of childhood's wanderings. Real country comes within easy walking distance of the home.

At the other extreme are the apparently almost unmodified rural communities beyond practical distance of daily travel to and from the city. A few hardened or desperate commuters manage to make the trip, but they are a mere trickle of population compared with the permanent residents. A more careful examination, however, reveals many evidences of the city's proximity and influence. The community is in the main beyond the bounds of its work, but not out of range of its pleasure. Thus road-houses and tea-rooms spring up to meet the needs of the motorist on his evening run. Perhaps some adventurous spirit has laid out an addition and advertised lots for sale. His venture has been unsuccessful, but he has truly expressed a lurking spirit in the community. It senses the fact that it will be a suburb in the future, though not yet. The type of farming around such a community has gradually changed. It caters to the immediate city markets and depends largely upon seasonal labor imported annually from the city. Finally, a small element of distinctly city population, of very distinct economic and social status, occupies a belt of outlying estates—at least as summer homes.

This fairly defines the limits of what President Kenyon L. Butterfield has called the "twilight zone" between farm and city. This "farming that is not farming," as he calls it, has probably only secondarily to do with food production; that is to say, with respect to the total food production of the nation it plays almost a negligible part. Contact with the soil, however, plays a very large part, says President Butterfield, in coloring the lives of people who inhabit this zone. The soil is the common denominator. The stained hands of the suburbanite and the farmer interpret the one to the other. "This twilight zone of farming does not at all solve the farm problem; perhaps it complicates it. It may help mightily to solve the city problem, for looking at it in the large, it promises not so much an economic gain for humanity as the evolution of a great welfare movement."[2]

While President Butterfield is chiefly interested in this type of land contacts because they involve improved methods of living, he does not despise the farm of from three to ten acres. "This small farm can support a family only where the market is good, the soil fertile, either naturally or under commercial fertilization, and where the family can do the work without hiring extra labor, except possibly for harvesting. In some cases

[2] Butterfield, "The Farmer and the New Day," p. 71.

RURAL SIDE OF SUBURBAN TREND

such a place will be occupied by a family which has partial support from other sources, but desires the country life and work for the sake of health or the better education of children, or just for sheer love of the country itself. . . . There is every reason to suppose that with the growth of cities and the resultant better markets and the increase in the price of land, very small farms will become a characteristic feature of American agriculture and will have a considerable influence upon certain types of production.''

This approach to the suburban problem from the standpoint of agriculture is unique. No previous speaker for the farmer has gone out of his way to understand the genuine affinities between large-scale agricultural production and the processes at work on the rural side of the suburbs, and no one previously has pointed out how the esthetic and economic motives intersphere in this intermediate zone.

Esthetic Aspects of Suburban Land Contacts

Out of the group of motives which have brought the commuter into intensive contact with the land the most inclusive one is the fact that he somehow likes it. His garden may be profitable, but rarely is. His real profits lie in the realm of intangible values. His manner of living repeats the fundamental formula of village life on the soil, both because it is good for his health and because it gives him esthetic satisfaction.

What we seriously insist upon is that suburban life works out into a typical psychology not primarily based upon the mere achievement of more spacious conditions of living. The suburbanite becomes land-minded through the experiences in miniature of a wide range of old and essentially rural processes. In brief, suburban life "gets one" and stamps him with its own image.

In the first place the suburbanite lives seasonally, exactly as the farmer does. Unlike the city dweller, his habits of life and his domestic occupations take on distinct complexion—spring, summer, fall, and winter.

The Suburbanite an Agriculturist

The suburbanite lives seasonally because he is a farmer on a diminutive scale. During the winter he gardens in his mind. In early spring he trims his trees, lights his brush-fires, and draws on his cherished compost heap for a dressing for the lawn. As soon as the season will let him he painstakingly prepares his seedbed or carefully transplants seedlings which he has started under glass.

His agricultural processes, whether expressed merely in flowers and shrubs or in a vegetable garden, also have to be planned exactly as a farm has. Every crop has its particular season. There must be a succession of fresh vegetables or a succession of bloom. The suburban gardener must learn intimately the likes and dislikes of each plant variety. He acquires a great fund of specialized knowledge and a wide range of specialized skills. He labors and rejoices, thinking garden quite as seriously as he does business or banking or even golf.

At the end of the season he puts the garden tenderly to bed for winter under a blanket of mulch. Whole chapters and volumes have been added to a life which is like the farmer's but very distinct from the city-dweller's.

The Suburbanite as Engineer and Mechanic

It has been humorously observed that the possession of the strength and skills necessary to operate a single-family house gives the suburban husband and father a standing with his own family not possessed by the apartment-dweller of similar status. His dignity and authority are maintained because they are dependent upon him for a wide variety of processes necessary to make life go smoothly. This the apartment-house dweller loses in favor of the janitor and elevator-man.

In their mechanical and engineering aspects these operating processes are of no little significance. They require labor with the hands and compel one to acquire a smattering of the specialized skills of carpenter, mason, electrician, and even plumber. The care of the furnace adds at least a cubit to the suburbanite's mechanical and moral stature. Outside of the house, in the upkeep of his walks and driveways, the management of drainage, and the disposal of refuse, he becomes something of the civil engineer. Finally, doctoring his own car tends inevitably to make him a man among men, inducting him into the great fraternity of garage-keepers and auto-mechanics and qualifying him to discuss the intricacies of farm machinery with the farmer himself.

It is seriously insisted that a manner of life which involves such experiences leaves its mark upon the mind and perhaps upon the temper and makes its contribution toward a distinct suburban psychology.

The Appreciation of Suburban Environment

The environment in which he lives does something to the suburbanite. He may not know exactly what and would likely scorn to call himself a lover of nature. Nevertheless, sky and landscape, unobstructed, come to have their way with him. There are also simple and subtle appeals to his affectional nature inherent in an environment based upon land contacts, especially if shared by childhood. Thus a careful census of wild birds in a suburban block frequently prove that the bird population is two or three times that of its human inhabitants. A single house-lot may be the nesting home of five or six species. One strangely enters into the mysteries of bird domesticity, into its fears and hopes, joys and distresses. Nothing can be more clownish than the antics of three or four fledglings trying to occupy the bird-bath at the same time.

Children's household pets involve an extension of parental care. One becomes profoundly concerned with the sicknesses of kittens and puppies. He has to mediate between the opposing interests of creatures, wild and tame, exactly as between quarreling children. All of this constitutes no mean exercise of the emotional nature. The suburbanite reaffirms some of the old virtues and kindnesses which evolved when men and animals were housemates in some prehistoric cave.

Environment then and its appreciation, with the inevitable reactions wrought by life in contact with no more of nature than the suburban houselot affords, are of almost inestimable significance in the shaping of the inner man. This is written in spite of acquaintance with suburbanites who know more about bridge than the most expert apartment-house dweller, whose only known garden implement is a golf-stick, and who get all their blisters from a tennis-racket. A not inconsiderable fraction of the suburban millions have their hands calloused in the performance of exactly the same types of work that the farmer does and find their outlooks touched by many of the farmer's most characteristic experiences.

A family sharing together such an environment tends to keep something of the solidarity of the country home. It enjoys a community of these experiences. What suburban childhood finds is not merely space for play, but a certain environmental content and feeling for life. A flushed young mother rakes autumn leaves; a baby rolls in them. This is to absorb distinctive sights and scenes. Daily living brings a multitude of little things but good, which cling to the heart and bless the imagination.

Economic Aspects of Intensive Land Contacts

In describing the extent of the suburban movement we noted the tendency of rural population to pile up on the outskirts of cities. We have also counted the little farms in New York City and smiled over the census of its cattle and poultry. Nevertheless, multiplying the facts thus suggested by all the cities of the land, one reaches an appreciation of the economic possibilities of the rural suburb going beyond even the candid recognition given it by President Butterfield.

The economic and social aspects of farming in the vicinity of cities, as distinguished from its technical processes, have been greatly neglected in official studies of agriculture. A single bulletin of the United States Department of Agriculture [3] has described this phenomnon for the city of Louisville, Kentucky.

Farming Near a City

Rapid changes in agricultural practice, it is shown, have accompanied the suburban development of Louisville. Old types of farming have gone and new types have come, based upon a much smaller average acreage.

The underlying economic fact is that the demand upon adjoining land for residence purposes has raised values to as high as from six hundred to seven hundred dollars per acre within five miles of the city, in contrast with farm-land values of little better than one hundred dollars per acre from ten to twenty miles out. The old type of intensive farming could not possibly pay upon such expensive land.

Certain lands lying in the river-bottom, undesirable for

[3] Arnold and Montgomery, "Influence of the City on Farming." Farmer's Bulletin No. 678 (1918).

residence because of low elevation, have also been brought into agricultural use. Their soils are particularly good for the trucking crops which are displacing grain farm-

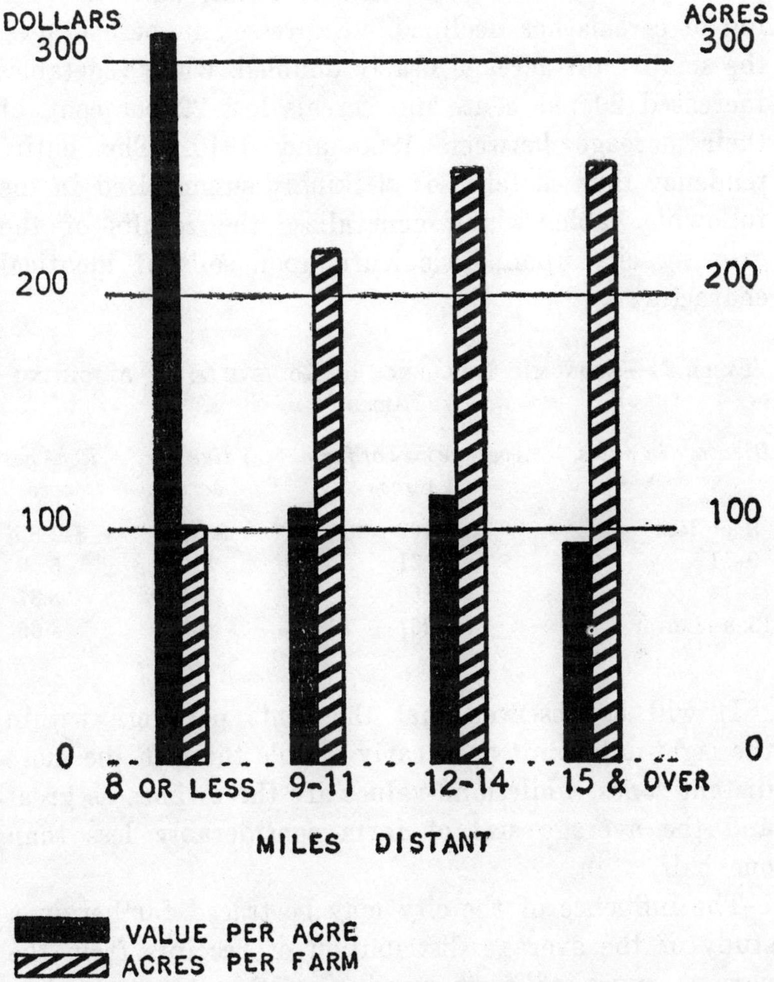

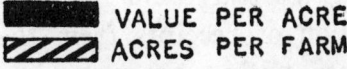

AVERAGE SIZE AND VALUE OF FARMS AS AFFECTED BY
THE PROXIMITY OF A CITY

ing and dairying along the whole agricultural line. Their relative increase has been slowly taking place ever since 1887. Dairying has been continuously pushed farther out into cheaper lands, and the raising of cereals has declined. Expressed in percentages, the small fruit acreage nearly doubled, while vegetables increased 29 per cent. and cereals lost 22 per cent. of their acreage between 1900 and 1910. The entire tendency thus sketched is strikingly summarized in the following table, which generalizes the results of the growing city upon agriculture upon soils of identical character:

TABLE 24—ECONOMIC INFLUENCE OF LOUISVILLE ON ADJOINING FARMS

Distance in miles	Average size of farm (Acres)	Value per acre	Rent per acre
8 or less	102	$312	$11.85
9–11	221	110	5.59
12–14	256	100	5.37
15 and over	257	95	4.66

It will be observed that the rents per acre within the eight-mile limit are nearly double those in the more distant zones, while land-values are three times as great and the average size of farm considerably less than one half.

The influence of the city may be traced farther in a study of the average distribution of receipts from the various types of farm produce within the suburban limit; truck crops here furnishing more than two thirds

RURAL SIDE OF SUBURBAN TREND

of the total income, whereas they furnished only about one third on farms between nine and fourteen miles distant, and only one fifth beyond fifteen miles.

TABLE 25—PERCENTAGE DISTRIBUTION OF AVERAGE RECEIPTS ACCORDING TO DISTANCE OF FARMS FROM LOUISVILLE

Distance in miles	Truck	Dairy	Other
8 or less	68	10	22
9–11	35	12	53
12–14	34	20	46
15 and over	20	27	53

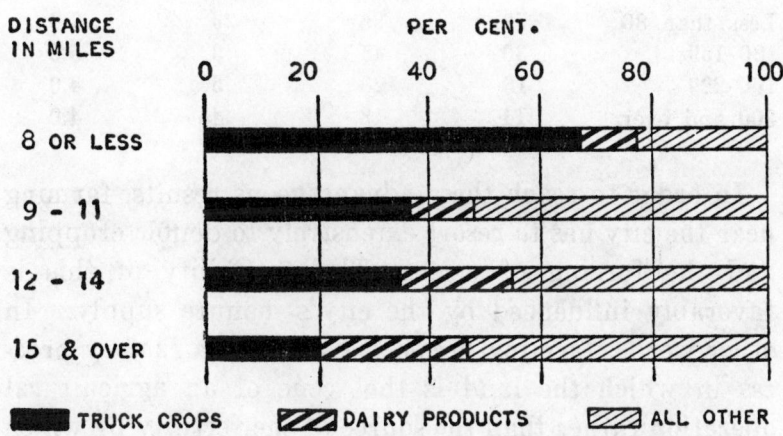

PERCENTAGE OF RECEIPTS DRAWN FROM DIFFERENT TYPES OF FARM PRODUCTS AS AFFECTED BY PROXIMITY OF A CITY

This very aptly shows the changed balance in agricultural production. Proximity to the city drives the farm to produce truck crops which are essential food for immediate urban consumption.

Only such crops can be raised upon land the price of which has been inflated by city growth. While the cost of farming operations is higher, net earnings and profits are also higher in the Louisville suburban area, as shown in the following table:

TABLE 26—EXPENSES, RECEIPTS, EARNINGS AND PROFITS PER ACRE, BY SIZE OF FARMS NEAR LOUISVILLE

Size of farm	Expenses per acre	Receipts per acre	Earnings per acre	Percentage of profit
(Acres)	(Dollars)	(Dollars)	(Dollars)	
Less than 80	73	96	23	7.0
80–159	36	45	9	5.6
160–229	15	20	5	4.0
300 and over	14	18	4	4.0

In order to reach these advantageous results, farming near the city has to resort extensively to double-cropping and the forcing of crops. The possibility of this is favorably influenced by the city's manure supply. In other words, farming becomes essentially a factory process in which the land is the scene of an agricultural operation rather than the source of the fertility by which the food is secured.

It is finally to be noted that agriculture near the city uses fewer animals per acre but more human labor. It therefore not only intensifies processes but adds population. Farming requires more people living on small acreages. In other words it assimilates agriculture to the suburban type.

RURAL SIDE OF SUBURBAN TREND

Similar Tendencies Near Other Cities

Very extensive statistical study would be necessary to determine how far the principles involved in the case of Louisville generally work in the same way with other cities, or whether other principles would emerge to complicate the case. Very similar tendencies have accompanied the rapid growth of Detroit, for example. In the adjoining county the acreage devoted to potatoes and vegetables has greatly increased, dairying slightly decreased, and land devoted to cereal crops considerably decreased in the last decade. This may probably be taken as the normal effect of city growth upon agriculture. Agriculture is conservative, however, and may not always respond quickly. At least it has not done so around the very rapidly growing but smaller city of Akron. Again, when the typical agriculture of a relatively new section is rapidly expanding, the demand of a small city for food grown near at hand may not be sufficient to change the general trend, even though this demand may be definitely registered in crop statistics. Such is the case of the agriculture adjoining Fort Worth, Texas, the main phenomenon of which is a vast increase in the acreage of cereal crops coupled with a much smaller increase in potatoes and other vegetables.

Numerous other exceptions would doubtless be found, none, however, disproving the general law that land rendered high priced by proximity to cities must be worked intensively and highly capitalized if its cultivation is to be profitable. This is most easily done by the production of food crops consumed by city people.

Such crops generally involve more human labor than extensive agriculture does, and themselves tend to increase the rural population in the vicinity of cities.

Phases of Suburban Agriculture

The particular type of agriculture which will develop in rural suburbs naturally depends partly upon climate and regional crop adaptions, as well as upon economic demands. Probably the most ubiquitous form of suburban agricultural undertaking is the poultry ranch, which flourishes north, south, east, and west, but reaches its highest development in some of the Pacific Coast suburbs. Here one finds a raw acre or two cut out of the forest, the inexpensive bungalow ranging from the two-room, unpainted shack to the neatly designed home of five or six rooms with open fireplace, electricity, tank, and pumping-engine, with garden-plot and rows of berries. Scores of such little suburban settlements are found upon the gravelly soil of the Puget Sound region.

Another characteristic form of suburban agriculture is fruit ranching. Good illustrations are the berry farms of the Puyallup Valley adjoining Tacoma, to say nothing of the famous fruit and nut ranches of Southern California. Much of the intensive land culture from which the Orientals are being evicted by adverse California legislation was suburban.

Still another interesting rural business largely suburban in location is the wholesale raising of cut flowers and of nursery stock. Still another aspect of suburban

RURAL SIDE OF SUBURBAN TREND

agriculture now finding increasing development is production for direct sales to motorists. Thousands of temporary counters or stands are set up at farm-yard gates within the range of the city's heavy pleasure traffic and quantities of fresh fruits and vegetables disposed of by this means.

Range of Economic Significance

From the standpoint of economic significance these various phases of suburban agriculture show wide variety. The working-man's garden, for example, affords him a not overtaxing variation of labor and contributes helpfully to the family living. Multitudes of small holdings are the partial support of families some of whose members have other occupations. This type of suburban agriculture, never as yet accurately measured in the United States but illustrated by the gardens of the World War years, is probably capable of very great permanent expansion. We have noted with surprise that 25 per cent. of the wage-earning population living on the farms of Kings County, Washington, are engaged in non-agricultural pursuits. If any such ratio pertains for other cities than Seattle it will be proof that America has already gone far toward developing that type of little farm so much talked about in European countries as the solvent of urban industrial problems.

Even this, however, is less significant economically than that type of complete agricultural enterprise which we have studied in the case of Louisville, Kentucky.

Here on diminished acreages the food of the city is being increasingly produced by a definite type of suburban agriculture which proves profitable beyond the average.

The small holding supplementing a factory job, together with intensive truck raising on the outskirts of cities, has been one of the chief outlets of the foreigner to the American soil. Everywhere on the margins of cities the former peasant of the Old World is breaking away from the tenement and reëstablishing his land contacts either in whole or in part. This is one of the most significant aspects of the suburban trend. It marks the decentralization of that stratum of urban civilization which has been most congested and problematical from the standpoint of social health and welfare. While we have seen the foreigner reëstablishing the slums on the outskirts of cities, one much more frequently finds the reassertion of some semblance of neatness and individual pride even in the cheapest of semi-rural homes. This, coupled with almost feverish industry and a consequent responsiveness of the soil in crop production, reads many lessons for the American farmer.

Of trivial economic significance relative to the total wealth and industry of America, but of distinct interest, are the rural homes of the professional classes where agriculture is carried on as an intelligent sideline. Not a few college professors and other brain-workers blessed with short working hours and long vacations, have found it possible to exercise their muscles and maintain their contacts with reality by doing a little specialized farming on the side. Their example has much to commend itself to others of their class.

In the case of professional classes, economic considerations are subordinate to and always merge with esthetic ones in the choice of a rural suburban home. It is interesting to note how similarly urban esthetic standards come to affect the purely rural producers within the range of the city. The hard-headed farmer learns to deck out his wayside tea-room in genuinely Greenwich Village style, and the displays of fruit and vegetables for the motorist trade closely imitate the window-dressing of city stores. Indeed, it would be almost possible to define the rural suburbs as the area over which urban esthetic standards show decisive influence.

Extensive Phases of Suburban Agriculture

Not all cities have suburbs. Many of the smaller ones, as we have noted, are exceedingly roomy and afford within their political limits all the space necessary for their suburban tendencies. With them, frequently, the type of farming generally characteristic of their region is found clear up to the city limits and even within them. Even the case of Louisville, Kentucky, did not show the extremes of intensification which our later illustrations suggest. Instead of limiting itself to three- or ten-acre farmlets, its strongly modified agriculture was being carried on on farms averaging more than one hundred acres in size. Sometimes the character of the soils surrounding a city is seriously adverse to crop intensification. We also find large-scale agricultural specialization adjacent to cities, as for example in the New Jersey fruit farms opposite Philadelphia.

Another radically different type of agricultural enterprise affected by cities is forestry. This naturally belongs to the farthest margins of their suburban zone where water-supplies are to be protected and municipal parks and playgrounds created. The "Plan of New York City and Environs," for example, assigns many thousands of acres in the outer suburban belts of the greater city to these uses; and, while only remotely connected with agriculture as popularly understood, this aspect of the use of land is being recognized as of increasing importance to the modern city. It is not too much to say that city planning hopes to provide every great city with a forested suburban belt from the standpoints of both sanitation and of recreation.

The Country Estate

The esthetic aspects of extensive land contacts in the suburbs are represented by the country homes of the wealthy classes. Increasingly the suburb for the very rich is not the true suburb in the sense of the community with single-family homes on villa plots, but is rather the rural suburb where many miles of estates generally join one another and absorb the greater part of extensive areas. The visit of the Prince of Wales in 1924 called attention to this type of suburban life as it flourishes on Long Island. Private polo-grounds, private golf-courses, private harbors and bathing-beaches are all symbols of the extensive command of land in such rural suburbs as the part-time residences and playgrounds of the very rich. Estates and country-clubs occupy 116,-

RURAL SIDE OF SUBURBAN TREND

000 acres of Long Island's area, or nearly half as much as all its farms.[4] The ten-o'clock club-car and the private motor are the commuting facilities of this class, and its influence upon the total suburban life of the regions affected by it is considerable and often perversive.

Community Life in the Rural Suburbs

The utmost exercise of the decentralization forces can carry only a small part of the city as far as the rural suburbs. In other words, they show extreme urban thinning out. Neither the means of maintaining close connections with the city over such distances, nor the resources for paying the cost of quantity transportation of men or of goods, exist.

One will therefore look for a much smaller variety of rural suburbs than of typical suburbs as described in Chapter III. Consequently one may generalize with fewer misgivings. The following paragraphs attempt to sketch the typical story of the rural suburbs from the community standpoint.

New Rural Suburbs

Since virtually all the occupied area of America not already devoted to cities was the seat of an old rural civilization, few rural suburbs have had a chance to grow from the ground up. In the Far West, however,

[4] "Long Island: The Sunrise Homeland," issued jointly by the Long Island Railway and Long Island Real Estate Board, 1923, p. 201.

home-seeking farmers, largely retiring from the lands of the Middle West, have often deliberately set themselves to establish rural suburbs within easy reach of cities. They have settled down on little poultry or fruit ranches such as we have described. Such movements result in a relatively unified social situation. There is an initial acceptance of proximity to the city as desirable and the purpose to live in dual relationships.

Having intentionally sought proximity to the city, such rural suburbs can have no fundamental quarrel with it.

The Struggle of Mutually Repellant Elements

Generally, however, the story of the rural suburbs is that of the well nigh impossible adjustment of radically diverse elements, often followed by the social disintegration of the old rural civilization.

On the one hand there is the suburban nucleus consisting of a few people who work in the city and who naturally find many of their other interests there. It is the center of their recreation and ideals, and their consciousness is colored by the easy sense of belonging to it. The majority of their neighbors, however, rarely go to the city. They work locally under a distinctive rural economy and suffer the familiar rural limitations of long hours and little cash returns. Consequently they have the smoldering sense of difference and more or less conscious inferiority.

Between these two groups a great gulf is fixed. The hard and set ways of rural conservatism, its aloofness,

cial cleavages are abolished, the landlord and the landless man of yesterday now finding themselves on the common level of failure. For another thing, quantities of agricultural land go out of use; for just as we found industry in the city spoiling for residential purposes more land than it can use for factories, so the rural outreach of the city spoils for old-style agriculture more land than it can immediately use for the new agriculture.

Where the social structure and standards of the old rural population are not finally utterly overborne, after a long and losing fight, there remain the social cleavages and animosities which we have already sketched. One or two additional aspects of the struggle require mention. For example, the clash of rural and urban standards most often comes over the question of public schools. The new suburbanites have come to the country for the sake of their children and intend to give them all possible educational advantages. The old rural population, with its ancient tradition of the one-room school, can see no rational ground of compromise with demands for school expenditure which it thinks extravagant and ruinous.

The next stage of the struggle frequently shifts to the question of incorporation. This is feared by the old element as a trick of the new invaders, a device which they understand and know how to operate as the original population does not. Consequently long periods of agitation and conflict frequently intervene before the divergent elements of the rural suburbs can get together on the simplest aspects of municipal housekeeping or community activity. While, therefore, in those voluntary groupings such as lodges and clubs, the divergent elements simply avoid one another, the battle rages in those phases of community life which compel common action of some sort to be reached. Long periods of conflict on such issues characterize the transitional phase of rural community experience. Worst of all, the conservatives are ultimately deserted by their own children, who imitate the new-comers and finally go over to them in sympathy and ambition. People under such conditions are not in a happy attitude toward one another. They cannot feel the cordial unity of purpose which makes a true community.

Economic and Social Realinements in the Rural Suburbs

The phase of evolution which we have just described is yeasty and unsettled in the extreme. In spite of it, however, and largely through the leaven working in it, a realinement of the economic and social elements on the rural side of the suburbs is taking place. Constructive forces are at work creatively on this utmost frontier of urban development.

Stabilization and Profits

In the first place, a condition of stabilization as between agriculture and industry has been reached. On all its margins the city has done its worst so far as farming is concerned. What is now going on is rapidly approaching the point of adjustment. Thus virtually all

RURAL SIDE OF SUBURBAN TREND

the farm laborers studied in an extensive investigation of Quaker farms surrounding Philadelphia had been engaged in factory or other city labor at some period of their careers. The majority were now engaged in producing food within sound of the factory whistle. They were on the land because they preferred to be there.

Again, as we have seen, the transformed agriculture on high-priced suburban land has required new capital and been made attractive by greater profits. This has added economic strength to the agricultural enterprise. Still farther, it employs more people and more forward-looking people. Aliens they may be, but the land to them is a renewal of opportunity, and their spirit puts to flight the stagnancy of a decadent rural order.

The City's Support of People on the Land

In the second place, the transformation of farming adjacent to cities means a widened economic opportunity for people dwelling on the land. We have previously insisted at length that ordinary suburban life is beyond the reach of the industrial classes because the small suburb cannot afford economic security, which rests on a variety of opportunities for employment. Such opportunities the open country has lacked even more than the suburbs. The majority of farm children have ultimately had to go away from home to find work.

Now, the proximity of the city brings to the farm many-sided industrial opportunity. We have found 25 per cent. of the employed farm population of Kings County, Washington, engaged in non-agricultural pursuits. Hundreds of depleted hillside farms in New England are still being worked just because the members of the family can find supplementary employment in nearby cities. Such farms could not stand by themselves alone. It is only as industry provides additional means of support that their families can be kept together on the land. Thus, after relationships are once stabilized, the city appears as a friend of near-by agriculture, both creating the demand for food products and affording variety of economic opportunity for rural workers.

INDUSTRIALIZATION OF AGRICULTURE AND MODERNIZATION OF DISTRIBUTION

Still again, as we have previously noted, suburban agriculture is increasingly applying factory processes to the soil. The soil is no longer the fertile mother of men with nourishment within her own bosom. It is here rather a mere receptacle into which imported plant food is poured and in which crops have root-space while they feed on raw material brought to them, exactly as do animals fattening in a pen. Agricultural production in the suburbs is thus coming at close quarters not only with the city as a physical fact, but with characteristic city processes. A new order of agricultural intelligence is being developed, drawing its precedents and methods from the industrial field. Farming is becoming essentially a factory process.

The proximity of the city also makes distribution a responsibility of the suburban farm equal with production. The suburban farmers' middleman is found in the city itself, in so far as he does not sell to the immediate consumer. He thus enters into extensive first-hand business relationships with the city. All this tends to naturalize even the outlying rural suburbs as parts of the essential life of the greater metropolitan district.

Yet all of this does not constitute a neat and comfortable solution of the problem of diverse elements in the more strictly rural suburbs. It does not immediately harmonize the conflicting points of view, and only gradually, if at all, passes over into the community-building process. The series of economic changes above sketched does, however, farther illustrate the unscrambling of the urban situation. The rural suburbs afford a better chance to make something worthy and satisfying out of these divergent elements than if they kept on seething in the caldron of the central city or merely dug themselves in as opposing forces in the old-time suburban country-side. Thus on the farther fringe, as well as in the more characteristic suburban middle-zone, the metropolitan scheme of civilization is simplified by increasing decentralization. Human and social problems are reduced to more manageable dimensions, and new grounds of hope appear for men of vision and good will.

Reserved Areas for Suburban Agriculture

Outside of Canada, the claims of the rural suburbs are virtually unrecognized either by the vision or the technique of American regional planning. Not a single title specifically on the subject, and originating with an expert resident in the United States, appears in Miss Kimball's monumental "Manual of Information on City Planning." A typical discussion of the matter dismisses the problem with a sentence to the effect that theoretically so many acres of land are necessary to feed one person, but that of course food is mainly not to be produced in the vicinity of the city. The extent to which cities draw farming population about them is not understood, and no well-worked-out economics of urban and adjacent agriculture has been developed as a basis for zoning as related to food production. Regional planners and agricultural leaders greatly need to get together on the basis of the facts in order to develop formulas of explanation and control.

CHAPTER X

THE DELIBERATE DECENTRALIZATION OF CITIES

NO unguided trend can be expected to work out in a completely satisfactory manner. While the story of American suburbs as traced through its major phases in the previous chapters has been pronounced hopeful in part, certain problematical and dubious aspects could not be denied. Such a development would naturally be unsystematic and largely accidental, and actually it has been very unbalanced and partial. It has shown many initial tragedies of conflict between old communities and the overmastering expansion of cities; many recurrent losses through abortive efforts, misjudgments, and uncontrolled social changes. The trend is strong and definite, but the outcome so far is incomplete and one-sided.

The City of To-morrow

One of the most stupendous dreams of the social control of civilization concerns the remaking of cities. It is proposed to decentralize them deliberately—to manage the suburban trend so as to secure far-reaching results in social welfare. Reason, it is recognized, did not originate the process, but reason is to rule its farther steps. Science could not start the suburban ball rolling, but science, it is hoped, may direct its farther course. By removing obstacles or interposing deflecting factors, the decentralization which is actually going on may be guided, accelerated, and focused upon ends "nearer to the heart's desire." This is the meaning of modern city planning as expanded to metropolitan and regional scale and directed to the problem of curing social evils, particularly those associated with congestion in living conditions.

The exact proposal is to break up that close concentration which seems the very genius of the city and to diffuse its forces over larger areas, loosening numerous of their ties from the big center of all and attaching them much more largely to minor centers.

City Planning

In virtually all its authoritative modern expressions, city planning implies the establishment of a definite social policy in behalf of the suburban trend. It has already involved much legislation, the gradual modification of the judicial point of view, and the reëducation of the courts on the subject of private property; also the development of a vast technical and administrative machinery. Many steps remain to be taken before the mobilization of social resources is complete or adequate to the task. Yet even now the permanent outlines of the scientific remaking of cities are possible. Experience has approved the technique of its major features. Planning boards and public works authorities of many varieties have the fundamentals of requisite power. The courts—though with some hesitation and frequent backward looks—increasingly maintain their authority. Experts are multiplying. Taxpayers are responding in piecemeal fashion, but they are responding. The modern city is bound to be remade. In the remaking it ought to be possible to make it more decentralized—and better, so far as decentralization itself means improvement. This implies the control of the present suburbs and the deliberate transformation of the adjacent country-side.

Can Cities be Controlled?

But is the city manageable to this extent? No wonder that "The New Republic" is reminded to quote, "Canst thou harness Leviathan?" Is the radical decentralization of cities within the scope of deliberate social decision and action?

The preceding chapters have virtually furnished the affirmative answer; and, though they have not hitherto acknowledged it, it has been a large part of their purpose to do so. Leviathan is already borne along by stupendous currents. To harness him is not to attempt to get him to go in another direction, but only to spur or check him or to swerve him a little to this side or the other in the line of his own movement. It was necessary to establish the suburban trend as a fact before using it as a groundwork for faith in the possibility of its deliberate and purposeful acceleration and ultimate dominance.

From Analysis to Advocacy

Up to this point the present study has dealt with the suburbs in a mood of inquiry and exposition. No rigid attempt has been made to disguise or suppress the writer's sympathies. There has been no pedantic withholding of comment. Judgments have been rendered not in accord with the colorlessness of strict scientific consistency; nevertheless, the point of view has been that of the interpreter rather than of the advocate. Suburban phenomena have been described and explained. Now, however, the book takes a positive position. Cities ought to be still more decentralized. The suburban trend presents a cause to be espoused, and if necessary a battle to be fought. The whole of urban life is at stake. By reinforcing the trend and farther rationalizing the process of decentralization, the suburbs may perhaps save the cities and themselves from the worst evils of both.

Science Controlling Cities

In the process of deliberate decentralization, science is ultimately to decide what elements in the present city ought to remain and what ought to go. Though natural economic competition has already settled the main trend, its results are not always either prompt or complete in detail. The present urban confusion and clutter is obvious and is certainly not entirely necessary. Why should industrial, commercial, and residential buildings be jumbled together in a way which involves a crossing and re-crossing of paths of traffic in a vast duplicative movement of people and goods with the consequent obstruction of the legitimate traffic? Why, with all its facilities, should urban life be physically so difficult as it has become? The present city is largely waste motion; man exhausts himself in getting about and keeping out of the way, and in the larger cities has virtually reached the point where he can no longer do either.

The Formula for Scientific Control

To rationalize and remedy the situation there must be a "proper adjustment of activities to areas," a "devotion of limited space to the highest possible uses." Things must be put where they belong.

The general principle is to prevent unnecessary processes and movements within the entire metropolitan area by locating all activities and populations conveniently and efficiently with respect to one another. Functions which continue to be centralized will still be more scientifically localized; for even after the suburbs have taken their full share, the problem of the systematic ordering of the city will be acute. Functions which can be decentralized will be performed by largely self-contained suburbs, "dependent only on the center for essentially central matters." This point of view is in radical conflict with that which would solve city problems by the improvement of transit facilities. Popular discussion assumes that when the city is twice as large it will have twice as many commuters. From our present point of view there may be fewer; what will they commute for when their work and interests are moved out near their homes?

Steps in Scientific Control of City Development

The first step is to analyze the nature and importance of the activities which the city carries on and which most profoundly *are* the city. Why is the city here in the first place? What original and essential service does it still perform? What other activities necessarily attach themselves to the primary one, so that they become equally basic even though not equally important? What secondary and subsequent activities have gathered around the city and become of its essence and idea? What are still secondary and less fundamentally related to the city? What are only loosely and incidentally attached or are quite accidental? Answering such questions constitutes a sifting of city elements, so that they can be arranged in a series beginning with those impossible to decentralize and ending with those which with but little persuasion can be moved to the suburbs.

The Study of Trends

All this remains a bare formula, a mere counsel of perfection like, "a place for everything and everything

DECENTRALIZATION OF CITIES 277

in its place," without a most painstaking study of what is actually happening in cities and why. The more significant facts have already been noted in previous chapters. Some functions, it was found, are actually remaining centralized; others are suburbanizing. Some are being crowded out of the city; others are doing the crowding. The movement is in certain directions and within certain limits.

Technical Inquiry

A full understanding of the situation involves a physical and topographical survey of the metropolitan area to see what limitations the site puts upon decentralization; also a study of its transit possibilities. "It is topography as modified by transportation which begins to yield the real data with which the economist must deal."

The industries of the city are massed in districts or else strangely diffused. In either case how did they come to be where they are? Are they located by reason of their space requirements, or grouped by their interdependence? Is it transit facilities or available power or the labor market which places them here rather than there? Which of the locating factors is inevitable and final, and which is subject to modification? How much of a change in their operation would be necessary to make a change of location by the industry pay?

Why are the stores of the city, great and small, where they are? Who trade at the great central stores, and can their prestige and economies be overcome by suburban counter-advantages? What neighborhood stores will naturally follow the decentralization of people?

Where must the people live who work in the industries and businesses which remain central? Who and how many of them must live near their work, and how many can be transported from the suburbs and back daily? What advantages effectively counterbalance the additional cost and loss of time? How far will partial decentralization in the radical suburban sense leave the city roomy enough to admit of limited decentralization for what remains? How many people, and who, will decentralize naturally if factories do, and who may be persuaded of the advantage of suburban life whether factories decentralize or not? Into what income classes are city people divided? How many are poor, how many rich, and how many rank between the extremes? What kinds of suburbs are within the economic reach of each, and how many of each economic class can be decentralized?

Answering such questions for each element in each city, one finally compasses the desirable possibilities of farther decentralization which social policy may facilitate. This is the basis of scientific management of metropolitan evolution.

Conclusions as to Central and Suburban Elements and Functions

Attempted management of city development, we repeat, cannot succeed if it finds itself in any essential conflict with the trends of evolution. Its conclusions

DECENTRALIZATION OF CITIES 279

therefore inevitably follow from the facts already traced.

The permanently central aspects of a metropolitan civilization are those which concern its basic functions. Most of the world's great cities are primarily ports where traffic is focused and goods transhipped from land to water or from sea to river. Here the first international merchantman, the sea-roving trader landed, frequently under the protecting shadow of a citadel or holy place,

> And on the strand undid his corded bales.

Around him the city grew up. The people of the port then—of its harbor, docks, warehouses, and their accompanying trade—are the first and most inevitable city men.

In the order of inevitability and originality of function, the second stratum of population is that which serves the first, which immediately functions in housing, clothing, feeding, and governing the people of the port. The two urban elements are inseparable; where one goes the other must follow.

Strangely enough the next most characteristic and central function of cities is performed for the benefit of minorities, and they largely strangers. It is illustrated by trade catering to people of leisure, culture, or large income, and to out-of-town visitors indulging in the novelty of a metropolitan experience involving the free expenditure of money. Cities must cater to this class in spectacular ways. They are the most impressionable and responsive patrons of art and fashion, and focus the efforts of artists, musicians, writers, actors and theater patrons, whose supreme efforts are largely supported by transient amusement-seekers. Still again, cities are centers of management of national and international industry and trade; that is to say, places where the ends of the earth meet and do business. At the center the market prices are made and registered; here the master words are spoken and disseminated. To house these various transients in the city vast hotels are necessary—another striking central feature.

Now, while many of the people associated with these essentially central functions become commuting suburbanites, the functions themselves are the permanent core of the city and permanently hold large populations close to themselves.

Industry Not Essentially Urban

Industry, on the contrary, is only incidentally attached to city centers, largely by the concentration of transportation facilities there. In smaller cities it naturally seeks the outskirts; and industries with large space requirements gravitate there for cheaper land.

Lighter industries organized on a relatively small scale, occupying manufacturing lofts and using electrical power, are exceedingly mobile, moving freely within cities as land values and transportation facilities shift. They are dependent, however, on a large labor supply and cannot easily decentralize except to go into rather large and varied suburbs.

DECENTRALIZATION OF CITIES 281

LIMITS TO SUBURBANIZATION

All such analysis is only to discover that diverse and sometimes conflicting forces are at work in the making of cities. Calculating their resultants as a basis for their remaking, one locates probable limits to the suburban trend. The cottage home ideal cannot be made the only ideal of urban populations. Perhaps we may hope for it for the majority, for nearly all who want it. But not all want it. Some millions of people, with incomes ample to pay the costs of suburban living and with transit facilities available, prefer the city. They do not want the inconvenience of operating a single-family house, nor to spend the time involved in commuting. Take away from the city all that can be taken away: the economic ties of many of them would be shifted to the suburbs. This might carry their homes also. But others would remain because they prefer to, because they are city-minded and would miss the complexity of the city if it were gone.

Others again, while choosing suburban life for themselves, wish to use the city on terms which make it necessary for others to live there.

Those who clean up the theaters and restaurants after the pleasure-seekers have gone home cannot be suburbanites. It is too late; there are no trains. These and millions of other caretakers and servants of the essential metropolitan functions must doubtless continue to find homes near their work; consequently near the center of the city. It will hardly be in single-family cottages, though it ought to be in a much roomier city, one healthier and more beautiful, and one greatly relieved of congestion both of streets and dwellings, through the decentralization of the elements which can go.

The Suburbs after Radical City Decentralization

But what will the suburbs be like after the cities have emptied themselves into the country? In Chapter II we anticipated this question to the extent of showing that there was room enough so that nobody need be crowded if all were properly distributed.[1] Physical space, however, only affords the possibility of saving the suburbs. No one imagines that population will diffuse evenly over the surface of the earth. The heavily populated suburbs of the future must have a structure permitting people to find their work and do it. This means the semi-centralization of functions in and around fairly large communities related to each other as well as to the central city.

The Maintenance of Suburban Character

How are the outward aspects and essential quality of suburban life to be assured under these circumstances?
In the first place, in nearly every metropolitan area, topography furnishes considerable areas of land which are not suitable for buildings or other city uses. These

[1] Pages 71 f.

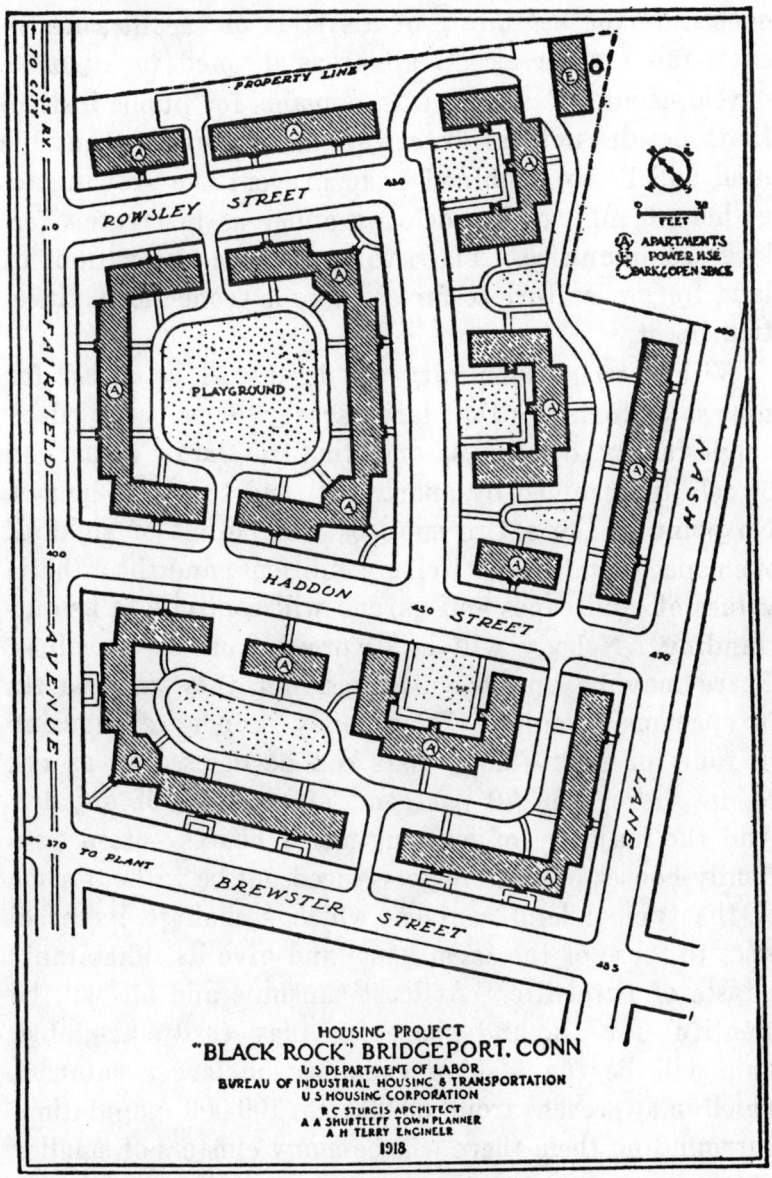

APARTMENT-HOUSE TYPE OF SUBURBAN DEVELOPMENT

constitute the beginning of a system of vacant zones to surround and break up all areas devoted to intensive development. Parks, forests, domains for public institutions, besides natural waterways and naturally unusable land will be so combined as to prevent the growing together of suburbs in such a manner as to create overlarge communities. These will reinforce reservations of land for agriculture so far as there is economic justification for it.

Within each community the land will be zoned for uses so as to assure that large areas will be occupied by single-family dwellings, and that no large areas can be solidly occupied by apartment- and tenement-houses. No point in the entire suburbs will be out of sight of open spaces and roomy living conditions; and the esthetic values of landscapes and garden will continue to be outstanding. Nobody will be divorced from these values. There may be apartment-houses, but they will be set in spacious grounds. Even fairly economical housing in four- or eight-family flats can be devised so as not to use more than 70 per cent. of the area of any lot. And the majority of working-men's houses—often two-family houses on shallow lots—need not be without some of the typical land contacts which assimilate its processes to those of the farm home and give its inhabitants a taste of rural life. At least sunshine and air will be plentiful for all, and space for play easily available. This will be the fashion even of the larger suburbs, which may reach from 50,000 to 100,000 population. Surrounding them there will be many clusters of smaller

DECENTRALIZATION OF CITIES 285

ones in which cottage homes for single families set on ample plots of land will almost exclusively prevail.

THE FUTURE AND THE NEXT STEPS

No one knows how far these conditions may actually be realized in fifty or a hundred years. But they ought ultimately to become the good fortune of the majority of urban people. City planners believe that it is not economically necessary for over 12 per cent. of the population to live in tenements. The cities may thus become primarily suburbs with only their purely central functions reserved, stressed, and probably even more glorified through being disentangled from the secondary and accessory ones.

So far we have been sketching the philosophy and the theory of the deliberate transformation of cities into metropolitan districts with primarily suburban character. The practical steps necessary to compass so vast a result must next be foretold.

PHYSICAL PLAN

First comes a general planning of each new community within the metropolitan area according to the ideals which we have previously indicated. As each comes to be developed it must be planned on detail. A compact statement of the technical steps involved is illustrated in the "Report of the United States Housing Corporation," especially Appendices IX and X.[2]

[2] Vol. II, pp. 497 and 505.

Social and Economic Plan

All functions and elements of community life will be planned for fairly and adequately. Zoning is not exclusive. It will not prevent the poor man from living where he can afford to, but will merely show him where he can afford to live and make suitable provision for him. It will not forbid industry where industry ought to be, but will arrange the space, transit facilities, and relations to labor markets so that industry will inevitably seek the location set apart for it. Actual zoning, of course, always provides means of revision of its decisions in the light of experience. Starting out, however, with the actual varieties of suburbs which have evolved, planning attempts to provide more satisfactorily for each type. It calculates the home requirements of each economic class and the space it can afford. It defends the general characteristics of communities and regions as they evolve. It helps actual tendencies to reach their best possibilities.

Particularly in the direction of providing for a balanced community is planning more democratic than many of the suburban communities that have evolved. Predicating that a community which evicts its own sons and daughters is not a good community, it frankly builds a limited number of small apartments for newly married people. Realizing that a man may still be a good citizen and neighbor at an age when he no longer cares to operate a furnace, it adds enough multi-family housing to take care of his case. Since there are to be tradesmen and domestic servants, the planned suburb

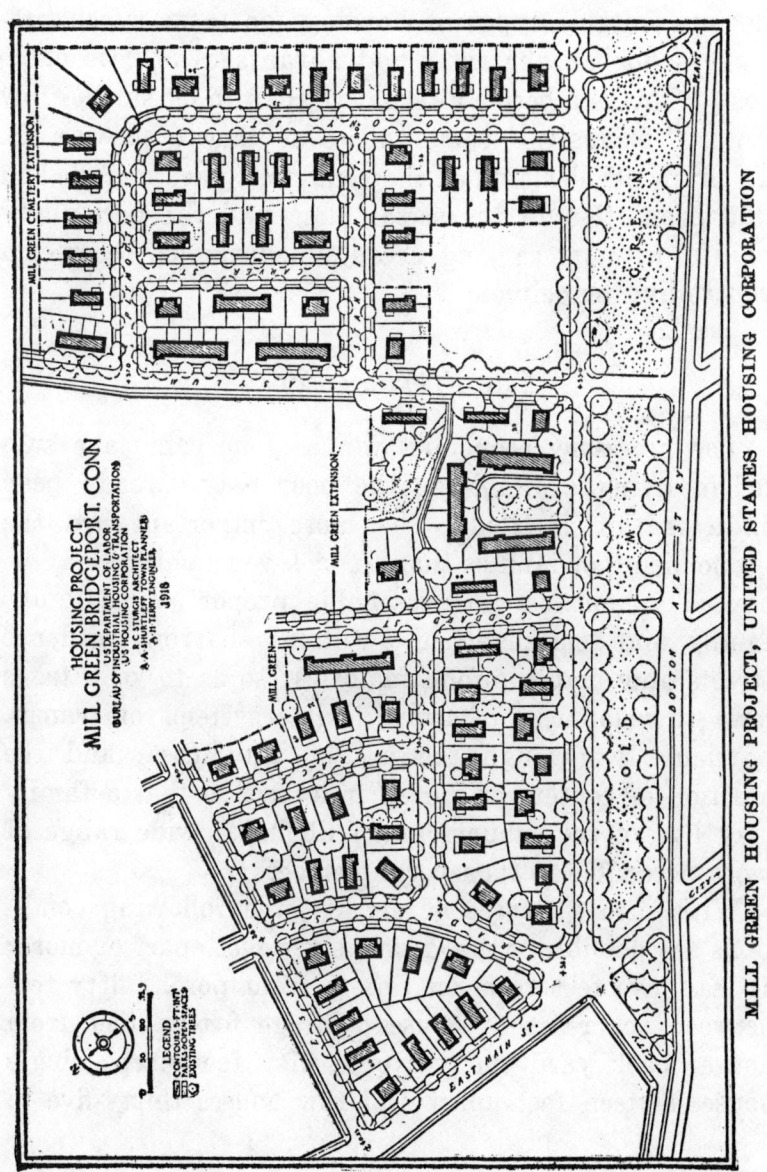

devises suitable types of housing for them which preserve suburban character and advantages at reasonable cost. This is a better alternative than to let slums grow up in "exclusive" communities as they otherwise do. In brief, all elements of the community are included in due proportion in the social plan, and the periodicity of life, with its varying needs and demands, becomes a controlling principle.

The Financial Plan

The necessary economies which alone can make suburban living available to the poor have already been indicated or implied. The more important are the economizing of land so that six or seven families may be housed on an acre; a reasonable proportion of multi-family and semi-detached dwellings; narrow residence streets and simple public facilities (so as to keep taxes low); development of more flexible systems of transit, particularly through the use of auto-buses; and the erection of centers of varied industry, so that a family may live in the suburbs and still find a wide range of work accessible to its several members.[3]

With such a degree of density, the following conditions are possible: house-fronts sixty feet apart or more; at least five feet from lot line to front porch; fifty feet between the rears of houses; garage fifteen feet from house; back yard thirty-five to fifty feet deep; single houses sixteen feet apart and row houses thirty-five to

[3] Pages 135 f.

DECENTRALIZATION OF CITIES

forty feet apart; an average of 4000 square feet of land per family.[4]

A Public Policy Facilitating Decentralization

The final step in effecting a general decentralization of cities is the more definite development of a group of related measures facilitating and accelerating it. All together they constitute a public policy favorable to the suburban trend.

Zoning

The predetermination within their corporate limits of the uses to which land may be put, and especially the limitation of possible congestion, is becoming habitual with American urban communities. Over twenty-two million people, constituting 40 per cent. of the urban population of the United States, lived in the 183 zoned communities in 1923.[5] Two thirds of this progress had been reached during the previous two years, thus marking a movement going forward by leaps and bounds. Thirty-six of the sixty-eight cities of 100,000 population and over had adopted zoning ordinances at that date. Of the States New Jersey leads with 34 places, followed by New York with 30, Illinois, 23, California, 17, Ohio, 13.

[4] "Report of U. S. Housing Corporation," Vol. II, p. 498.
[5] "Zoning Progress in the United States," report of the U. S. Department of Commerce, Division of Building and Housing, 1923.

These laws originate in the police powers of municipalities as relating to the health, safety, and general welfare of their people. In detail they have suffered a rather severe pruning back by the courts in defense of the rights of private property. Thus a man who wants to start a store on his own lot in a district zoned for residence use only has frequently found judicial decisions on his side. Nevertheless, the main lines of zoning control hold and are continuously strengthened. Uses of private property are greatly limited by police-power regulations and will be still more in the future.

The chief deficiency at present is the lack of legislation extending zoning to rural areas between towns and cities and the strong tendency of communities to zone against one another. More than 300 separate municipalities are concerned in the area covered by the single "Plan of New York and Its Environs." Obviously territory adjacent to incorporated places should be zoned in harmony with their intended or inevitable development. Regional planning hence must succeed city planning. City planning in the United States now stands on the threshold of this new suburban trend.

Stiffening Building Requirements

Requirements as to air-space, sun-light and fire protection, the regulation of construction and operation of city tenements can legitimately be pressed to the extent of discouraging that type of housing investment. The dangers to health and morality are so obvious that very high standards may well be adopted which shall have the effect of penalizing such over-intensive use of land. This will greatly facilitate the suburban trend.

Higher Taxes for Over-Used Land

The principle is already well established that the real estate under a sky-scraper may be taxed at higher rates than the same area under a two-story building next door. By the same logic, a city might systematically assess all similarly located plots in proportion to the intensity of use made of them. If the law allowed an eight-family tenement as the maximum burden of a lot, such use might bear the highest rate of assessment. If only a four-family tenement was put on it, it might be assessed for less, and still less if used for only a two-family house. The improvements in either case would be assessed on their true values. Tenement property in the past has got off lightly with respect to taxation compared with smaller dwellings, and it is only fair to equalize in the interest of decentralization.[6]

The Temporary Exemption of Improvements from Taxation

Coupled with administrative measures against the overuse of land, such expedients as the exemption of new structures from taxes for a period of years would tend to turn building to the suburbs. Such exemptions have been declared legal for limited areas and are in

[6] "Plan of New York and Environs," Report of Progress, 1923; p. 26.

actual operation; and there is no reason why public policy should not offer them in such a way as to get houses built where public policy finds it good for them to be.

Excess Taxation of Unused Land

Quite apart from the broader implications and claims of the single-tax theory, even very conservative economists concede the justice of taxing land so as to encourage its use. Otherwise society creates values by building all around the vacant lot, and its owner takes their unearned increment, thus reaping where he has not sowed. The speculative land-holding of suburban areas is nothing less than a vast conspiracy to reap benefit from others' risks and labors. An equalization of taxes would prick the bubble of inflated prices and relieve owners who are putting their property to present use.

Transit Facilities

More and more public policy controls the suburban transit situation, through franchises and the rate-making power of the State, if not through public ownership. Not only can the suburban trend be facilitated by rapid transit to and from the city, but also and especially by the creating of transit routes tributary to and between minor suburban centers. Sometimes this method will need to be used in advance of any present economic demand. Motor-bus routes make this possible as never before without excessive first costs. People need facilities for keeping away from the city as well as for getting to it. The building up of self-contained centers, offering wide range of employment, themselves fairly roomy and surrounded by residential suburbs for industrial workers, hinges, more than upon anything else, upon a deliberate transit policy intended to produce this effect.

Direct State Aid in Housing Construction

Other than the brief history of the United States Housing Corporation, we have no national precedent for deliberate governmental measures accelerating the suburban trend. Neither have state experiments gone far. The Massachusetts Homestead Commission has done a slight amount of pioneer work in furnishing direction and credit for housing schemes. North Dakota under Non-Partizan League control legalized state assistance in home construction as part of its rather radical legislative program. California has land settlements in operation primarily for farmers and ex-soldiers. Neither of these experiments has been without its vicissitudes and limitations. However, even these rather feeble beginnings constitute precedents. The logical distinction between public credit extended more and more liberally to assist the farmer to secure land, and public credit extended most gingerly to assist the worker to own a house, is that the first is for productive property, while the use of a home is mere consumption. This, however, is to overwork an economic distinction. The

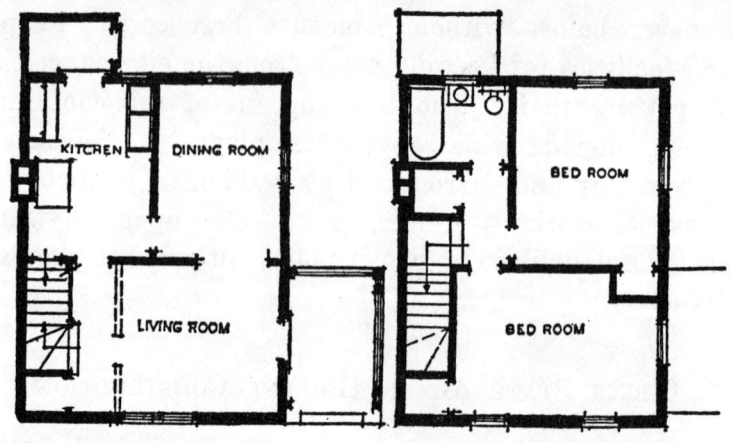
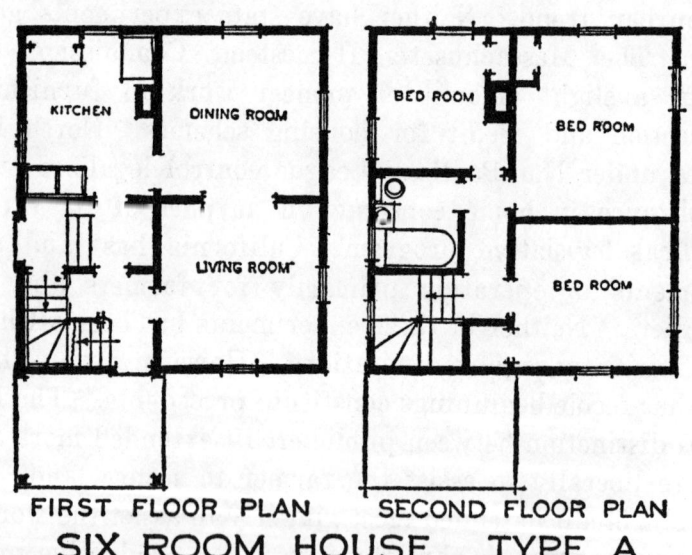

STANDARD TYPES OF INDUSTRIAL HOUSING
United States Housing Corporation. Five- and six-room houses.

DECENTRALIZATION OF CITIES

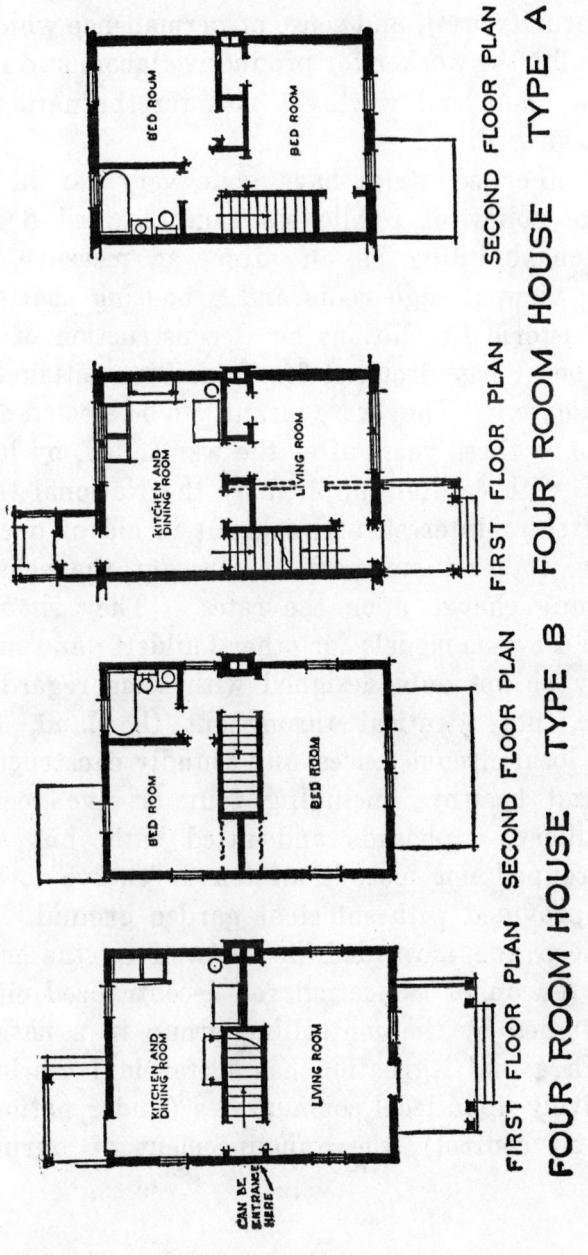

STANDARD TYPES OF INDUSTRIAL HOUSING
United States Housing Corporation. Four-room houses.

comfort, security, rest, and sense of permanence which a home gives fits the worker for productive labors and may easily be as good and worthy a risk for the nation to take as farm credit is.

Certain other countries have gone very far in accepting the policy of public assistance toward decentralized home-building as an after-war measure, especially in view of high rents and a housing shortage. Thus the historic Resolutions on Reconstruction of the British Labor Party declared for "a million cottages of the Great Peace." They were meant "to be erected during the two or three years after the war ended, by local authorities, with capital supplied by the National Government, free of interest, and a grant in aid of one or other form at least sufficient to prevent the scheme involving any charge upon the rates. [They should] be fitted to serve as models for other builders; and must accordingly be not only designed with some regard to appearance, not identical throughout the land, but adapted to local circumstances, and soundly constructed, spacious and healthy; including four or five rooms, larder, scullery, cupboards and fitted bath, but also suitably grouped not more than ten or twelve to the acre; and provided with sufficient garden ground."

This voiced the most definite as well as the most daring expression of aspiration for decentralized cities ever entertained by the controlling group in a nation. And though actual legislation has so far laid the burden exclusively upon local communities (under national stimulus and control), the announcement of purpose marks an epoch. On our side of the Atlantic, Canada is actively at work in providing housing through public credit and is connecting it with definite planning in the interests of deliberate decentralization.

Considering its own beginnings and these powerful examples, the next acute crisis may easily find the United States permanently committed to a direct backing of the suburban trend.

Suburban Development through Organized Private Effort

Hitherto in the United States industrial employers have chiefly been looked to for the creation of residential suburbs in connection with the housing of their workers. It has been more congenial to the national temper to depend upon such "enlightened selfishness" in the interest of increased labor efficiency. In response to this motive, very appreciable results have been secured. Corporations have broad credit, and they can buy land and materials at wholesale, plan consistently, build in quantity, and create conditions which make community facilities inexpensive. All these economies count greatly. The various housing developments of the United States Steel Corporation, for example, present some excellent instances like Fairfield, near Birmingham, Alabama, and Morgan Park, Duluth, Minnesota. As industries increasingly find it advantageous to decentralize, more and more cases of planned "model" suburbs are to be expected as a concomitant process. This tendency will go far toward the goal of healthy and uncrowded living for the masses.

"Own Your Own Town"

It is to be pointed out, however, that it is the workers primarily, and not the corporations, who create the economic and social values in such new communities. The land around or within reach of the factory enjoys a potential demand as the site of workers' homes. The more homes are built the more valuable it becomes. Either the corporation may buy up the land, build the homes for rent or for sale, and reap the benefit; or private speculative builders may do the same, though generally much less economically. Or finally the workers may organize coöperatively and do it for themselves, reaping the advantage of increased values, converting them to community improvements and the reduction of taxation, and in the end owning their own town.

Why should they not do so more frequently, as they are beginning to do in England? In the United States both the workers themselves and the interests who would have to advance them credit are unaccustomed to coöperation in this realm and on the scale necessary. The success, however, of small-scale building and loan associations and the rapid growth of coöperative ownership apartment-houses in cities foretell the not-distant time when the coöperative development of residential additions or entire cottage communities will be within the bounds of experience and will constitute a real alternative.

DECENTRALIZATION OF CITIES

New Units of Government

Both from the standpoint of planning and administration, new political integrations must take place within the metropolitan area. Whether people with common problems finance themselves through the ordinary processes of municipal borrowing, or function as part of a state-aid scheme, it is important that all the territory legitimately concerned, and just that territory, should have means of political expression. A drainage area may easily set itself up as a special district, issue bonds, and levy taxes to pay for its improvements. Why, then, should not an area whose population movements flow within a given area and toward a common center be allowed also to set itself up as a political unit for planning and community development, both physical and social?

The present slow process of annexation takes care in time of the more thickly settled areas, but the very unspoiled open areas which most need to be occupied rationally are not included in the plans of the incorporated parts. Settlement frequently starts wrong from the beginning. The political fragment therefore needs to be taken up into the social whole and a form of government devised according to the facts of metropolitan relationship and growth.

This is what Detroit is just now attempting. Its problem is to combine a city, a county, twelve villages, twenty-one townships, and 122 school districts of varying jurisdictions—a total of 160 separate governments lying within a fifteen-mile radius from the center—into a single government "for certain purposes which cannot be undertaken satisfactorily by cities and villages individually." As recommended by the Detroit Bureau of Governmental Research, Inc., these would include water-supply, sewerage, rapid transit, and port development, and possibly ultimately police, health, and education. In these matters it would supersede the original governments, which would retain more limited functions.[7]

Summary of Social Policy of Decentralization

Thus by zoning, by the pressure or relaxation of taxation from various angles, by direction of transit development, by provision of credit either by state aid or by corporation or coöperative action, a community which is given a logical unit for government to function in may very greatly accelerate the suburban trend. Communities should do so as a deliberate social policy.

The Correction of Suburban Deficiencies

It is not to be expected that decentralization will drag no problems in its train or that some of the urban evils will not follow the city as it disperses itself among the suburbs. Some of these symptoms already appear. Thus a recent conference on child labor, called in Philadelphia by Dr. Royal Meeker, state secretary of labor and industry, heard the charge that work on ready-

[7] "The Detroit Metropolitan Area"; Report by the Detroit Bureau of Governmental Research, Inc., for the Detroit Board of Commerce, January, 1924.

DECENTRALIZATION OF CITIES 301

made garments is now jobbed out to families in the suburban and rural districts and collected by motor-trucks, instead of being made in the factories from which the garments are sold. It was conceded that city sweatshops have been placed under fairly rigid control, and practical restraints against the employment of children under legal age are enforced in the factories. But under suburban conditions law enforcement has increasing difficulties because the constant vigilance required has to be spread over a so much larger area.

The gains of decentralization consequently are not all gains. Pure air and sunshine, however; remoteness from contagious disease; family privacy and the control of children by the mother within her own premises; opportunity for back-yard plays for domestic pets and a garden—these constitute such profound advantages that scarcely any price would be too high for them. Add to these the esthetic and moral gains of the suburban environment with its land contacts linking life with that of the farmer and laborer, and one ends with the recovery of most of the ultimate objective goods of life.

The Reintegration of Suburban Life

The conscious and deliberate spreading out of city elements which this chapter has described is, however, even more significant as an internal rebalancing of elements of experience and a consequent reintegration of life. That characteristic suburban splitting of daily experience into widely sundered halves—one devoted to production, the other to consumption—is to be remedied by the relocation of both in single communities in which the responsibilities of citizenship may be exercised with respect to both. Social organization and fellowship are again to be between people, both phases of whose existence are known to their fellows, as they are in the little town or small city. Mother and children will now be acquainted with the father of the family as he is at work, not merely as he is at rest or at play. All sides of a man will be involved in his life within his own community.

Such a situation will not forbid his continuing relation to the great center. Man is capable of, and must learn the art of, cherishing multiple loyalties. He can do so only by achieving a scale of relative frequencies and values. These enlarging relationships to the city must be limited to appropriate and essentially central matters. The rivalry of evenly balanced tendencies will then be gone. The reorganized suburb, recognized as a governmental unit and magnified in the consciousness of its inhabitants, will be large and varied enough to supply most of the needs and afford most of the satisfactions of its people. It will have its theaters, its galleries. Out of the more closely associated lives of its people, and away from the over-specialization and professionalism of the city, may spring up forms of amateur expressions of the creative arts. In the semi-independent community one may hope for more singing and dancing, more painting of pictures and writing of books with and for one's neighbors, and with less dependence upon high-priced specialists and geniuses.

DECENTRALIZATION OF CITIES

To hear and see the best in the world is poor recompense for the habit of passivity and lack of initiative on the part of the masses. This is the city's great shortcoming. It is all so vast and complicated that multitudes are content to stand on the side-lines while a handful play. Within the decentralized city, the reorganized suburbs are everybody's chance to get into the game.

These are some of the more immediate ends which imagination and ideals discern beyond the physical decentralization of cities. Enlarging the suburbs will both enlarge and equalize privilege for the many and help to recover lost or imperiled values of life for all.

CHAPTER XI

THE SUBURBAN EVANGEL

Jerusalem shall be inhabited as villages without walls, by reason of the multitude of men and cattle therein.—ZECHARIAH II, 4.

THE prospect that the expanding city may permanently overflow into village forms and contain cattle as well as men is one of the most heartening evangels of future civilization.

Up to the present, the city is civilization's Great Adventure, but by no means a wholly profitable or happy one. Indeed, it has been so little a success that the quest of an alternative has become one of the primary concerns of our age. No set of questions is more thrilling for speculation nor more momentous for human welfare than those which relate to the manner of distribution of mankind over the face of the earth, the pattern of his concentration and diffusion, the balance between city and country, the probable shifts and compromises between them, and the possible relatively final stabilization in mediating type of social organization and culture which shall be essentially suburban.

THE REVULSION FROM CIVILIZATION

A mood of reaction and doubt which constitutes part

THE SUBURBAN EVANGEL

of the terrible back-wash of the World War, marks the attitude of the present toward the future. There had been temperamental pessimists before; to-day's pessimists are disillusioned optimists, men who yesterday believed that material progress and science were near to ushering in the Golden Age. There is a revulsion from civilization which has as its climax a condemnation and repudiation of the city as its most characteristic and fatal vehicle and expression.

The Indictment of the City

Even the most conventional and emotional expressions of this attitude find fresh force and poignancy. Cities have long been symbolized as Towers of Babel rearing themselves in ruthless energy. It is only repeating "old stuff" which Arnold Bennett gibes at us about the Woolworth Building:

Anybody in America will tell you without tremor (but with pride) that each story of a skyscraper means a life sacrificed. Twenty stories—twenty men snuffed out; thirty stories—thirty men. A building of some sixty stories is now going up—sixty corpses, sixty funerals, sixty domestic hearths to be slowly rearranged, and the registers alone know how many widows, orphans and other loose by-products.[1]

This is the voice of pity and indignation in rebellion against what the city assumes as a necessary evil.

[1] Arnold Bennett, "Your United States," p. 39.

World-weariness fully as much as moral revolt inspires the following outburst from Sherwood Anderson:

> At times all Chicagoans grow weary of the almost universal ugliness of Chicago and everyone sags. One feels it in the streets, in the stores, in the homes. The bodies of the people sag and a cry seems to go up out of a million throats: "We are set down here in this continual noise, dirt and ugliness. Why did you put us down here? There is no rest. We are always being hurried about from place to place, to no end. . . . We are tired, tired. What is it all about? Why did you put us down here, mother of men?"

Quoting these words, a reflective book reviewer is moved to add:

> If it is that bad in Chicago, what must the sag be like in the average American city?

One knows that such plaints are rhetorical or moody; yet, even so, they are symptoms of the discontent of a chastened and discouraged world with urban assumptions of success and superiority. And even as minor symptoms they have a certain scientific value.

Specific Evils

In such a generalization as the present chapter attempts, it will not be necessary to add the weight either of story or of statistics to the revelation of specific evils of city living made or implied in previous chapters. In the nation's thirty-two largest cities more than twenty-two millions of people inhabit an area which

THE SUBURBAN EVANGEL

would suffice for only 10,000 American farm families on farms of average size. Even though every one of them were asleep and with no conscious contacts going on, the unsettled dust of the day and the effluvium of their lungs would go on polluting the common air. Biologists discern congestions of germs to match congestions of people and animals. From all the incredible roominess of the world in which they exist, these microscopic organisms marshal themselves into unseen, parasitic cities unimaginably more populous than ours. Disease colonizes and settles down with the urban race of men. Sunshine which might destroy or neutralize it cannot penetrate into dark rooms or scant air-shafts.

The noise of the city is nerve-racking. The feverish life of the streets; the inevitable exposure in tenement hallways and windows of things which should be private; the impossibility of maintaining family discipline, standards, or culture when life is habitually led within crowds of mixed elements; the cruel lack of space for childhood in which to play and to exercise the most creditable instincts and initiative; the consequent conflict with authority which creates criminals by circumstance and by definition in addition to those who become predatory or vile; the artificiality, unwholesomeness and final terrible apathy in the presence of it all—all these are the commonplaces of recognized city evils.

ECONOMIC INEFFICIENCY

A newer indictment of the city charges its supposedly efficient facilities and economic advantages with being frauds. Henry Ford says that cities have become too difficult to carry on industry in and that they should be scrapped as out-of-date machinery. If in self-congratulation one thinks, "My automobile takes me to the city in half an hour," he soon gets jammed in traffic which creeps forward by inches; or, while he is imagining, "This express elevator will get me up to my office almost instantly," he is waiting indefinitely for the elevator and is crowded off when it comes. Hitherto the city has seemed to keep a little ahead of the thousand inconveniences and strains essentially of its own creation. Now, many feel, even its mechanics has broken down. Its vast roaring, moving, conflicting masses are virtually deadlocked so far as going where they want to go is concerned. At least cities are continuously taking more out of the strength and nerves of their people till the breaking-point is in sight for facilities and nerves alike.

The City against Man

Probing still deeper, the social philosophers see in the city the final expression of a discrepancy between human nature and environment which is wrecking the race. The caveman, they say, is trying to live in modern New York, Chicago, and San Francisco. There has been no essential change in human nature, and the modifications of attitude and behavior which artificialized city life demands are too much for him. An impossible complexity has come upon man, not of foresight or volition, but as a fatal cumulative result of material inventions.

THE SUBURBAN EVANGEL

One device requires another till the earth is cluttered with them.

Particularly is man in cities in sad misadjustment with himself because they do not call for nor permit the exercise of his entire nature, either physical or emotional. Machines do too much for him on the former side, and conventions allow too little play on the latter. His instinctive and impulsive life is not allowed for. If they are suppressed he becomes mentally unstable and abnormal; if they are not, he is in criminal conflict with his world.

Virtually all forms of mental derangement, it is pointed out, occur much more frequently among urban populations. This is ascribed to specialization in occupation and to the physical and social limitations of city life. These find place for only part of human nature. But the growth of cities means still more of specialization and limitation; and no end is in sight.

This is equivalent to saying that civilization is running away with itself. It is on the downgrade and its brakes are not working. It is falling apart with overstrain, and a crash is imminent.

The actuality of the tendencies on which extreme judgments like this are based have become almost commonplace with sober and thoughtful men. Graham Wallas confesses that the plan for a Greater Chicago impressed him as "suited for giants and not men, or at least only to the gigantic qualities of mankind."[2] Unfortunately in man's mind such qualities are bound up with a tough set of older dwarf instincts with which

[2] "The Great Society," p. 56.

the gigantic qualities must keep on living. If, by reason of environmental strain, a rift is opened between the two, instability and final insanity results, and the giant is laid low.

THE SYSTEMATIC DETERIORATION OF THE RACE

Such is the tragedy of cities. Schematizing what they are continually doing for the race, one may conceive it as a terrific in-draft which sucks up the best blood and brawn of the rural regions. The urbanizing process itself is essentially a down-draft which reduces the best of this generally high-grade material to a lower level of vitality and morality (though selecting its finest minds for highly specialized services which they have not bodies able to sustain long), and consigns the worst to a social scrap-heap of terrific and ever-increasing dimensions. The consequence is "folk depletion" in the open country, mental and social overstrain and abnormality in the cities, and a bad time all around.

"BACK TO"—WHAT?

It is not strange that a race moving forward with so doubtful a prospect should begin to look backward. This has always been man's resort when he dared not look forward. There have been many myths of primitive excellence, of a heroic age which it would be salvation to recover. The looking backward of our more scientific and sophisticated age, however, cannot really

THE SUBURBAN EVANGEL

bring itself to be enthusiastic over a return to primitive savagery. For one thing, its method of securing food obviously could sustain only a meager fraction of the world's present population. In other words, no one really proposes that the race go clear back to its beginnings as a remedy for civilization.

Man's Limited Capacity for Adaptation

Nor is such a complete return necessary. Human nature, all agree, is capable of a certain measure of adaptive elasticity. Village life, which was its typical form of civilization up to the beginning of the era of steam-driven machinery, little more than a century ago, was not, so far as determined, an undue strain upon it. The city does overstrain human nature, and relief must be looked for in the direction of the village. Just how far back, then, is it necessary to go? Perhaps no farther than the suburbs, and to a different balance between the urban and rural elements in civilization. One cannot prove just where the broken ranks of civilization will hold even if it is possible to rally them again. But it is worth trying along this line.

The City Subordinate to the Suburbs

It is, then, the little home, surrounded by land, and not the cave of the primitive man, which is to replace the Tower of Babel as the symbol of man's new attempt at mastering the art of living. This is what British labor so wistfully looks forward to in its "million cottages of the Great Peace." In the background of the imagination, as one must admit, always lurks the image of a chastened and relatively diminished city. Literally speaking, man is not yet convinced that he can really get along without it, though he is pretty definitely rallying for a fresh effort of adjustment in which this his upstart and mechanical master shall be reduced to his proper place as a servant. And if it is objected that the suburbs have been shown sophisticated and dependent, part and parcel of the city in fact though of the village in form, it yet remains that their life has a distinctive quality which separates them from the latter. They have their own overtones played upon from the standpoint either of form or of substance.

The logic of the suburban evangel is that the salvaging of civilization for its next eon of experiment may well be a case of

> The little more, and how much it is;
> The little less and what worlds away!

Even the relatively slight acceleration of the suburban trend by such means of social control as are in sight, may set up changes in the structure and relationships of modern society which, when sufficiently reinforced, may save the day for the human race.

Specific Issues

It is clear that the traits of human nature are less at war with the suburban environment than with the

of working hours and relationships.³ Yet these comprehend the average man's most definite and concrete contributions to society, and whatever promise of the future leaves them out lacks something of the quality of a genuine evangel.

In turning, therefore, to ask finally whether humanity is really likely to try the experiment of a suburbanized civilization, one finds at the bottom of his curiosity and interest the query whether or under what conditions there might come along with it new zest for work. Will life be better motivated as well as better served from the standpoints of convenience and health? Will man, as a creature with a unified nature, be happier?

Prophetic Trends Toward a Suburban Civilization

Is mankind really likely, as its next epochal effort, to try out the experiment of a suburban civilization? Moving along the "borderland between experience and prophecy," one may discern tendencies which are likely to make the suburban phase of civilization at least relatively more important in the future. These promise to make our evangel of quantitative as well as qualitative significance.

The Prospect of a Crowded World

The first is vast prospective increase of population. Whether one considers our own country only, or the

---

³ Taylor's evidence in "Satellite Cities," including Miss Jane Addams's Reflections upon the Pullman Experiment, proves that frequently they do not.

entire globe, the story is the same. Mankind has multiplied during the past century at a rate entirely unique in history.[4] If the recent rate of increase continues, the hundred and odd million people of the United States in 1920 will be over one hundred and sixty million by 1950, and the billion and three quarters of the present human race will be hanging out a "standing-room only" sign before the end of two centuries. And whether the present increase fully continues or not, there is every prospect of a more and more crowded habitable globe.[5]

It is not intended to assume that increase of population will inevitably go on indefinitely to the point that war, plague, and famine will be probable and preferable alternatives. The secret of making synthetic food may be discovered, or mankind may be able to provide for a new eon of subsistence by wholesale stocking and husbandry of the seas with animal and possibly also with edible plant life. Deliberate limitation of human increase through birth-control is already operating as a partial check. All that is meant is to point out the immense momentum of the present swing of the pendulum, which is probably to continue till the civilized portion of the race faces the very sharp necessity of more intensive cultivation of land to keep from having to reduce its planes of living. This is quite within the range of practical social policies. Current discussions of the future often hinge upon the fear that nations will have to go to war to get more territory on which to raise food, or else starve. The United States Depart-

[4] Giddings, "Studies in the Theory of Human Society," p. 241.
[5] East, "Mankind at the Crossroads," pp. 66 f.

ment of Agriculture is most seriously engaged in making an inventory of the food-production resources of the nation against the not-distant day when it will not be able to feed itself without a radical change in the type of farming,[6] while highly scientific evidence is offered to prove that human beings now living may survive to see the day when the entire world has reached the limit beyond which it is impossible to increase food sufficiently to keep up with population.[7]

Crowding is already finding its first focusing in the vicinity of cities, but, with decentralization continuing, might proceed until the total filling in of the earth's area would give the whole a less rural and more suburban aspect.

The Larger Destinies of Agriculture

The finger of prophecy points to the suburbs rather than to the cities themselves as the next important theater of the process for a very specific reason already suggested: the pinch for which a crowded world must look forward is the lack, not of goods enough to go around, but of food. Economic analysis is accustomed to point out that with mechanical power and tools— and continuously better ones operated with improved technique—population, no matter how vast, can keep ahead of its need for manufactured goods, raw material

[6] See Baker and Strong, "Arable Land in the United States," year-book of the United States Department of Agriculture, 1918, pp. 433–441.

[7] East, "Mankind at the Crossroads," p. 69.

being given. Indeed, it is this capacity of the new-found tools of civilization to produce faster than consumption requires which has made our unparalleled growth of population possible. So far as they are concerned, the future prospect is for a continuously decreasing work day—six, five, or even four hours being sufficient to supply the world with necessary industrial products.[8]

Not so with food. It is likely to take more labor and longer time to produce a bushel of wheat a century from now than it does in America to-day, because more of it will have to be raised on poor land and the remainder by intensive methods which increase work faster than they do yield.[9] Both alternatives will be practised in areas contiguous to present cities as well as elsewhere, and indeed will probably have increasing emphasis there where they have already started. When the same number of dollars per acre will build up a depleted farm as would reclaim one from the desert and the two show equal promise of being profitable, the farm near the city is most likely to be chosen first. The phenomenon

[8] The proclamation of this prospect by "practical" men of affairs is no longer a surprise. Thus the New York "Sun" (October 2, 1924) reports:

"The third annual meeting of the American Construction Council opened at the Hotel Biltmore yesterday and will be concluded to-day. James Hartness, President of the American Engineering Council and former Governor of Vermont, who spoke on 'Prosperity Through Industrial Teamwork,' listed a number of 'fundamental facts' relating to industry, among which he included a prediction that eventually workers would have a five-hour day."

[9] Carver, "Principles of Rural Economics," p. 122 f.

THE SUBURBAN EVANGEL 319

of war gardens shows the natural lines of effort to meet food shortage. The great bulk of the newly required food will doubtless be raised on more extensive farms, but there will be every incentive to produce crops for immediate human consumption in the near vicinity of concentrated bodies of consumers. This means large rural suburbs; gaining upon cities as food production takes more workers relative to manufacturing.

Who Will Produce the World's Food?

When the five-hour work day becomes able to produce all the manufactured goods the world needs, it is mathematically immaterial from the mere standpoint of production whether fifty out of every one hundred workers transfer from industry to agriculture, or whether all of the hundred continue to work half a day in the factory and the other half in the fields. The question, of course, is how to make the fields available and how to organize the alternatives economically. No one would expect that it would literally be by half-days. Agriculture is a seasonal occupation. Its possible alternatives with industry in the use of a common labor force would largely follow seasonal rhythm. This is essentially Henry Ford's solution, which a factory organization of agriculture applying intensive methods makes quite conceivable.[10] Probably no industry is capable of more economies than farming. Pressure for food will make every possible efficiency compulsory. Such economical

[10] Interview reported in "Automotive Industries," September, 1924.

organization is most likely to originate in the vicinity of cities and to involve populations whose members are in touch with both agriculture and industry, as now in the environs of Seattle. At any rate and however the working out of these factors is visualized, it implies an acceleration of the suburban trend. And while not certain, it at least becomes possible that the very workers who produce goods will produce part at least of their own food or be intently associated with those who do, both living in the border-land between city and country.

This may sound unconvincing to those who note how poorly present "back-to-the-farm" movements have worked. But humanity is likely to change its mind about farming if it comes to pass, as foreseen by Professor East, that a single year's crop shortage might starve to death fifty million people in one famine.

The Prospect of "Giant Power"

The much-proclaimed decentralization of electrical power, which now appears almost imminent, may appear at first glance to favor not a suburban type of diffusion of population, but a still more extremely open and rural type. Through the substitution of electricity for steam and the combination of present electrical systems into giant systems, it is proposed to bring power to every village and to every farmer's door. Not only may scattered families have it cheaply for assistance in mechanical tasks, but small-scale village industries may spring up wherever there is raw material, and their concentration in city centers be greatly checked.

THE SUBURBAN EVANGEL

This would tend to the industrializing of the countryside and the upbuilding of small independent communities.

When the actual prospect is sifted, however, it is obvious that here again is a situation which points to large suburban development as its first phase. What is really proposed is to hitch up the existing electric systems, which center in cities, into regional systems covering areas already highly urbanized, the Appalachian and Atlantic seaboard system always being first thought of and mentioned. Within such areas, the decentralizing process will logically work out in the development of a network of communities until many of the present cities will be but minor concentrations within a great and continuous suburban structure, both physically and socially. There will be much farming within its borders, but most of it will be within communities of the rural suburban type, rather than in independent agricultural communities.

Natural Limits to Diffusion

One does not know to what ultimate diffusion the pressure of population upon food resources may drive humanity; but the world's harbors will not be removed. Its river highways will remain, and its mountain barriers stand fast. Deserts will not be inhabited beyond the available resources of irrigation. Equal diffusion over the face of the earth or diffusion based on agricultural resources primarily is not really conceivable. Typography and geography will continue to furnish the ground pattern for society. There will be concentration of population at the strategic points of intercommunication and along the great trade routes, which may be widened out and complicated by crossroads on land and in the air, but which cannot be obliterated.

If finally the coal of the United States should become exhausted and manufacturing actually had to shift to the region of the major water-power resources (located in the Rocky Mountain and western coast ranges), population would congest in hot valleys or on the high range country, where in either case irrigation would be necessary for food production. But it is just this collocation of industry and agriculture on small acreages which would most certainly create a suburban situation.

Either version therefore of the decentralization of electrical power is likely to hasten a suburban rather than an urban or a rural civilization.

WORK, HAPPINESS, AND ENVIRONMENT

Our concluding interest is to discover whether and under what conditions in such a world a better motivation of work and great all-round happiness for workers might be reached.

With its industrial pressure relatively relieved and its pressure for food production increased, with the in- 'ustrial worker and the food producer at the same time ser together in space and increasingly masters of the ꞉ tools and technique, a world which is wise will al-

THE SUBURBAN EVANGEL

most surely employ the same labor force on the two tasks. A recent interpreter of Henry Ford's industrial anticipations summarizes them as forecasting "such changes in farming, transit and manufacture as will break up cities, narrow farming down to a twenty-five day year, and make producing villages, with their clustered homes and plants, the foundation stones of a new structure for American life and labor." [11]

But Henry Ford (who habitually prophesies in fragments and not by complete visions) speaks also of "a great many more small cities rather than a few bigger ones. Instead of centralizing in one city," he says, "there'll be ten cities." This is necessary to complete the more likely picture. The "producing villages" will be suburbs of the "more small cities." Farming, however, is undoubtedly not going to be narrowed down to twenty-five days per year. Not being an economist, Henry Ford apparently has not reckoned with the necessary outcome of rapidly increasing population in terms of the food supply. So long as arable land is limited, the law of diminishing returns ordains that additional crop yield can only be secured at the cost of disproportionately larger amounts of cost and labor.

Such a condition is commonly dreaded as involving a lowering of the plane of living; but if the labor necessary to manufacture goods is correspondingly reduced, no such misfortune is necessitated. Nor need there be

---

[11] Kellogg, "The Play of a Big Man with a Little River," "Survey Graphic," Vol. IV. No. 6, p. 637.

a real lowering of the standard even when such labor can no longer be correspondingly reduced, provided sufficient motive is obtained to make the additional work required intellectually and spiritually interesting and rewarding.

Not Less Work but More Satisfying Work

If, for example, the worker of the future has his own home on the land ("owned" ultimately if need be by society, but his to hold non-speculatively on permanent tenure), if his daily hours of mechanical labor are reduced to four or five, if his domestic burdens are lightened by electrical power available for home, garden, and farm, if he can universally have immediate land contacts and the whole laboring population can participate —at least seasonally—in food production or be within the economic partnership of family groups some of whose members do so—he may look forward without dread or the sense of burden to as much expenditure of energy in work as the human race is now accustomed to. All this is assuming that he will like his work better, that its monotony is relieved, that he has more freedom in it— as is habitual even in peasant labor on the land—and that the incentives of industrial initiative and the enlargement of the self through the enjoyment of a personal home and goods and a neighborly society can be achieved.

Such a happy consummation the present suburban trend and its probable future developments at least make more possible.

THE SUBURBAN EVANGEL

The Suburbs of the Future

Let us try to visualize the suburban civilization of the future. Most of the area of the nation will be covered with villages and farm lands such as one now finds in the more thickly populated portions of Europe, though there also may be detached villas and farmsteads of moderate dimensions. Most of these villages will be clustered about minor centers which, together with them, constitute the suburbs of cities of moderate size. These cities will perform the metropolitan functions for their districts. Much of the work as well as the recreational interests of the people will lie in the minor centers. These minor centers must be large enough to afford some considerable variety of employment for residents, who will chiefly live on uncrowded house-lots; though there may be multi-family apartments in reasonable proportion to house single people, the aged, and perhaps young married couples. There may be also considerable populations of commuters. Perhaps, however, the bulk of the population will live on the land, functioning both as agricultural producers and as industrial workers in nearby factories. The two interests will be seasonally adjusted, though the greatly reduced industrial work-day may run through the year except for the farmer's busy season. Heavy industry may have to be carried on on the edges of the cities; but all lighter industry, in which the manufacture of "parts" for Ford cars may still have honorable place, will be relegated to the villages. Each nation of the world being forced to a self-sufficing economy with respect to food, the transportation of goods between different parts of the world is likely to be reduced. Still the world's harbors are likely to be rimmed by supercities—though of relatively smaller size than now—in which the arch-metropolitan functions of civilization will have their seats. Government may be more decentralized, art diffused, and radio and aëroplane may all but annihilate space; but the unity of life and of mankind is probably dependent upon its possession and perpetuation of places which gather up and epitomize the more diffused forms of civilization. These must almost certainly still be cities in whose intercourse the creative common thinking and sentiment of mankind are likely to be wrought out. In this sense an urban core may still constitute the glowing center of a suburban civilization and a Holy City still symbolize the consummation of human hope.

Even so, this consummation will never be reached unless some version of suburban or rural life shall have normalized human experience, found molds for civilization more congruous with the original nature of man than those of the present are, and utilized his inner impulses in due proportion. "Jerusalem shall be inhabited as villages without walls." Along the golden streets shall be trees and water, and man shall walk in gardens in the cool of the day.

The suburban trend—broadened and enriched especially on its rural side and plastic to changes in world economics due to larger population—thus genuinely leads out into an evangel of hope. Something of what may betide in the next centuries we have "seen in a mirror darkly." Mankind must at least turn backward toward the cottage home and toward the land. This locates him first in the suburbs. A crowded world must be either suburban or savage. Which it shall be can be determined only by trial and error, but what we have seen makes us believe that the suburbs must furnish the gyroscope for the next Great Experiment.

THE END

APPENDIX I

PER CENT OF INCREASE OF POPULATION OF ADJACENT TERRITORY (SUBURBS) OF CITIES OF 100,000 POPULATION AND OVER 1910–1920 (14TH CENSUS)

City	Per Cent	City	Per Cent
Detroit	228.9	Toledo	26.5
San Antonio	125.0	Nashville	25.4
Los Angeles	106.4	Washington	25.2
Cleveland	86.0	Portland, Ore.	24.3
Akron	80.6	St. Louis	23.9
Seattle	79.9	Pittsburgh	23.8
Chicago	73.8	Kansas City (Mo. and Kan.)	22.6
Youngstown	54.3		
Bridgeport	52.4	Dayton	22.4
Birmingham	48.7	Houston	21.3
Fort Worth	48.2	Denver	20.9
Atlanta	47.7	Springfield	20.1
San Francisco	41.7	Boston	18.9
Norfolk	35.9	Providence	18.3
Milwaukee	35.2	Salt Lake City	17.8
Buffalo	33.9	Columbus	16.6
Trenton	33.2	Minneapolis—St. Paul	16.3
Philadelphia	32.9	Syracuse	16.2
New Haven	31.1	New Orleans	15.3
Wilmington	29.6	Scranton	13.4
Hartford	28.8	Louisville	13.1
Dallas	28.3	Lowell	13.0
New York	27.7	Fall River—N. Bedford	12.9

APPENDIX

Spokane	12.8	Memphis	3.6
Des Moines	10.1	Cincinnati	2.4
Worcester	7.9	Grand Rapids	1.5
Indianapolis	7.2	Rochester	—13.5
Reading	6.9	Richmond	—17.2
Albany	4.8	Omaha	—30.3
		Baltimore	—38.7

APPENDIX II

NUMBER OF INCORPORATED SUBURBAN CITIES AND TOWNS LOCATED WITHIN METROPOLITAN DISTRICTS OF CITIES OF 100,000 POPULATION AND OVER BY SIZE GROUPS

Cities of 200,000 Population and Over	Total	25,000 and Over	15,000-25,000	10,000-15,000	5,000-10,000	2,500-5,000	1,000-2,500	500-1,000
Akron	7	0	1	2	1	1	1	1
Atlanta	8	0	0	0	2	2	1	3
Baltimore	1	0	0	0	0	0	1	0
Boston (and Cambridge)	55	12	9	7	12	4	9	2
Buffalo	17	0	2	1	3	6	4	1
Chicago	67	6	1	5	7	11	20	17
Cincinnati	34	4	0	0	4	7	7	12
Cleveland	28	2	0	0	1	6	10	9
Columbus	12	0	0	0	0	1	5	6
Denver	6	0	0	0	0	1	2	3
Detroit	15	2	0	1	1	4	7	0
Indianapolis	8	0	0	0	0	0	6	2
Kansas City (Mo. & Kan.)	7	0	0	1	1	1	2	2
Los Angeles	28	2	1	2	3	7	9	4
Louisville	8	0	1	1	0	2	1	3
Milwaukee	20	0	1	1	5	4	7	2
Minneapolis-St. Paul	16	0	0	0	1	4	6	5
New Orleans	3	0	0	0	1	1	1	0
New York [1]	129	17	10	3	26	30	30	13

[1] Plus 4 cities of 100,000 and over included in the metropolitan area.

Cities of 200,000 Population and Over	Total	25,000 and Over	15,000-25,000	10,000-15,000	5,000-10,000	2,500-5,000	1,000-2,500	500-1,000
Phila. (and Camden)	57	2	0	2	6	16	26	5
Pittsburg	71	1	5	5	21	16	19	4
Portland	10	0	0	1	1	0	7	1
Providence	21	3	4	3	5	6	0	0
Rochester	23	0	0	0	1	5	14	3
St. Louis	25	1	1	1	3	5	10	4
San Fran.-Oakland	22	2	1	0	2	7	5	5
Seattle	6	0	0	0	1	1	2	2
Toledo	6	0	0	0	0	1	2	3
Washington	13	0	1	0	0	2	4	6

Cities of 100,000-200,000 Population	Total	25,000 and Over	15,000-25,000	10,000-15,000	5,000-10,000	2,500-5,000	1,000-2,500	500-1,000
Albany	26	2	2	2	1	5	12	2
Bridgeport	10	0	0	2	2	1	4	1
Birmingham	10	0	1	0	1	1	4	3
Dallas	4	0	0	0	0	0	2	2
Dayton	4	0	0	0	0	1	3	0
Des Moines	6	0	0	0	0	0	1	5
Fall River-New Bedford	19	1	0	0	3	6	8	1
Fort Worth	2	0	0	0	0	1	0	1
Grand Rapids	3	0	0	0	0	0	2	1
Hartford	24	1	1	1	4	8	9	0
Houston	4	0	0	0	0	1	1	2
Lowell	23	2	1	0	5	4	8	3
Memphis	0	0	0	0	0	0	0	0
Nashville	0	0	0	0	0	0	0	0

APPENDIX

Cities of 100,000-200,000 Population	Total	25,000 and Over	15,000-25,000	10,000-15,000	5,000-10,000	2,500-5,000	1,000-2,500	500-1,000
New Haven	17	0	2	1	4	3	7	0
Norfolk	6	2	0	0	2	1	1	0
Omaha	3	1	0	0	0	0	0	2
Reading	11	0	0	0	0	2	7	2
Richmond	0	0	0	0	0	0	0	0
Salt Lake City	3	0	0	0	0	1	2	0
San Antonio	0	0	0	0	0	0	0	0
Scranton	27	0	3	3	7	7	3	4
Spokane	3	0	0	0	0	2	1	0
Springfield	21	2	1	3	4	4	4	3
Syracuse	22	0	0	0	2	5	11	4
Trenton	8	0	0	0	1	2	2	3
Wilmington	7	0	0	0	2	1	2	2
Worcester	24	0	0	2	4	7	8	3
Youngstown	15	1	1	2	2	2	4	3
Total	1025	66	50	52	152	216	324	165

BRIEF ANNOTATED BIBLIOGRAPHY OF SUBURBAN LITERATURE

I GENERAL AND QUANTITATIVE ASPECTS

1. Fourteenth U. S. Census, "Cities and Their Suburbs," Vol. I, pp. 62–75.
   The source of practically all current quantitative information.
2. Weber, "The Growth of Cities in the Nineteenth Century." New York, 1899.
3. Whitbeck, "The Selection of Urban Sites" (in "Land Economics," Institute for Research in Land Economics, Madison, Wisconsin, 1922).
4. Hurd, "The Structure of Cities," Alexander Hamilton Institute, New York, 1910.
5. Burgess, "The Growth of the City" (in "Publications of the American Sociological Society," Vol. XVIII, pp. 1–17).
6. Thompson, "Growth of Population in Outlying Parts of Metropolitan Districts" (in "Journal of the American Statistical Association," Vol. XVIII, pp. 57 f.).
   Doubts whether the census data prove a "tendency toward living in the less congested parts of our metropolitan areas."
7. Ford, George B., "Regional and Metropolitan Planning" (in "Proceedings" of Fifteenth National Conference on City Planning, 1923, pp. 1–45).
   Reviews and summarizes the most recent tendency to include entire metropolitan areas in city planning processes.
8. Bailey, "The Twentieth Century City," "American City," Vol. XXXI, p. 142.
9. Lindeman, "The Community." New York, 1921.

Compares suburbs with other types of communities.

10. "New York Walk Book." American Geographical Society, New York, 1923.

Geography, topography, geology, history, and esthetic appreciation of a metropolitan district combined in a practical handbook for the pedestrian.

II Types and Varieties of Suburbs

1. Kimball, "Manual of Information on City Planning." Harvard University Press, 1923.

   Elaborate annotated bibliography. Includes "Short List of Typical City Plan Reports," pp. 43–46, classified according to types of communities and including industrial and residential suburbs.
2. "Report of the U. S. Housing Corporation." U. S. Department of Labor, 1919 (2 vols.).

   Vol. II includes numerous plans and illustrations of suburban industrial housing, with cost-accounting and details.
3. Nolen, "The Industrial Village." National Housing Association, Publication No. 50 (1918).
4. Taylor, "Satellite Cities: A Study of Industrial Suburbs." New York, 1915.

   Descriptive, with strong emphasis on social welfare aspects of suburban development.
5. Wood, "The Housing of Unskilled Wage Earners." New York, 1919.

   A survey of the field, including both European and American movements.
6. Ford, James, "Residential and Industrial Decentralization" (in Nolen, "City Planning," Chap. XV, New York, 1916).

   A lucid summary of the social and economic factors involved.
7. Piquet, "Is the Big City Doomed as an Industrial Center?" "Industrial Management," Vol. LXVIII, p. 139.

III Economic and Social Aspects

1. Bureau of the Census, "Financial Statistics of Cities," 1922.

   Includes data for individual cities of 30,000 population and over, but not separately tabulated for suburbs.

BIBLIOGRAPHY 337

2. Ely and Moorhouse, "Elements of Land Economics." New York, 1924.
3. Arner, "Outlying Land Values," Lecture IV, pp. 133 f. (in "Urban Land Economics," Institute for Research in Land Economics, Madison, Wisconsin, 1922).
4. Hurd, "Principles of Land Values." New York, 1903.
5. National Industrial Conference Board, "The Building Situation," Special Report 29, 1924.

   A nation-wide survey showing very poor current prospects for the provision of good homes for the working classes upon voluntary private initiative.
6. Purdy, "Own Your Own Town" (in "Proceedings" of Seventh National Conference on Housing, 1918, pp. 273–284).
7. Massachusetts Homestead Commission, Reports 1914–20.

   Duties of the commission since transferred to the Department of Public Welfare, State House, Boston.
8. "Plan of New York and Its Environs," Report of Progress, 1923, pp. 39–63, and subsequent monographs.

   Summary of preliminary reports by specialists in the economic and social aspects of metropolitan city planning.
9. Fourteenth Census, Vol. II, p. 1298, "Statistics of House Ownership."
10. Byington, "Homestead" (volume in "The Pittsburgh Survey," Russell Sage Foundation); also "Sharpsburg: A Typical Waste of Childhood," pp. 279–304 and Appendix II.

    Intimate studies of home and family life in industrial suburbs.
11. Detroit Bureau of Governmental Research, "The Detroit Metropolitan Area" (January, 1924, 25 p.).

    Reports a plan of metropolitan government to the Detroit Board of Commerce.
12. Hamilton, "Improving Our County Government." "American City," Vol. XXX, No. 3 (March, 1924).

    Exposition of the proposed new charter unifying the suburban communities of Westchester County, New York, in a single government.
13. Hamlin, "Low-Cost Cottage Construction in America: A

Study Based on the Housing Collection in the Harvard Social Museum." Publications of the Department of Social Ethics, Harvard University, 1917.
14. Magnusson, "Employers' Housing in the United States." United States Bureau of Labor Statistics, "Monthly Review," Vol. V, pp. 869–894 (November, 1917).

IV RURAL ASPECTS

1. Galpin, "Replanning the City as a Place not to Live," Chap. IX of "Rural Social Problems," New York, 1924.
Advocates leaving the city entirely to business, and would make all homes of city people suburban.
2. Butterfield, "The Farmer and the New Day." New York, 1919, pp. 70–83.
3. Arnold and Montgomery, "Influence of a City upon Farming," U. S. Department of Agriculture, "Farmer's Bulletin 678" (1918).
The most adequate research study of the underlying problem of the rural suburbs.
4. Adams, "Reserving Productive Areas within and around Cities: A Proposal to Substitute Agricultural Wedges for Zones," "Journal of American Institute of Architects," October, 1921, pp. 316–319.
5. Kimball, "Manual of Information on City Planning" (see No. 1 under Sec. II), titles under "Rural" and "Regional Planning."
6. "Select Bibliography of Country Planning," No. 67, Russell Sage Foundation (October, 1924).
Titles chiefly under general sociology, parks, farm management and rural church surveys. A few community-planning titles applying to suburbs.

V CITY PLANNING ESPECIALLY AS INVOLVING THE SUBURBS

1. U. S. Department of Commerce, "Zoning in the United States." Report of the Division of Building and Housing, 1923.

BIBLIOGRAPHY 339

2. "Plan of New York and Environs" (see No. 7 under Sec. III). Also maps and diagrams, 1923.
3. Nolen (editor), "City Planning." New York, 1916.
   Especially Chap. XV, Ford, "Residential and Industrial Decentralization" (see No. 6 under Sec. II).
4. "Proceedings of Fifteenth National Conference on City Planning," "Regional Planning."
   Planning expanded so as to include the suburbs, in many aspects. See especially Ford, "Regional and Metropolitan Planning," pp. 1-25, and Whitten, "Regional Zoning," pp. 85-114.
5. "Metropolitan, County and Regional Planning," "Landscape Architect," Vol. XIV, p. 98 (January, 1924).
   A brief summary of the present status of the movement.
6. Williams, "How to Get Garden Suburbs in America" (in "Proceedings of Seventh National Conference on Housing," pp. 273-284).
7. Bassett, "Present Attitude of the Courts toward Zoning" (in "Proceedings of Fifteenth National Conference on City Planning," pp. 115-135).
   Reviews the extension of legislation empowering zoning outside of municipal boundaries.
8. "Zoning Notes." Monthly Department in "The American City," New York.
   A review of current legislation and legal happenings in this field from month to month.

VI FUTURE CIVILIZATION AS INVOLVING THE SUBURBS

1. Ogburn, "Social Change." New York, 1922.
   Expounds the thesis that human nature cannot endure current civilization and must have something simpler or break under the strain.
2. East, "Mankind at the Crossroads." New York, 1923.
3. Carver, "Principles of Rural Economics." Boston, 1911.
4. Baker and Strong, "Arable Land in the United States," Year-Book of the U. S. Department of Agriculture, 1918.

Estimates the future capacity of the nation to support population through agricultural production.
5. Ford, Henry, "My Life and Work."
Prophesies general industrial decentralization and the decline of cities.
6. "Giant Power," "Survey Graphic," Vol. IV, No. 6.
The prospect of electrical super-power systems and the probable consequences for city and country.